Second Edition

Metro 2

James Styring | Nicholas Tims | Christina de la Mare

OXFORD UNIVERSITY PRESS

Contents

Welcome to Metro

W Life online and offline

Music styles

1 Label the styles of music.

classical hip-hop jazz metal pop ~~R&B~~ rock

0 R&B 1 ________ 2 ________ 3 ________ 4 ________ 5 ________ 6 ________

Movies and TV

2 Complete the words.

Streaming What are you going to watch this weekend?

TV shows

0 r e a l i t y s h o ws

1 t__ __k s__ __ws

2 s__ __ __ __s s__ __ws

3 s__ __p o__ __ __as

Movies

4 a__ __ __ __n m__ __ __ __s

5 c__ __ __ __ies

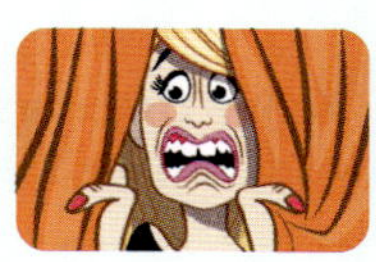

6 h__ __ __ __r m__ __ __ __s

7 s__ __ __ __ __e f__ __ __ __ __n m__ __ __ __s

Online activities

3 Choose the correct options.

0 (post) / take comments on websites
1 chat / look up information
2 chat / download with your friends
3 read / take news about sport online
4 read / share videos and pictures
5 look up / write a blog about your life
6 download / write music to your phone
7 have / take quizzes online

4 How often do you do the activities in exercise 3? Write sentences using the expressions below or your own ideas.

every day never once a week once or twice a month sometimes three or four times a day twice a week

0 I post comments on websites once or twice a month.
1 ____________________
2 ____________________
3 ____________________
4 ____________________
5 ____________________
6 ____________________
7 ____________________

Simple past: regular and irregular

1 Complete the chart with the simple past form of eight regular verbs.

~~camp~~ carry do escape feel go leave live play pull put read say share take walk wear

Simple past: regular		
+ -ed	+ -d	-y + -ied
0 camped	4 ______	7 ______
1 ______	5 ______	
2 ______	6 ______	
3 ______		

2 Write the irregular verbs in exercise 1 and their simple past forms. If you need help, use the list at the back of the book.

0 do did
1 ______ ______
2 ______ ______
3 ______ ______
4 ______ ______
5 ______ ______
6 ______ ______
7 ______ ______
8 ______ ______

Simple past: affirmative and negative

3 Write sentences with the prompts. Use the simple past form of the verbs.

0 I / do / my homework
I did my homework.
1 we / not watch / a horror movie
______
2 she / see / her friends
______
3 you / not have / breakfast
______
4 he / play / his guitar
______
5 they / not camp / on the beach
______
6 Tom / hang out / with his friends yesterday
______
7 I / not find / my math book.
______
8 he / wear / his new T-shirt last night
______
9 we / go / to the park this morning
______

Simple past: questions and answers

4 Order the words to make questions.

0 go on vacation / did / Where / you / ?
Where did you go on vacation?
1 you / How / travel / did / ?
______
2 any new food / Did / try / you / ?
______
3 go with / did / Who / you / ?
______
4 take / a coat / you / Did / ?
______

could / couldn't

5 Complete the sentences with *could* or *couldn't*.

0 
1 
2 
3 
4 
5 

0 Could you play the piano when you were 11?
Yes, I could.
1 I ______ speak English when I arrived in the U.S.
2 Abigail ______ ski before she started school!
3 Dad ______ remember where his glasses were.
4 ______ your brother ride a bike when he was four?
No, he ______.
5 You ______ draw very well when you were small.

6 Your turn Work with a partner. Ask and answer questions with the words in the chart.

Did you	share any photos online watch any reality shows	yesterday? last weekend?
Could you	play the guitar ski swim	when you were five? last winter?

Did you share any photos yesterday?

Yes, I did.

Could you swim when you were five?

No, I couldn't.

W Outdoor adventure

Adventure sports

1 Complete the list with *do*, *go*, or *play*, and the sports.

bungee jump karate sailing ~~scuba diving~~ skydiving surfing tennis volleyball

What are your life goals?

0 go scuba diving in Australia
1 ________________ without an instructor
2 ________________ with a *sensei* (teacher) in Japan
3 ________________ in the Caribbean
4 ________________ in Hawaii
5 ________________ at Wimbledon, London (U.K.)
6 ________________ at Miami Beach
7 ________________ in New Zealand

Adventure: verbs

2 Read the advice and choose the correct verbs.

When animals attack ...

Elephants

Elephants can run at 25 km/h, so don't try to [0] **follow / escape**. [1] **Look for / Escape** a tree and [2] **climb / jump** it!

Bears

Are you [3] **following / camping** in an area with bears? Don't sleep and cook in the same place. [4] **Carry / Pull** a small bell. Bears hate the sound.

Bees

Don't [5] **jump / sail** into a river or lake. You can't breathe underwater, but bees can wait! Run and [6] **carry / pull** your shirt over your head.

Life events: verbs

3 Complete the profile with the verbs. There is one extra verb.

bought found got ~~grew up~~ had left went were

THE LION WHISPERER

Kevin Richardson is a South African lion expert. He [0] grew up in Johannesburg and he always loved animals. He [1] ______ high school at 18 and [2] ______ to college to study zoology, but he left after two years. At 23, he [3] ______ a job at a wildlife park. He helped with all the animals, but his favorites were the lions. Some of the lions [4] ______ born at the park and now he is part of their family. Kevin [5] ______ married in 2007 and he [6] ______ two children, Tyler and Jessica.

Adjectives of feeling

4 Choose the correct options.

0 Is there any pizza? I'm **hungry** / **scared**.
1 You look **freezing** / **thirsty**. Here, have my jacket.
2 Are you **boiling** / **excited** about your birthday tomorrow?
3 I don't like this horror movie. I'm **scared** / **tired**!
4 Sara is **bored** / **worried** about her history test.

was / were: affirmative, negative, and questions

1 **Complete the text with *was, were, wasn't,* or *weren't*.**

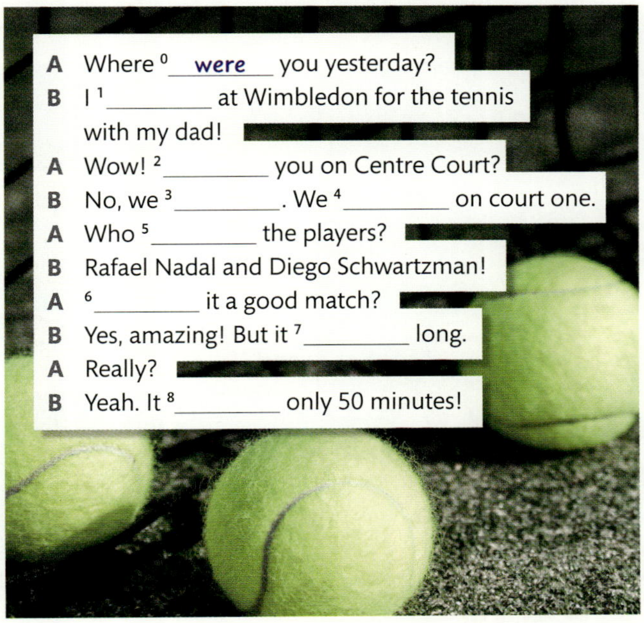

A Where [0] were you yesterday?
B I [1] ________ at Wimbledon for the tennis with my dad!
A Wow! [2] ________ you on Centre Court?
B No, we [3] ________. We [4] ________ on court one.
A Who [5] ________ the players?
B Rafael Nadal and Diego Schwartzman!
A [6] ________ it a good match?
B Yes, amazing! But it [7] ________ long.
A Really?
B Yeah. It [8] ________ only 50 minutes!

Past progressive

2 **Look at the pictures. Write affirmative and negative past progressive sentences.**

0 Evan / read / swim
Evan was reading. He wasn't swimming.
1 Bella / walk / run
____
2 Carter / do parkour / ride a bike
____
3 Daisy / kick the ball / throwing it
____

3 **Write past progressive questions about the pictures. Answer the questions.**

0 What / Bella and Daisy both / wear?
What were Bella and Daisy both wearing?
They were wearing shorts and T-shirts.
1 Where / Evan / read?
____
2 What / Daisy and Bella / play?
____
3 Who / jump?
____
4 Who / not exercise?
____
5 What / Evan and Carter both / wear?
____

4 **Your turn** **Write questions with the prompts.**

0 what / you / do / yesterday / ?
What were you doing yesterday?
1 what / you / wear / ?
____
2 who / you / talk / to / ?
____
3 what / you / think / about / ?
____
4 how / you / feel / ?
____

5 **Ask and answer the questions in exercise 4 with a partner.**

What were you doing yesterday?

I was watching a movie.

Food: count nouns and non-count nouns

1 **Complete the food wheel with the words.**

burgers butter cake cereal cookies eggs ham hot dogs juice ketchup mangoes nuts ~~oranges~~ pineapples potato chips strawberries

Food and drink

fruit (e.g. ⁰ *oranges*,
1 ______,
2 ______,
3 ______) and
vegetables (e.g. broccoli, asparagus), 4 ______

bread, rice, pasta, and 5 ______

6 ______, milk, yogurt, cheese

7 ______, meat (e.g. 8 ______,
9 ______,
10 ______),
fish, beans, and 11 ______

food and drinks with a lot of sugar and/or fat (e.g. soda, 12 ______,
13 ______,
14 ______,
15 ______)

Transportation, habitats, and places in a town

2 **Look at the view of the island. Label the habitats and the forms of transportation you can use.**

Habitats

beach forest lake river ~~town~~ village

Transportation nouns

drive a car ride a motorcycle sail on a ferry take a bus take the subway take a train

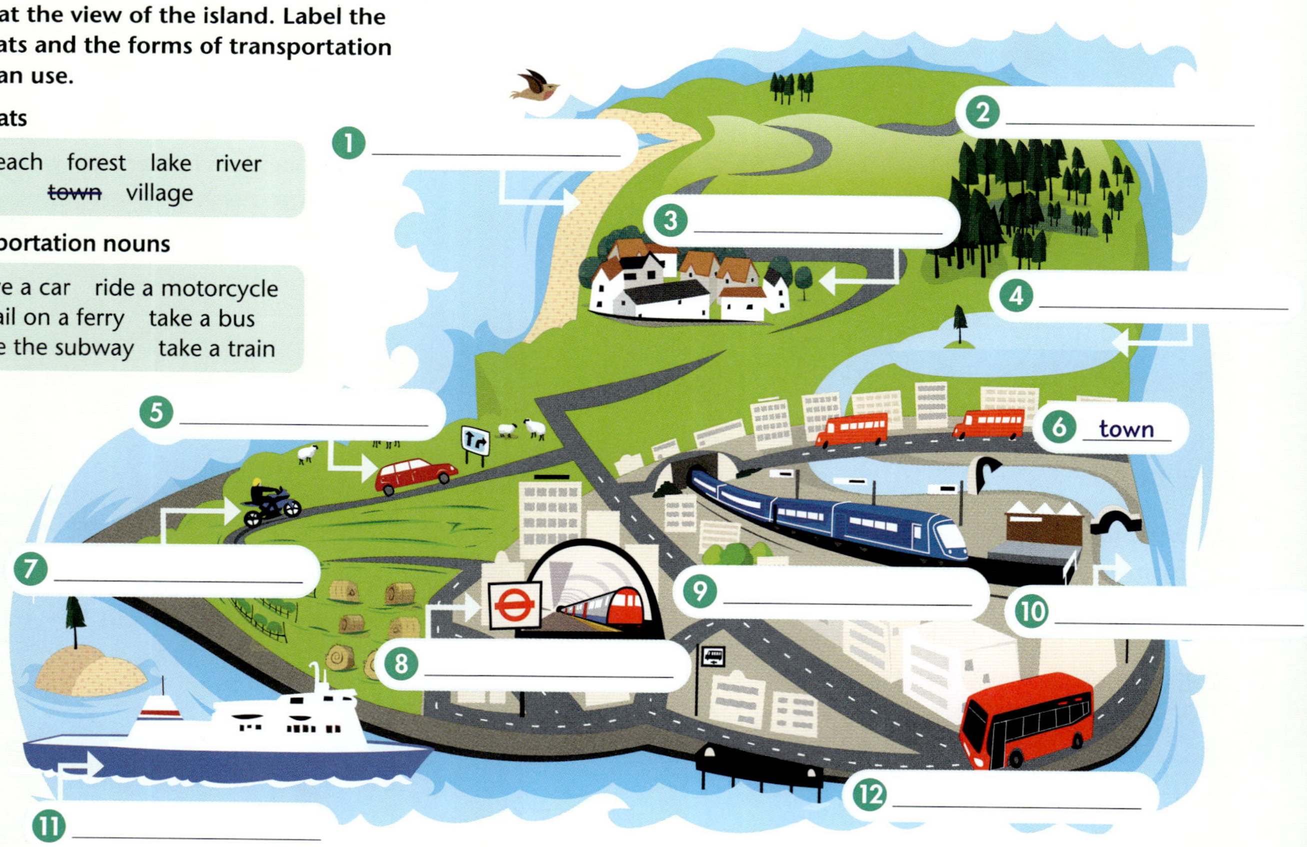

1 ______
2 ______
3 ______
4 ______
5 ______
6 *town*
7 ______
8 ______
9 ______
10 ______
11 ______
12 ______

there is / there are + count nouns: *a / an, some, any*

1 Complete the sentences with the correct form of *there is / there are*. Add *a, an, some,* or *any* if necessary.

0 "___Is there___ a burger for me?"
"No, ______________. Sorry. We ate them all!"

1 ______________ tomatoes, so we can't make tomato salad.

2 "______________ nuts in this?"
"No, ______________."

3 ______________ amazing cake in the classroom. It's Mrs. Carson's birthday.

4 ______________ potato chips in the kitchen. Please eat them!

Non-count nouns

2 Choose the non-count nouns.

sugar **(oil)** mango orange salt bread strawberry water juice cookie

How much / How many + quantifiers

3 Choose the correct options.

A Wow! [0] **(There's)** / **There are** a lot of sugar in ketchup.
B Is there [1] **many** / **any** oil in it?
A No, there [2] **isn't** / **aren't**. But there [3] **is** / **are** some salt.

A How [4] **many** / **much** juice is there?
B There's [5] **a lot of** / **many** apple juice, but there isn't [6] **a little** / **much** orange juice.
A And how [7] **many** / **much** oranges are there?
B There are [8] **a lot of** / **much** oranges. Let's make [9] **any** / **some** juice!

A How much water [10] **is** / **are** there? I have a headache.
B There isn't [11] **much** / **few** water, but we can buy [12] **some** / **any**.
A Where? There aren't [13] **many** / **much** stores near here.
B There are [14] **a little** / **a few** restaurants over there. Let's ask them.

Comparative adjectives

4 Lucy and Amy are on vacation in Montreal, Canada. Complete the conversation with the comparative form of the adjectives. Add *than* if necessary.

Lucy It's our first day! What do you want to do?
Amy Let's go out. It's [0] ___sunnier than___ (sunny) at home!
Lucy Yes, it's great! Do you want to go to the park?
Amy Yeah! All the parks here are [1] ______________ (big) at home!
Lucy What about some food?
Amy Definitely. The food here is [2] ______________ (delicious) ...
Lucy ... than at home? Yes, I know. And it's [3] ______________ (cheap), too!
Amy And I want to go clothes shopping. I think some things are [4] ______________ (expensive) at home. But that's OK.
Lucy How do you want to travel?
Amy On the subway? I think it's [5] ______________ (fast).
Lucy What? Than at home?
Amy No! Than the bus!

Whose + possessive pronouns

5 Read the sentences. Write matching questions with *Whose* and answers with *hers, mine, ours, theirs* or *yours*.

0 It's my passport.
___Whose is the passport? It's mine.___

1 It's her hot dog.
____

2 They're your books.
____

3 Those bags belong to them.
____

4 This house belongs to us.
____

6 Your turn Think of a place you often visit on vacation. Answer the questions below in your notebook.

1 What habitats are there?
2 What forms of transportation are there?
3 What food do you usually eat there?
4 How is it different from your hometown?

7 Describe the place to a partner. Use your answers to the questions in exercise 6.

We often go to Fortaleza. There are amazing beaches there and it's near some beautiful villages. In Fortaleza, you can take the bus or take the subway, ...

W What are you up to?

Weekend activities

1 What are the plans for this weekend? Match the activities with the pictures.

0 "I need to buy some new trainers."
"Do you want to go **out for a meal** / **shopping** on Saturday?"

1 "Let's go to **an amusement park** / **a football match**!"
"Great idea! I love going on exciting rides."

2 "Would you like to have a **cookout** / **party** on Sunday?"
"Sounds good! I can buy some hot dogs and burgers."

3 "Do you want to **hang out with your friends** / **have a sleepover**?"
"Yes! We can talk all night and eat pizza and cookies!"

4 "I don't want to cook tonight."
"Why don't we **have a cookout** / **go out for a meal**?"

5 "I love looking at art."
"Me too! Let's **go to an exhibition** / **see your relatives** this weekend!"

Personality

2 Complete the descriptions with the adjectives. Then write about your best friend, using three of the adjectives in the box.

brave cheerful friendly ~~funny~~
helpful honest lazy shy smart

What's your best friend like?

My best friend Luis is very [0] _funny_ and always makes me laugh. Luis is always [1] ________ and helps us to smile when we're feeling sad. He's really [2] ________ and loves going on big rides at the amusement park!

My best friend Fletcher is very [3] ________ and always tells the truth. He's [4] ________, too. When we need more burgers for a cookout, he always runs to the supermarket! He's very [5] ________, and he likes talking to everyone!

My best friend Amelia is very [6] ________ and always gets good grades. She studies hard – not like me: I'm a bit [7] ________! Amelia is [8] ________ and is a bit nervous with new people. But I know she's a great person.

My best friend ________________________

____

____

____

Weather

3 Match the weather words with the pictures.

cloudy foggy hot ~~icy~~ raining
snowing sunny warm windy

0 icy

1 ________

2 ________

3 ________

4 ________

5 ________

6 ________

7 ________

8 ________

Simple present vs. present progressive

4 Choose the correct options.

Ben Hi Elsa, what [0] **are you doing** / **do you do**?
Elsa Hi Ben! I [1] **hang out** / **'m hanging out** with some friends in the park. What about you?
Ben I'm in town with my sister. We [2] **'re going shopping** / **go shopping** a lot on weekends.
I [3] **look for** / **'m looking for** a new sweater.
Elsa I hope you find one! Hey, [4] **are you going** / **do you go** to art exhibitions?
Ben Yes, I do. I [5] **'m loving** / **love art**. Why?
Elsa Well, there's a new exhibition at the art academy. Would you like to go next week?
Ben Yes, great!

Future time expressions

5 Choose the correct options.

0 I'm going to my friend's house **later** / **morning**.
1 Are you going to Evan's party **on** / **this** evening?
2 We're going out for a meal on Saturday **evening** / **tonight**.
3 Julian is seeing his cousins **later** / **next** week.
4 Is Hannah having a cookout **Sunday** / **tomorrow**?
5 I'm going to a soccer game **on** / **tomorrow** Wednesday.

Present progressive (future)

6 Complete the mini dialogues with the verbs.

do / not work get back / meet ~~go away~~ / ~~see~~
hang out / go take / not swim travel / not take

0 A Are we going away this weekend?
B Yes, we're seeing your cousins.
1 A What ________ we ________ this weekend?
B I don't know. Dad ________ so we can go out.
2 A ________ you ________ at the mall later?
B No! I ________ to a comics exhibition.
3 A How ________ the girls ________ to Joe's house?
B They ________ the subway. They're walking.
4 A What time ________ Mom ________ tonight?
B About 10 p.m. Dad ________ her at the airport.
5 A ________ you ________ your phone to the beach?
B Yes, I am. And I ________, so you can leave yours with me.

7 Your turn Complete the planner with the activities below. You can do them at any time on any day.

do a bungee jump go camping hang out with friends
have a cookout have a sleepover make a cake
play volleyball see the new horror movie

Monday		Friday	
a.m.	p.m.	a.m.	p.m.
Tuesday		**Saturday**	
a.m.	p.m.	a.m.	p.m.
Wednesday		**Sunday**	
a.m.	p.m.	a.m.	p.m.
Thursday		**Notes**	
a.m.	p.m.		

8 In pairs, ask and answer questions about your diaries from exercise 7. Use the future time expressions from exercise 5. See how many 'yes' answers you can get!

Are you doing a bungee jump on Saturday?
No, I'm not.
Are you doing it on Sunday?
Yes, I am!
That's a yes for me!

1 On vacation

Maira 42 minutes ago
Paris is the best city for sightseeing! I love visiting museums in new cities, just like Natalie.
42 Reply

A Video 01 **Watch or listen. Check the places Natalie visits.**

0 ☑	museum	3 ☐	ferry	6 ☐	bookstore	9 ☐	monument
1 ☐	art gallery	4 ☐	market	7 ☐	library	10 ☐	park
2 ☐	river	5 ☐	mall	8 ☐	movie theater	11 ☐	beach

B **Watch or listen again. Choose the correct options.**

0 Natalie visited Paris with **family** / **friends**
1 She didn't go inside the Louvre because it was **closed** / **full**.
2 Natalie thinks L'Orangerie is **busier** / **quieter** than the Louvre.
3 From the Centre Pompidou Natalie **can see a lot** / **can't see much** of the city.
4 Natalie **climbed** / **looked at** the Eiffel Tower.

C **Answer the questions.**

1 Do you think Natalie's vacation sounds fun? Why? / Why not?
2 What would you like to see or do in Paris?

Vocabulary

LO Talk about vacation activities

10 cool *vacation ideas!*

Vacation activities

1.2k 22

Try new food. What about cheese with fries? They're very popular in Canada.

______. The Tower of London is full of British history and has millions of visitors every year!

______. Try the V8 Hotel in Germany. Your bed is a car!

______ for family and friends. This market in Hong Kong sells a lot of great things.

______. You can walk along the Appalachian Trail in the U.S.

______. Why not try the Ithaa restaurant in the Maldives? It's under the ocean!

______. What about Melbourne's graffiti? It's great for a selfie!

______ in Ecuador. This one on the Galapagos Islands is beautiful.

______ – but remember to protect your skin!

______ in New York City. There are a lot of things to see in Manhattan!

1 02 **Look at the pictures in the text. Complete the vacation ideas with the activities. Listen and check.**

buy gifts eat out go hiking go sightseeing go to the beach stay in a hotel sunbathe take photos ~~try new food~~ visit museums

2 03 **Listen and repeat.**

3 **Look at the activities in exercise 1 and complete the chart in your notebook for you.**

It's interesting	It's boring

4 **Read the sentences about summer vacations. Choose the correct options.**

0 A lot of our vacations are in my grandparents' house. But occasionally we **stay in a hotel** / **sunbathe**!
1 My dad always gets very brown because he **sunbathes** / **takes photos** a lot.
2 On vacation, I **go to the beach** / **take photos** a lot and put them on Instagram.
3 My sister often **buys gifts** / **goes sightseeing** for her friends in stores. But I think it's boring!
4 I often **go hiking** / **try new food** on vacation. But some things taste disgusting!
5 We rarely **eat out** / **go to the beach**. My mom cooks a lot on vacation – but I want to go to a restaurant!
6 Mom and Dad often **stay in a hotel** / **visit museums**. But I don't like buildings full of old things!
7 When we **buy gifts** / **go to the beach** my sister and I always swim in the ocean – we love it!

5 **Your turn** **Plan your perfect vacation with a partner. Ask and answer questions.**

Do you want to buy some gifts?

No, I don't. That's boring!

International English
Weak forms

Natalie is British. She uses weak forms of words like *a, the, and, I, on, than, was*. These words are not stressed in affirmative sentences.

My name is Natalie and I recently visited Paris.
Here are the top five things I did with my friends.

D **Video** 04 **Read the International English box. Watch or listen to the example.**

E **Video** 05 **Watch or listen to the sentences from Natalie's vlog. Complete them with the weak forms.**

0 Number one, we visited the Louvre Museum.
1 It's ______ really popular museum, so it ______ full.
2 It's ______ lot more peaceful ______ quiet ______ ______ Louvre.
3 There is ______ big market along ______ river.
4 It's very different ______ ______ Champs-Élysées, ...
5 My friends ______ I ate our lunch ______ ______ park ...
6 I had ______ wonderful time in Paris.

Pronunciation p.124 Workbook p.128

 LO Read a quiz about vacation destinations

A quiz

1 06 **Read and listen to the quiz. Which countries are the people in?**

1 Paulo is in the U.S.
2 Ellie is in ______.
3 Jack is in ______
4 Masayo is in ______.
5 Tom is in ______.

2 07 **Take the quiz. Listen and check.**

3 **Read the quiz again and choose the correct options.**

1 The T-shirt is for Paulo's **cousin** / **friend**.
2 Uluru is very **new** / **old**.
3 Jack **doesn't want to** / **wants to** see the monster in the lake.
4 Masayo and her friends are traveling around a **city** / **country**.
5 Tom is eating boxty for the **first** / **second** time.

4 Your turn **Order the activities in the quiz by preference. 1 = favorite activity. Compare your list with a partner and give reasons for your answers.**

Number 1 is Uluru. It looks like an amazing place. Number 5 is trying boxty. It looks disgusting!

Really? Boxty is my number 1! I always try new food on vacation.

The vacation quiz

1

I'm in Venice Beach, California in the U.S., and I like shopping! I'm buying a T-shirt for my best friend. The price is ...
a €15. **b** £15. **c** $15.
Paulo

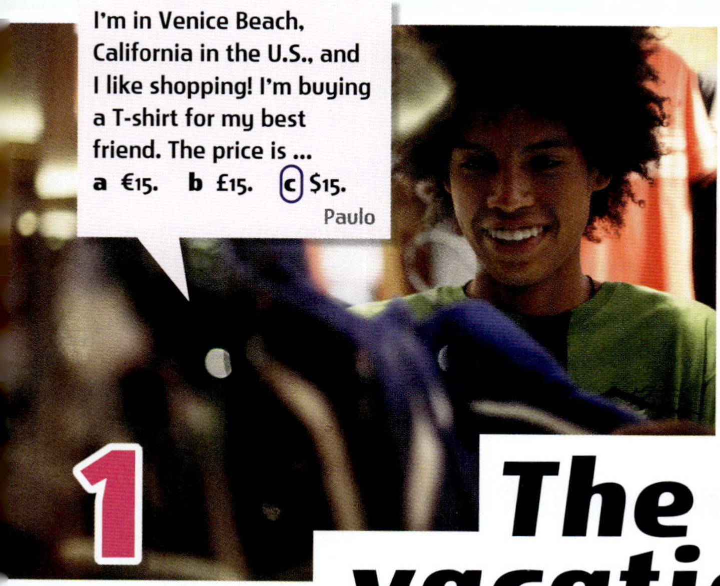

2

I love sightseeing, and today I'm standing in front of a very special place in Australia. It's an enormous rock called Uluru and it's very important to the country's Aboriginal people. Uluru is 600 million years old and it's in the ... of the country.
a center **b** north **c** south
Ellie

3

I love going hiking in the U.K. Today I'm hiking around a Scottish lake with a group of friends – and we're looking for a very famous monster! The name of the lake is ...
a Loch Lomond. **b** Loch Ness.
c Loch Morar.
Jack

4

I'm on a bus tour in Madrid, Spain with two of my friends. They like the royal family and taking photos of the royal palaces! King Felipe and Queen Letizia live in ...
a the Royal Palace of Madrid.
b the Palace of Zarzuela.
c the Royal Palace of Aranjuez.
Masayo

5

My family and I love eating out, and today we're at a restaurant in Ireland. I'm trying a new food: boxty! Its main ingredient is ...
a potatoes. **b** pasta. **c** rice.
Tom

Grammar **LO** Use *like* + *-ing* to talk about activities you like and don't like

like / love / hate + -ing

1 08 **Read and listen to the Grammar in context. Who is the boy in the photo: Jack or Emile?** ______

Grammar in context — **Present and Practice**

Jack Do you like **going hiking**?
Emile No, I don't. I **hate walking**.
Jack Really? Why?
Emile It's slow and boring! I **like running**. I often go running in the mountains. What about you?
Jack Oh, I **don't like doing** exercise. But **I love taking** photos. That's why I go hiking! I went to Scotland recently and I took some great photos!

Grammar notes p.129

2 **Complete the chart with words from the Grammar in context.**

Affirmative		
	I **love** / He **loves**	[0] taking photos.
	I **like** / He **likes**	[1] ______.
Negative		
	I **don't like** / He **doesn't like**	[2] ______ exercise.
	I **hate** / We **hate**	[3] ______.
Questions		
	Do you **like** / **Does** he **like**	[4] ______ hiking?

Stop

Most verbs: + *-ing* — *play* → ***playing***
Consonant+ *-e*: ~~e~~ + *-ing* — *dance* → ***dancing***
One vowel + one consonant: double the consonant + *-ing*: *jog* → ***jogging***

3 **Choose the correct options.**

0 David doesn't **like** / **likes** taking photos.
1 We hate **eat** / **eating** out.
2 My brothers **doesn't** / **don't** like going to the beach.
3 I hate **buying** / **buys** gifts.
4 "**Do you like** / **You like** trying new food?" "No, I don't."
5 "Does your sister like sunbathing?" "Yes, she **does** / **likes**."

4 09 **Listen and check.**

5 **Look at the pictures and write sentences with prompts.**

0 Otis / try / new food
Otis hates trying new food.

1 Milagros / visit / museums
______

2 Max and Toby / go / sightseeing
______

3 I / hike
______

4 Dad / buy / gifts
______

5 your grandma / like / sunbathing / ?
______

6 **Complete the text. Use the prompts in the word pool.**

hate / be   like / go / hiking   like / swim   love / go / sightseeing   love / spend   ~~not like / go~~   not like / visit

Family vacations

A lot of teenagers [0] don't like going on vacation with their parents. They [1] ______ museums or going sightseeing. They [2] ______ far from their friends, and they don't want to spend time with their parents. I'm one of those teenagers! My mom is great, but our vacations are often difficult. Mom [3] ______ through forests, and she [4] ______ in the local town. But I [5] ______ in the pool, and I [6] ______ time on my phone! What are your vacations like?

7 **Your turn** **What do you and your family *like* / *love* / *hate* doing on vacation? Tell a partner.**

Workbook p.129 Metro Express p.108

1 Vocabulary LO Talk about my feelings

Feelings

1 🔊10 **Look at the pictures and complete the sentences. Listen and check.**

angry with ~~bored of~~ crazy about disappointed with happy about interested in nervous about proud of scared of surprised by

0 He's *bored of* sightseeing.

1 I'm ________________ our hotel.

2 She's ________________ ice cream!

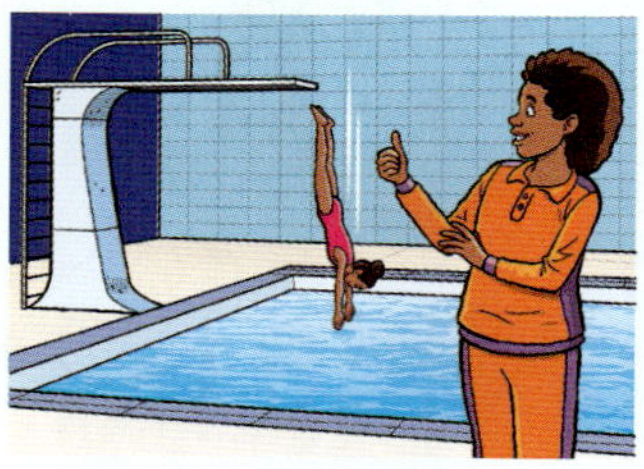

3 I'm ________________ my daughter!

4 I'm ________________ flying.

5 He's ________________ being on vacation.

6 She's ________________ the boy.

7 He's ________________ surfing.

8 She's ________________ the magazine article.

9 I'm ________________ you!

2 🔊11 **Listen and repeat.**

3 Complete the sentences with the correct adjective + preposition from the parentheses.

0 My dad is *proud of* me. I ordered my meal in Portuguese! (**angry with** / **proud of**)

1 My parents are ________________ our meal. They think it's terrible! (**disappointed with** / **interested in**)

2 I'm ________________ sightseeing. I love discovering new places! (**crazy about** / **surprised by**)

3 My sister is ________________ the dark. She sleeps with a light on. (**happy about** / **scared of**)

4 I'm ________________ trying new food. Last time I got sick! (**bored of** / **nervous about**)

Listening Skills

LO Listen to descriptions of a family vacation

Let's go on vacation!

1 🔊12 **The Jones family are on a driving vacation in the U.S. Listen and match the descriptions 1–4 with the pictures A–D.**

A ____

B ____

C *1*

D ____

2 🔊12 **Listen again. Choose the correct options.**

1 Dad is **nervous about** / **scared of** driving. Yosemite is **an easy** / **difficult** place to find.

2 Mom is **angry with** / **surprised by** Dad because he isn't listening to her. She doesn't like **driving** / **map reading**!

3 Daisy is **bored of** / **disappointed with** traveling. She's **happy about** / **scared of** seeing the bears in Yosemite!

4 Aiden is **interested in** / **crazy about** swimming. He wants to go swimming in a **lake** / **pool**.

Workbook p.128

Superlative adjectives

1 13 **Read and listen to the Grammar in context. What can you see in Yosemite National Park?**

____

Grammar in context — **Present and Practice**

Yosemite National Park is one of **the biggest** parks in the U.S. It is home to some of **the largest** trees in the world. One of **the most beautiful** animals in the park is the mountain lion, or cougar. Summer is **the busiest** time at the park. **The best** times to visit are in May and September.

Grammar notes p.130

2 **Complete the chart with words from the Grammar in context.**

Short adjectives	
the* + *-est* or *-st	
old	**The** old**est** national park in the world is in Mongolia.
large	Yosemite is home to some of ⁰ the largest trees in the world.
the* ~~y~~ + *-iest	
busy	Summer is **the** bus**iest** time of year.
the* + double consonant + *-est	
big	It's one of **the** big**gest** parks in the U.S.
Long adjectives	
***the most* + adjective**	
beautiful	One of ¹ __________ animals is the mountain lion.
Irregular adjectives	
good	² __________ times to visit are in May and September.
bad	Winter is **the worst** time to go.

3 **The Jones family are looking for Yosemite National Park. Complete the dialogue with the superlative form of the adjectives in parentheses.**

Dad Where is this park? Yosemite is ⁰ the most difficult (difficult) place to find!
Mom You need to turn right here. Right! Not left! I'm giving you ¹ __________ (easy) instructions!
Dad What? Oh, you really are ² __________ (bad) map reader. You're taking us ³ __________ (long) way!
Mom Look at the signs! ⁴ __________ (big) one says "Yosemite National Park!"
Daisy When do we arrive? This is ⁵ __________ (boring) trip! I want to see the bears! They're ⁶ __________ (good) part of this vacation!

4 14 **Listen and check.**

5 **The Jones family are comparing hotels in Yosemite. Look at the information. Write sentences with the words in parentheses.**

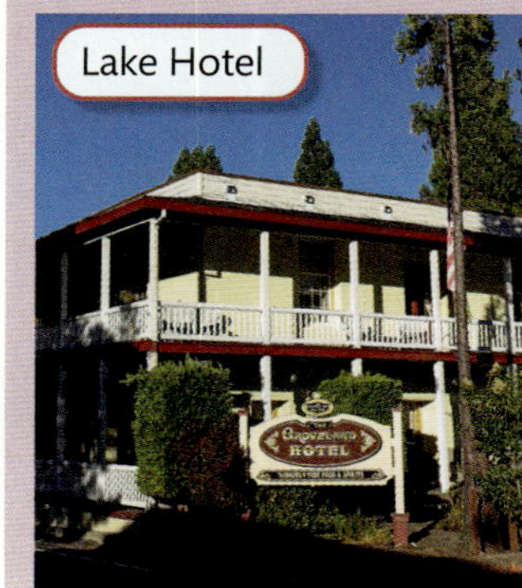

	Mountain Lion Lodge	Lake Hotel	Yosemite View Hotel
Room size	11.5 m^2	51 m^2	37 m^2
Price	$85 a night	$130 a night	$380 a night
Food	★★	★	★★★★

0 Lake Hotel has the biggest rooms. (big / rooms)
1 ______________________________ (small / rooms)
2 ______________________________ (expensive / hotel)
3 ______________________________ (cheap / hotel)
4 ______________________________ (good / food)
5 ______________________________ (bad / food)

6 **Your turn** **Write questions with the prompts and superlative adjectives. Then ask and answer with a partner.**

0 where was / your / exciting / vacation?
Where was your most exciting vacation?
1 what is / beautiful / place you know?
____
2 what was / your / long / trip?
____

Where was your most exciting vacation?

My school trip to Paris!

Workbook p.130 Metro Express p.108

1

Listing Skills

LO Listen to people talking about vacations and identify the purpose of a text

Top vacations

Active Listeners
Identifying purpose

Active listeners check the purpose of a text first and then listen for more detail.

1 15 **Read the tip. Then listen to the people talking about vacations. What are they trying to do?**

1 ☐ complain 2 ☐ persuade 3 ☐ teach

2 15 **Listen again. Check (✓) the activities you can do on each vacation.**

	1	2	3
sunbathe	✓		
go to the beach			
go hiking			
go shopping			
go sightseeing			
watch movies outside			
stay in a hotel			

3 15 **Complete each sentence with one word or number. Listen and check.**

0 The Siesta Beach Hotel pool is __22__ meters long.
1 The hotel has ________ restaurants.
2 On the Summer Camp vacation you can ________ and sunbathe.
3 The Summer Camp vacation is one or two ________ long.
4 The Discover South America advertisement mentions ________ different countries.
5 The Discover South America website has a ________ with more information.

4 Your turn **Discuss the three vacations with a partner.**

I like the ... because I love ... I don't like the ... because I'm not crazy about ...

I prefer the ... vacation because it's the cheapest / most interesting / ...

Reading Skills

LO Read comments and scan them for key words

Readers' comments

1 **Read the four texts quickly. Match 0–3 with a–d to make true sentences.**

0 Sam is __d__
1 Amelie is ___
2 Francisco is ___
3 Ryan and Becky are ___

a taking a long walk.
b exploring a city.
c eating and painting.
d making food.

Active Readers
Scanning for key words

Active readers read questions carefully. What information do they ask for? Think about the key words you need to look for. Then scan the text quickly to find them.

2 **Read the tip. Then read the questions in exercise 3. What information does each question ask for?**

a distance a feeling ~~an activity~~ an object
a part of the day a place food and drink

0 __an activity__
1 ________
2 ________
3 ________
4 ________
5 ________
6 ________

3 16 **Read and listen to the texts again and answer the questions. Write four words maximum for each answer.**

0 What is Sam doing on social media?
__He's watching cookery videos.__
1 How did he feel about the bread last time?
____
2 What item of technology does Amelie use?
____
3 What time of day are Ryan and Becky at the café?
____
4 What can you eat and drink at the café?
____
5 Where did Francisco go hiking?
____
6 How far did he hike?
____

4 Your turn **With a partner, brainstorm five things you can do in your town on a staycation.**

You can go swimming or play tennis at the sports center.

Yes, I think the sports center is the best place to go in our town! You can also play tennis there.

Great – we have two things on our list then. ..

Staycation: *the stay-at-home vacation!*

Are you ...
At home for the summer?
Bored of sitting indoors?
Try these cool staycation ideas!

I like watching cooking videos. Right now I'm making bread, but it's the most difficult thing to make! The first time I tried I was very disappointed with the bread. But I'm happier about it this time!
Sam, U.S.

I'm interested in the history of my city, so I'm walking around it and I'm using an app on my phone to learn more. The app shows you a historical map of the area you're standing in and photos and information from many years ago. It's the most interesting way to learn about my city!
Amelie, U.K.

My sister and I are crazy about art, so today we're painting in a café. You can paint a plate, cup, or other item. And you can have tea and cake, too! This is the nicest way to spend an afternoon in the school holiday. Also, the best gifts for family and friends are the ones you make yourself!
Ryan and Becky, U.K.

I love being in the countryside, and today I went hiking. It's the healthiest staycation activity! My walk was 20 km. I recorded it with my exercise app, and I finished it in my fastest time. I took some great photos, too!
Francisco, U.S.

International English
🇬🇧 holiday = 🇺🇸 vacation

Workbook p.131 Writing Skills p.100

Make, accept, and refuse invitations

1 🔊17 **Read and listen to the phone conversation. What are Kayla and Avery doing on the beach tomorrow?**

Kayla Hey Avery, it's Friday, so how about going to the beach after school? I want to take photos for my art project.
Avery That sounds awesome, but I can't go. I have a lot of homework.
Kayla Do you need to do it all tonight? You have all weekend!
Avery I hate leaving things till the last minute. I'm sorry, but it's the worst thing for me!
Kayla Seriously, Avery, you need to take a break sometimes. Do you want to go tomorrow? Then you can do your homework tonight.
Avery OK, that sounds good! Thanks, Kayla!
Kayla Let's take a snack with us.
Avery Great idea!

2 🔊18 **Listen and repeat.**

Active Speakers
Invitations

Active speakers make, accept, and refuse invitations politely.
They use these expressions to make invitations:
How about ... -ing? Do you want to ... ? Let's ...
They use these expressions to accept:
OK, that sounds good. Great idea!
They use these expressions to refuse:
That sounds awesome, but ...,
I'm sorry, but ...

3 🔊19 **Read the tip. Complete the conversation below with the correct words. Then listen and check.**

A Do you [0] want to watch a movie at my house?
B [1] ________ sounds awesome, but I can't come. I have chores to do.
A You can do them later! You need some free time, too.
B I'm sorry, [2] ________ I don't like leaving them.
A OK. How about a movie tomorrow instead?
B OK, that [3] ________ good!
A Great! [4] ________ buy some soda and snacks.
B Great idea!

4 **Politely refuse the invitations below. Use your own ideas and the expressions in the tip box.**

1 Hey, do you want to play soccer after school today?
____
2 Let's visit that new market on Saturday.
____
3 How about watching a movie tonight?
____

Global Skills
Making time for work and play

3 GOOD HEALTH AND WELL-BEING

It's important to do your homework, chores, and other tasks. However, you don't need to do it all at the same time. It's fine to divide a big task into smaller tasks. That way, you can accept invitations from friends and enjoy your free time, too.

5 **Read the Global Skills box. What was wrong with Avery's study plan? How did Kayla try to help Avery?**

____
____

6 **Complete the table with tasks you *need* to do this week, and fun activities you *want* to do this week.**

Tasks	Fun activities
homework	go to the beach

7 **In pairs have a conversation about tasks and fun activities. Use the model below and your ideas from exercise 6.**

How about ... ? / Do you want to ... ?
↘ I'm sorry, but ... / That sounds awesome, but ...
↙ How about ... ? / Let's ...
↘ OK, that sounds good. / Great idea.
↙ Let's ... / How about ... ? Do you want to ... ?
↘ ... sounds good. / Great idea.

Watch LO Understand and reflect on a video about a famous city

Miami, Florida

Before you watch

1 Match the words with the pictures.

~~a café~~ big houses clothes stores a stadium

0 a café

1 ______

2 ______

3 ______

2 Where in your town, city, or country can you see the places in exercise 1?

In my town there are big houses near the beach.

While you watch

Active Viewers
Using visual clues

You can use visual clues about buildings, popular activities, and transportation to learn about a new place.

3 Video Read the tip. Watch the video with the sound off. What do you see? Choose the correct options.

0 **old** / **(tall)** buildings
1 **boats** / **airplanes**
2 people at the **beach** / **pool**
3 people playing **tennis** / **volleyball**
4 people on **skateboards** / **bikes**
5 a sports **stadium** / **store**
6 **restaurants** / **movie theaters** and coffee shops
7 people **surfing** / **shopping**

4 Video Watch again. Complete the notes.

basketball ~~beach~~ boutiques cafés coconut football stores sunbathe swim volleyball

Place	Notes
South [0] Beach	a good place to [1] ______, [2] ______, walk, play [3] ______, ride a bike
Tenth Street	great restaurants, [4] ______, hotels
American Airlines Arena	Miami Heat play [5] ______ here
Sun Life Stadium	home of Miami's American [6] ______ team
[7] ______ Grove	[8] ______, restaurants, [9] ______

After you watch

5 Complete the chart with notes about buildings, popular activities, and transportation in a city in your country. Then compare in pairs.

	Notes
Buildings	
Popular activities	
Transportation	

Project p.108

2 Material world

Metro VIDEO

Documentary
Volcano adventure

Cole 1 hour ago
Would I like to sleep next to a volcano? Hmmm, not sure! Everything looks dangerous, but Sam isn't scared of anything.

A Video 20 **Watch or listen to the video. Why does Sam make videos inside volcanoes?**

a for his studies at university b to teach people about volcanoes c for Hollywood movies

B **Watch or listen again. Are the sentences T (*true*) or F (*false*)?**

0 Lots of people do Sam's job. T ☐ F ☑
1 Ambrym is an island with a lot of volcanoes. T ☐ F ☐
2 Sam travels to Ambrym by helicopter. T ☐ F ☐
3 The weather on Ambrym is windy. T ☐ F ☐
4 The drone can't film inside the volcano. T ☐ F ☐
5 Inside the volcano, Sam's phone works well. T ☐ F ☐
6 Sam's suit protects him from the lava. T ☐ F ☐

C **Answer the questions.**

1 What are two good things about Sam's job?
2 What are two bad things about it?
3 Do you want to do Sam's job? Why? / Why not?

Vocabulary **LO** Talk about different materials

Materials: nouns

1 21 **Look at the online post. Match the words with the objects. Listen, check, and repeat.**

canvas cardboard cotton ~~glass~~ leather metal paper plastic rubber stone wood wool

Stop

Materials nouns also function as adjectives.

*A **plastic** bag* → *A **cardboard** box*

When we use *wool* and *wood* as adjectives we change them.

wool – ***woolen*** → *wood* – ***wooden***

2 Read the blog post and choose the correct options.

What do I bring to school every day? Every day I wear a [0] **cotton** / **stone** T-shirt and pants to school. On cold days I wear a [1] **cardboard** / **woolen** sweater or denim jacket, and I often wear [2] **paper** / **plastic** sunglasses, too. I carry my school books in a [3] **canvas** / **glass** backpack. I also carry a [4] **metal** / **woolen** tennis racket and a [5] **rubber** / **leather** tennis ball. I usually have a novel in my backpack. Some people like reading on their phones or tablets, but I prefer [6] **metal** / **paper** books!

3 Your turn **Make a list of objects you touch every day and the materials they are made of.**

A T-shirt – cotton

4 In pairs. Tell your partner the items in your list. Your partner guesses what they are made of.

My shoes

Um, maybe they're made of leather?

International English
Stressing key words

Sam is from the U.S. He speaks quickly, but he stresses the key words in sentences. These are usually nouns, adjectives, verbs, and adverbs. Focusing on these words can help us to understand.

We've **got** to get **started**.

D Video 22 **Read the International English box. Watch or listen to the example.**

E Video 23 **Watch the video again or listen to the sentences. Underline the stressed words.**

0 Ambrym has lots of volcanoes.
1 His videos are useful for other people who would like to learn about volcanoes ...
2 We got as close as we could to the lava.
3 Just had an amazing day of climbing.
4 This is what it's all about.
5 It's the end of one more day in a volcano.

Pronunciation p.124 Workbook p.132

2 Reading Skills

LO Read a magazine article about an unusual house

A magazine article

1 24 **Read and listen to the magazine article. How did Cara Brookins learn how to build a home?**

2 **Read again. Where do you find the answers to the questions below? Write the paragraph letter (A–E).**

0 Why didn't Cara buy a house? B

1 What kind of home would people like to live in? ____

2 What is the house like? ____

3 What did Cara use to build the house? ____

4 When did Cara and her children work on their house? ____

3 **Read the article again and answer the questions.**

0 Who did Cara talk to about her idea?
She talked to her children.

1 What materials did Cara use to build her home?

2 Where did Cara and her children go during the day?

3 How long did it take to build the house?

4 How many bedrooms does the house have?

5 How do the Brookins family feel about their home?

We built our own house

A We'd all like to live in our perfect home. Maybe it's an apartment with amazing views, or an enormous house with beautiful gardens and a pool. But would you like to build one?

B Cara Brookins wanted a nice house for her and her four children. She didn't have the money to buy a house, but it was cheaper to build one. After a conversation with her children, Cara made the biggest decision of her life: she decided to build her own home!

C Cara bought the materials: wood for the walls and doors, glass for the windows, plastic tubes for the bathroom and kitchen, and metal cables for the electricity. She had no experience with building, so she and her children learned about it from YouTube videos!

D During the day Cara went to work and her children went to school. And in the afternoons and evenings, they watched the YouTube videos and worked on their new home. Eventually, after nine long months, it was finished.

E The Brookins house is amazing. It's a large, comfortable five-bedroom home on two floors, and includes a library and a garage for three cars! Many people are proud of their homes, but for the Brookins family, it's an extra-special feeling.

would like

1 25 **Read and listen to the Grammar in context. What is Kye's ideal house like?**

Grammar in context — **Present and Practice**

Kye What's that magazine on your coffee table?
Alicia It's an architecture magazine. **Would** you **like** to see it?
Kye Yes, I **would**! I love architecture.
Alicia What kind of home **would** you **like** to have in the future?
Kye **I'd like** to have a big house with a big yard.
Alicia That sounds nice.
Kye But I'**d like** a really modern house. I'**d like** one that looks different from all the other houses!
Alicia Hmmm ... there aren't many houses like that!
Kye I know. I'**d like** to build it myself!

Grammar notes p.133

2 Complete the chart with the words from Grammar in context.

Affirmative			
I / You / He / She / We / They	**'d / would** ⁰ like	a nice home to have a big house.	
Questions			
Would	you / he / she / they	¹ ________	a snack? ² ________ see it?
Short answers			
Yes, ...		No, ...	
I / he / she / we / they	³ ________ .	I / he / she / we / they	**wouldn't.**

3 Choose the correct options.

0 We'd (like) / **like to** a new house.
1 Would you **like** / **like to** a glass of water?
2 She'd **like** / **like to** have a private bathroom.
3 He'd **like** / **like to** build a wooden sauna in his bedroom.
4 Would your parents **like** / **like to** a bigger house?
5 Would you **like** / **like to** see that movie tomorrow?

4 Complete the conversation with the missing words.

Luiz Where would you ⁰ like to live when you're older?
Marcia I'd like ¹ ________ live in the countryside, near the beach.
Luiz ² ________ you like an apartment or a house?
Marcia I think ³ ________ like a house.
Luiz Who would you like ⁴ ________ live with?
Marcia I'd ⁵ ________ to live with a group of friends! My best friend Ana and I always talk about it.
Luiz ⁶ ________ you like to have a pool?
Marcia Ana would like ⁷ ________ have one. But I like swimming in the ocean!

5 26 **Listen and check.**

6 Write questions and short answers with the prompts.

0 you / go / swimming ✓
Would you like to go swimming? Yes, I would.
1 he / a bigger bedroom ✓
____
2 she / have / a pool ✗
____
3 they / some / pizza ✗
____

7 **Your turn** **Write a list of things for an ideal home.**

private movie theater, pool, library

8 Ask a partner about their ideal home. Use your list in exercise 7.

Would you like to have a private movie theater in your house?

Yes, I would.

Workbook p.133 Metro Express p.109

2 Vocabulary

LO Describe different materials

Materials: adjectives

1 27 **Match the adjectives below with their opposites. Listen, check, and repeat.**

dark dirty hard light ~~synthetic~~ thin

0 natural synthetic
1 heavy ______
2 clean ______
3 pale ______
4 thick ______
5 soft ______

2 Complete the sentences with the correct pairs of adjectives from exercise 1.

0 This material isn't natural. It's synthetic.

1 This wood isn't ______. It's ______.

2 These windows aren't ______. The glass is very ______!

3 This bed isn't ______. It's ______.

4 These stones aren't ______. They're ______.

5 Her jacket isn't ______. It's ______.

3 Your turn **Find five things around you that you can describe with an adjective from exercise 1. Write them down in your notebook. Then share your ideas with a partner.** A heavy bag

Listening Skills

9 INDUSTRY, INNOVATION AND INFRASTRUCTURE

LO Listen to and do a quiz about unusual uses of materials

Materials quiz

1 Look at the pictures. Which materials do you think they are made of?

2 28 **Do the quiz. Then listen and check your answers.**

0 The Modern Seaweed house is on a Danish island. One of its main materials is ...
   (a) wool. b cotton. c paper.
1 The Wikkelhouse is in the Netherlands. It's made of thick ... and it only takes a day to build!
   a cardboard b wood c plastic
2 The Billion Euro House is a house made from ... in Ireland.
   a cotton b paper c canvas
3 In a park in New York City you can see a car made of ...
   a stone. b metal. c rubber.
4 In 1966 women enjoyed wearing dresses made of ...
   a canvas. b paper. c plastic.

3 28 **Listen again. Choose the correct options.**

0 The materials on the wool house are (**natural**) / **synthetic**.
1 The cardboard in the Wikkel House is very **heavy** / **strong**.
2 Frank Buckley's house was very **cheap** / **expensive** to build.
3 The car is in New York City. An **artist** / **engineer** built it.
4 Paper clothes were popular in the **U.K.** / **U.S.**

4 Your turn **Which of the objects in exercises 2 and 3 do you find the most unusual or interesting? Explain your reasons to a partner.**

I find the paper dresses the most unusual, because they probably got dirty very easily!

Workbook p.132

Grammar

LO Use indefinite pronouns to talk about people, places, and things

Indefinite pronouns: words with *some*, *any*, *no*, and *every*

1 29 **Read and listen to the Grammar in context. What can you do at the festival?**

Grammar in context | **Present and Practice**

Would you like to go **somewhere** exciting next winter? At the Harbin Snow and Ice Festival in China, there's **something** for **everyone**. From January to March every year, there are enormous buildings and sculptures **everywhere** – and **everything** is made of ice! **No one** goes home bored. You can eat out there, buy gifts, or go swimming in an ice lake! Is there **anything** better?

Grammar notes p.134

2 Complete the chart with *some-* and *any-* words from the Grammar in context.

	Affirmative	Negative / Question
Person	someone / somebody	anyone / anybody
Place	0 somewhere	anywhere
Thing	1 ______	2 ______

3 Choose the correct indefinite pronouns to complete the sentences.

0 There's somebody on the phone for you. (**anyone** / **somebody** / **something**)
1 I'd like ______ to eat. (**anything** / **something** / **somewhere**)
2 Where are my sneakers? I know they're here ______! (**anything** / **someone** / **somewhere**)
3 I need a new summer jacket. I want ______ light. (**anywhere** / **anything** / **something**)
4 Do you have ______ to drink? (**anything** / **anywhere** / **somewhere**)

4 Complete the chart with *no-* and *every-* words from the Grammar in context.

	All	Zero
Person	everyone / everybody	0 no one / nobody
Place	1 ______	nowhere
Thing	2 ______	nothing

5 Complete the mini-dialogues with the words from the chart in exercise 4.

1 A 0 Everyone is buying those thin cotton T-shirts.
B Yeah! There are people wearing them 1 ______!
2 A These bags are really heavy. We can't carry 2 ______!
B I know. And 3 ______ is helping!
3 A I want one of those thick canvas backpacks, but there's 4 ______ in the stores.
B I know! I looked 5 ______ for them.

6 30 **Listen and check.**

7 Read the blog post and complete the sentences.

Blog

All about oobleck

Does 0 anyone / **anything** remember oobleck? It's a popular science project in elementary schools [1] **anywhere** / **everywhere**. Oobleck is a liquid that goes hard when you touch it, but then becomes a liquid again. In the past, [2] **no one** / **nowhere** understood it, but now [3] **something** / **everyone** is talking about it. Oobleck doesn't really cost [4] **anything** / **someone** to make. It's a mix of water and a natural cooking ingredient called corn starch. But scientists say it can be very useful in industry. It can fix holes in roads. You can even build robots with it – is there [5] **anything** / **nowhere** you can't use it for? Here's [6] **anyone** / **something** interesting: Oobleck gets its name from a 1949 children's book, by Dr. Seuss. But now we know, it's a lot more than child's play!

8 Your turn Complete the questions with indefinite pronouns. Then ask and answer.

0 Does anyone in your family play a sport?
1 Is there ______ to play a sport near your house?
2 Does ______ in your family play a musical instrument?
3 Does anyone do ______ else?

Does anyone in your family play a sport?

My sister plays basketball. She's good!

2

Listening Skills

LO Listen to a podcast and identify the audience

What's in my phone?

Active Listeners
Identifying the audience

Active listeners think about who a text is for.

1 31 **Read the tip. Listen to the podcast about phones. Who is it for?**

a technology experts b the general public

2 31 **Listen again. Choose the correct answers.**

0 Ethan ...
- a broke his phone yesterday.
- b broke Ava's phone yesterday.
- c dropped his phone yesterday.
- d got a new phone yesterday.

1 The glass on phone screens is ...
- a thin.
- b thick.
- c heavy.
- d synthetic.

2 Inside a phone there ...
- a are heavy metals.
- b are one or two types of metal.
- c is only one kind of metal.
- d are lots of different types of metal.

3 Ethan's phone is ...
- a metal.
- b plastic.
- c heavy.
- d dirty.

4 Plastic protects the phone and ...
- a helps it to work better.
- b doesn't get hot.
- c looks cool.
- d is stronger than everything else.

3 Your turn **Check (✓) the sentences that are true for you. Then compare them with a partner.**

1 ☐ My phone is very light.
2 ☐ My phone always works well.
3 ☐ I rarely drop my phone.

Reading Skills

LO Skim-read a blog post to understand the main idea

A blog post

Active Readers
Skim-reading

Active readers look for the general idea of a text before they read it in detail. Read the title and look for key words – this is called "Skim-reading".

1 32 **Read the tip. Read and listen to the blog post about craft projects. What is the general idea? Choose the correct answer.**

- a Projects that cost a lot of money and time.
- b Projects that are cheap and easy to do.

2 **Read the blog post again. Complete the table.**

Project	Materials needed
1 clean your sneakers	toothpaste, ______
2 build a shelf	______
3 make a bag	______
4 make a phone holder	______
5 build a plant wall	______
6 make some speakers	______, ______

3 **For each question, choose the correct answer.**

Project 1
- a Toothpaste is bad for leather sneakers.
- b Toothpaste stops the odor in sneakers.
- c Toothpaste makes your sneakers cleaner.

Project 2
- a This shelf is good for your bedroom.
- b You need to use new cardboard for the shelf.
- c The shelf can hold a lot of heavy objects.

Project 3
- a You can put a lot of different things in the bag.
- b The bag is a good way to carry your scarf.
- c You need to buy something to make the bag.

Project 4
- a The holder only works with light phones.
- b You need to watch a video before you build the holder.
- c The holder stops your arms becoming tired.

Project 5
- a New plastic bottles are prettier than old ones.
- b You can grow different plants inside the bottles.
- c Fill all the bottles with water first.

Project 6
- a You only need three items to make the speakers.
- b Plastic cups are better than cardboard tubes.
- c Everything works better with a plastic phone.

4 Your turn **Which project would you like to do? Tell a partner.**

12 RESPONSIBLE CONSUMPTION AND PRODUCTION

You can do it!

1

Are your white leather sneakers dirty? Do they smell bad, too? Try these two easy cleaning methods! Clean your sneakers with toothpaste (yes, really!) and put a lot of old newspaper inside. The paper stops the bad odor!

2

Would you like something new for your bedroom? This cardboard shelf is easy to make and doesn't cost anything! All you need is some clean cardboard, some scissors and some tape! It's quite strong, but don't put anything heavy on it!

3

Would you like a new bag? With this idea, you can make one from an old cotton scarf. You don't need to cut anything, and it can hold everything!

4

Do you watch a lot of videos? It's great to have something that holds your phone. This phone holder is made from wooden lollipop sticks. It's very light, but it works really well, and it costs nothing to make!

5

Would you like to make your garden prettier? You can do this with some old plastic bottles. Make some holes in them, attach them to the wall, and put plants in them. You can grow everything in a plastic bottle! Just remember to give them water!

6

Do you need some new speakers for your phone? Here is the solution! You can make them with two plastic cups and a cardboard tube. Everything sounds better. Seriously!

Workbook p.135 Writing Skills p.101

2 Speaking & Global Skills

LO Take turns in a discussion

Group discussion

1 🔊33 **Read and listen. Why doesn't Megan like Jose's idea?**

Grace OK! We need ideas for the school magazine. José, what's your opinion?
José Well, I'd like to write about a new laser keyboard. It's a small metal device and it turns any table into a keyboard!
Megan Can I say something? We always have articles about computer technology. We need something different.
José I disagree. Technology is cool! And you can use the laser keyboard everywhere. Grace, what's your opinion?
Grace Hmm, I agree with José. The keyboard for my tablet is really heavy and I hate carrying it! Do you have any other ideas, Megan?
Megan No, I don't have anything to add.

2 🔊34 **Listen and repeat.**

Active Speakers
Taking turns

Active speakers use the following phrases to take turns in discussions:
What's your opinion?
Can I say something?
I don't have anything to add.
I agree (with ...)
I disagree (with ...)

3 🔊35 **Read the tip. Complete the conversations below with expressions from the tip. Then listen and check.**

0 A Does anyone have any other ideas?
B No, I don't have anything to add.
1 A We need another idea. Hayley, ______________________ ?
B ______________________ you! We need to get some more ideas.
2 A ____? I'm not happy about this idea. It's a boring topic.
B ______________ The students like reading about it.

Global Skills
Body language in taking turns

Everyone uses body language. But be careful! Body language can mean different things in different countries.

4 **Read the Global Skills box. Look at the poster about polite body language. Is body language similar in your country?**

5 **In groups of three, read out the conversation in exercise 1. Use the body language from exercise 4.**

6 **You are having a meeting for your school magazine. You need to choose a simple craft project for an article. In your group, choose two of the ideas from page 29 or use your own ideas.**

7 **Use the diagram to have a conversation between three people in a meeting. Use your ideas from exercise 6.**

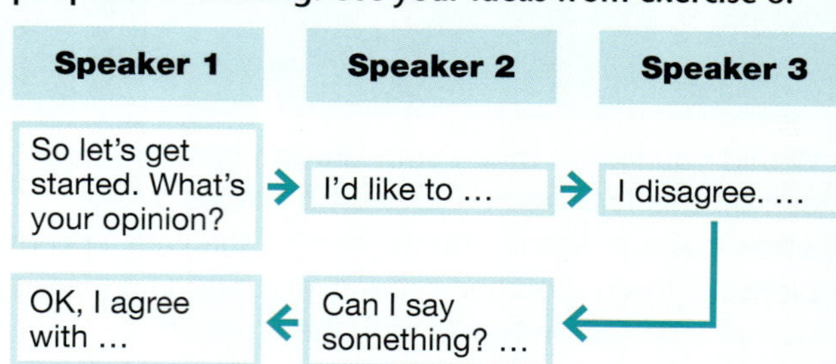

Surfers against sewage, the U.K.

14 LIFE BELOW WATER

Before you watch

1 Look at the two photos. What problem and solution do they show?

Active Viewers
Inferring

Active viewers make guesses about the things that they see or hear in videos. This is called inferring.

2 Video Read the tip. Then watch the video with the sound off. Answer the questions with your own ideas and give reasons.

0 Which country can you see?
I think it's the U.K. because the writing on the bags is in English and the weather is cold.

1 What is the age of the people doing the beach cleans? ______

2 What time of year does the video show? ______

3 What days of the week does this activity happen on? ______

While you watch

3 Video Watch again. Put the sentences about the video in the correct order.

____ We can all stop using plastic.
____ Everyone can collect litter for two minutes.
__1__ Our environment is getting very dirty.
____ Beach cleaners usually collect the same materials.
____ A group is trying to clean our rivers and beaches.
____ People use social media to discuss beach cleaning.

4 Video Watch again. Answer the questions with a maximum of four words.

0 What does the group *Surfers against sewage* clean?
beaches and rivers

1 How many volunteers do the beach cleans? ______

2 What are their hats and boots made of? ______

3 How many tons of trash did they collect last year? ______

4 Where is the idea popular now? ______

5 What materials does the group usually find on the beach? ______

International English
rubbish = trash

After you watch

5 Discuss the questions with a partner. Give reasons for your answers.

1 Do you think that groups like *Surfers against sewage* can make a big difference in our environment? Use the points in the table and your own ideas.

For	Against
Everyone can do it. Lots of volunteers. Social media can make more people join.	Job of governments, not individual people. Lots of beaches. What about trash in the ocean?

Project p.109

A Review

Vocabulary

1 Look at the pictures. Write the vacation activities.

0 b u y g i f t s

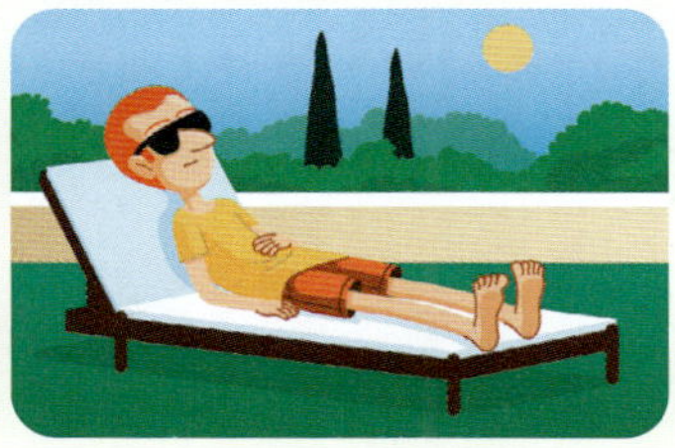

1 s___ ___ ___ ___ ___ ___ ___

2 eat o___ ___

3 t___ ___ new f___ ___ ___

4 go h___ ___ ___ ___ ___

5 g___ to the b___ ___ ___ ___

6 s___ ___ ___ in a h___ ___ ___ ___

7 g___ s___ ___ ___ ___ ___ ___ ___ ___ ___ ___ ___

2 Choose the correct options.

0 I got the best grade in my class. My parents are really **proud of** / **happy about** me.
1 Ana was **surprised by** / **disappointed with** the price. It was really cheap for a tablet.
2 Juliana is **angry with** / **scared of** water, so she never goes swimming.
3 The boys were really **disappointed with** / **interested in** the amusement park. It was terrible!
4 We go camping every year. We're **nervous about** / **bored of** it and we want to stay in a hotel!
5 Our hotel isn't very nice. Mom and Dad aren't **happy about** / **nervous about** it, so they're complaining to the manager.
6 My sister is **angry with** / **proud of** me because I lost her games console.
7 Joel is really **nervous about** / **crazy about** his new sneakers. He thinks they're perfect for basketball.

3 Complete the sentences with the words in the box.

canvas cardboard cotton glass leather plastic ~~rubber~~ wood

0 When I was four, my favorite birthday present was a ___rubber___ ball from my grandparents.
1 Rock stars often wear black ___________ jackets.
2 This backpack is made of strong ___________.
3 In summer, I wear ___________ T-shirts every day.
4 When we moved house, we put all our things in ___________ boxes.
5 My dad built this table with ___________ from an old tree in our yard.
6 Yesterday, my brother broke the ___________ in his bedroom window.
7 I have one ___________ water bottle, and I use it every day.

4 Read the two reviews. Choose the correct adjectives.

dark dirty hard ~~synthetic~~ thin

Don't stay in this hotel!

I stayed in the Riviera Hotel and it was terrible! The bed sheets were [0] ___synthetic___, the bed was very [1] ___________ and uncomfortable, and the duvet was really [2] ___________ – I was cold all night! Also, my room was [3] ___________ all day because the windows were really [4] ___________! Don't stay in this hotel!

light natural pale soft thick

I love my new sweatshirt!

My new sweatshirt is a beautiful [5] ___________ pink. It's made from 100% [6] ___________ materials, so it's very [7] ___________ next to my skin. It isn't [8] ___________, so you can wear it under a jacket. It feels very [9] ___________, but it keeps me warm and comfortable all day!

Grammar

1 Complete the sentences using *love, like,* or *hate* + *-ing*.

0 They ___hate sunbathing___. (hate / sunbathe)
1 I ______________. (not like / dance)
2 ______________? (you / like / hike)
3 My mom ______________. (love / jog)
4 He ______________ on weekends. (hate / study)
5 We ______________. (not like / swim)

2 Look at the pictures. Then write affirmative and negative sentences and questions with *would like*.

0 I / try / some new food
___I'd like to try some new food.___

1 we / not sleep / on a cold hard floor
____

2 you / live / in a wooden house / ?
____

3 she / eat / out tonight / ?
____

4 my brother / buy / that cotton T-shirt
____

5 they / visit / a museum
____

3 Complete the sentences. Use the superlative form of the highlighted adjectives.

0 Science is interesting, but I think geography is ___the most interesting___ subject.
1 The history exam was hard, but it wasn't ______________ exam. The math exam was worse!
2 This ice cream is good, but Gino's Deli makes ______________ ice cream.
3 Tina's funny, but she isn't ______________ person in our class.
4 Relax, you aren't bad at soccer. I think I'm ______________ player in the team!
5 Skateboarding and skiing are exciting, but I think surfing is ______________ sport.

4 Choose the correct options.

0 The beach is very busy. There are people (**everywhere**) / **nowhere**!
1 Did you go **anyone** / **anywhere** nice on vacation?
2 I want to buy **anything** / **something** in the gift store.
3 **No one** / **Nowhere** was at the hotel when we arrived.
4 I can't choose! I love **everyone** / **everything** on the menu!
5 We're lost! Let's ask **someone** / **no one** for help.

Look back: Units 1 and 2

Read the dialogue. Then choose the correct answers.

Jess Hey, how was your vacation! Your skin looks very [0] ___pale___!
Pablo Yeah I know. I didn't go to the [1] ______________.
Jess But you love [2] ______________! Were you sick?
Pablo No, the weather was terrible. I wore a [3] ______________ sweater for the entire vacation!
Jess Did you stay in a hotel?
Pablo Yes, but it was horrible. On the third night Dad ate [4] ______________ bad in the restaurant and was really sick.
Jess I'm sorry to hear that.
Pablo [5] ______________ you like to know the [6] ______________ part?
Jess Tell me.
Pablo All the museums ... we [7] ______________ about 100!

0	**a** heavy	**b** light	**c** pale
1	**a** beach	**b** gifts	**c** hiking
2	**a** sunbathe	**b** sunbathes	**c** sunbathing
3	**a** wooden	**b** woolen	**c** rubber
4	**a** anything	**b** nothing	**c** something
5	**a** Do	**b** Would	**c** Did
6	**a** the worst	**b** worst	**c** worse
7	**a** stayed	**b** went	**c** visited

CLIL A p.116

3 Responsible shopper

Metro VIDEO

Documentary
Our clothes

12 RESPONSIBLE CONSUMPTION AND PRODUCTION

Cole 3 hours ago
It's great that our old clothes have another life in Ghana!
But what's going to happen to traditional Ghanaian clothes?

42 Reply

A Video 36 **Watch or listen. Which clothes are cheaper? Choose the correct answer.**

a secondhand (old) clothes from Europe   b new clothes from Ghana

B **Watch or listen again. Choose the correct options.**

0 The presenter finds **good-quality** / **bad-quality** secondhand clothes in Ghana.
1 People in Ghana **pay for the clothes** / **get the clothes for free.**
2 Some workers make the clothes look **comfortable** / **new** before they sell them.
3 Traditional clothes in Ghana teach people about **reading and writing** / **the country's history**.
4 The historian is worried about the future of **traditional** / **secondhand** clothes.
5 Today **European** / **Ghanaian** clothes are becoming more popular in Ghana.

C **What is the message of the video? Choose the correct answer. Do you agree? Why? / Why not?**

a It's important to keep traditional things and remember your country's history.
b Modern things are always better, so we don't need to learn about the past.

Vocabulary LO Talk about money

Money

Super saver or big spender?

Check (✓) the sentences that are true for you!

A
- ☐ I save my money.
- ☐ I earn my own money.
- ☐ I lend money to friends.
- ☐ I spend my money on things I need.
- ☐ I pay for friends when they don't have money.

B
- ☐ I buy things I can't afford.
- ☐ I waste money on things I don't need.
- ☐ I borrow money from friends.
- ☐ I owe people money.
- ☐ I order a lot of things online.

1 37 **Look at the quiz. Match the highlighted verbs with the definitions. Listen, check, and repeat.**

0 ___pay___: to give money so that you can buy something
1 ____________: to get something from someone for a short time
2 ____________: to get money for doing work
3 ____________: to give something to someone for a short time
4 ____________: to keep money so that you can buy something later
5 ____________: to not buy or do something because you don't have the money
6 ____________: to use in a bad way
7 ____________: to use money to buy something
8 ____________: to need to give back money that someone gave you
9 ____________: to buy something online

2 Do the quiz. Go to page 126 to read your results. Then compare your answers with a partner.

3 Complete the conversations with the words in the box. There is one extra word you do not need.

borrow ~~can't afford~~ lend order owe spend waste

0 "Those sneakers are awesome, but I ___can't afford___ them."
"Don't worry. I can ____________ you some money."
1 "Can I ____________ some money for a soda?"
"No! You ____________ me $10 from last week!"
2 "Thanks for the birthday money! I want to ____________ it on something nice!"
"OK. But don't ____________ it on things you don't need!"

4 Your turn **Discuss the questions.**

1 What do you usually spend your money on?
2 What do you think you waste money on?

I spend my money on clothes!

Really? I prefer to save my money and spend it on something I really want!

International English
The schwa /ə/

Ade is from the U.K. He pronounces the vowels in unstressed syllables with the schwa sound /ə/. The historian, Osei-Bonsu, is from Ghana. He uses full vowel sounds.

Ade *So, are traditional prints still as popular, not just Kente, but the traditional clothing?*

Osei-Bonsu *Secondhand clothing brought in from Europe and America ... It's cheaper, far cheaper.*

D Video 38 **Read the International English box. Watch or listen to the examples. Which accent is easier to understand? Why?**

E Video 39 **Underline the schwa /ə/ sounds in the highlighted words. Then watch the video or listen and check.**

You've [0]gotta love this place. There's a guy just [1]over there who's turning [2]trousers into skirts. You've got this guy here, who's adding dye to jeans, making old [3]secondhand jeans look brand new.

Workbook p.136

12 RESPONSIBLE CONSUMPTION AND PRODUCTION

Instructions

1 40 **Read the instructions about saving money. Match the headings a–e with the steps 1–5. Then listen and check.**

- **a** Find the lowest price for things you want.
- **b** Think before you spend.
- **c** Sell the things you don't use.
- **d** Don't spend all your money!
- **e** Make a list of things you waste money on.

HOME | ADVICE | CONTACT

5 steps to becoming money smart

Step 1: _e_

Buy a notebook and start a money journal. There are apps for this, too! Write all the things you buy – and why. At the end of the week, check your journal. Did you waste any money? Make a plan: next week, I'm not going to spend any money on …

Step 2: ___

Use the 50:50 method to save money. Every time you get some money, save half of it. Of course, that doesn't mean you need to spend the other half! We're going to look at that next …

Step 3: ___

Don't go to malls on weekends or spend time on your favorite shopping websites. Before you need to go shopping, make a list of things you are going to buy. Always ask yourself these questions: Why do I want this? Do I need it? Can I afford it?

Step 4: ___

If you really need to buy something, be a smart shopper. Read reviews of the things you like, and then look online or in stores for the best price. Can you buy it secondhand for a lower price? People sell their old stuff every day. In fact, …

Step 5: ___

Look around your bedroom. Do you wear all those clothes? What about those books and toys? You can sell them online – it's a great way to earn money!

2 Complete the summary of each step with the words.

earn ~~learn~~ look for save waste

- **0** Use a notebook or an app to _learn_ how you spend money.
- **1** The 50:50 method means you ________ half of all the money you get.
- **2** Plan your shopping trips so you don't ________ your money and only buy the things you need.
- **3** Use the internet to ________ reviews and the best prices for things.
- **4** Sell your old stuff and ________ money at the same time!

3 Your turn **Discuss the questions.**

1. Do you use any of the tips in the article?
2. Which is the easiest step?
3. Which is the hardest?
4. Do you sell old things you don't use? How?
5. Can you think of another tip?

I use step 3. I always find the cheapest price online before I buy something!

Oh really? I just go to the mall!

Grammar

LO Use *be going to* to talk about plans and intentions

be going to (plans and intentions): affirmative and negative

1 41 **Read and listen to the Grammar in context. Is the sentence T (*true*) or F (*false*)?**

Pedro thinks he wasted his money on the jacket. T ☐ F ☐

Grammar in context — Present and Practice

In my money journal this week I wrote: *"On Tuesday 11/8 I bought an expensive new jacket – I need one for winter ..."* It looks great, but it's very thin. I think **I'm going to** return it. **I'm going to** spend half of the money on a better jacket and **I'm going to** save the rest. **I'm not going to** spend it on things I don't need. My friend Ava **is going to** do the same. We **aren't going to** waste our money!

Grammar notes p.137

2 Complete the chart with words from the Grammar in context.

Affirmative	Negative
I [0] *'m going to* return it.	I [1] ______ spend it on things I don't need.
You**'re going to** save some money.	You **aren't going to** wear the jacket.
Ava [2] ______ do the same.	She **isn't going to** buy things she can't afford.
We / You / They **are going to** meet at the mall.	We / You / They [3] ______ waste our money!

3 Pedro is talking to his mom about his plans for the weekend. Choose the correct options.

Pedro This weekend, [0] I **'s** / **('m)** going to do things differently. I'm not going to [1] **go** / **going** to the mall!

Mom Really? What are your plans?

Pedro Ava and I [2] **are going** / **going** to look in secondhand stores. Ava is going to [3] **look** / **looks** for some clothes, and I'm going [4] **buy** / **to buy** some books!

Mom Well, that sounds great. I'm ... surprised!

Pedro Yes! We [5] **aren't** / **don't** going to waste our money. We [6] **'re going** / **go** to be money smart!

Mom I like the sound of that!

4 42 **Listen and check.**

5 It's the end of the weekend. How did Pedro do? Use the prompts below to complete his journal.

Saturday:

I bought some secondhand jeans for $8! My old ones were too short for me. [0] *I'm going to wear* (I / wear) them to school. [1] ______ (I / not use) them for special occasions. I bought some books, too, for $3. [2] ______ (I / give) one to my brother for his birthday!

Sunday:

Ava and I went to a burger bar. But next week [3] ______ (we / not buy) any food in cafés or restaurants. [4] ______ (Ava / meet) me in the park for a picnic. In total, I only spent $18. [5] ______ (I / not spend) more than $20 each weekend. [6] ______ (I / save) my money and spend it on a new bike!

6 Read the introduction. Then complete the sentences with the affirmative or negative form of *be going to* and the verbs.

~~borrow~~ buy do waste

TeenSurveys: Summer is coming. Everyone has plans, but fun activities are often expensive! We asked students how they are going to save for the summer. Here are the best ideas.

0 I *'m going to borrow* some games from a friend.

1 I ______ any money on snacks.

2 We ______ any new clothes.

3 I ______ a lot of chores at home.

7 Your turn **Imagine you want to save money. Make sentences with the affirmative or negative form of *be going to*.**

I'm not going to drink any soda for a month.

3 Vocabulary

LO Talk about shopping

Shopping

1 🔊43 **Complete the conversations with the words. Listen and check.**

bargain cash change counter coupon ~~credit cards~~ discount price receipt sale

2 🔊44 **Listen and repeat.**

3 **Complete the sentences with the words. There is one extra word you do not need.**

0 Do you always check your ___change___ at the ___counter___? (credit card / counter / change)

1 Do you look for ____________ that give good ____________? (coupons / receipts / discounts)

2 Do you check ____________ on ____________? (credit cards / receipts / prices)

3 Do ____________ in your country offer good ____________? (bargains / cash / sales)

4 Do you use paper money – ____________ – or do you pay with a ____________? (credit card / cash / counter)

4 **Your turn** **Discuss the questions in exercise 3.**

> I never check my change because I always pay by credit card!

Listening Skills

LO Listen to conversations about shopping

At the store

1 🔊45 **Listen to the first part of a conversation. Choose the correct picture.**

2 🔊45 **Listen again. Complete the sentences with numbers.**

0 The T-shirt cost $40, but now it is only $ __20__.

1 Leah wants to borrow $____.

2 The coupon gives her a ____% discount.

3 Leah has $____.

3 🔊46 **Listen to the second part of the conversation. Choose the correct summary.**

a Leah can buy the T-shirt because Isaac lends her the money.

b Leah can buy the T-shirt because it's in the sale.

c Leah can buy the T-shirt because she uses the coupon.

4 🔊46 **Read the sentences. Listen again. Then complete the sentences.**

0 Leah takes the T-shirt to the __counter__.

1 She shows the ____________ on Isaac's phone to the sales clerk.

2 Leah can't use the coupon for clothes in the ____________.

3 Leah ____________ some money from Isaac.

4 Isaac's ____________ can buy Isaac's jacket because he's coming to the ____________ tomorrow.

5 Leah ____________ Isaac $5.

Pronunciation p.124 Workbook p.136

Grammar

LO Use *be going to* to ask about plans and intentions

be going to (plans and intentions): questions and short answers

1 47 **Read and listen to the Grammar in context. Choose the correct option.**

Leah's new T-shirt **is** / **isn't** OK for Hayleigh's party.

Grammar in context — Present and Practice

Isaac	When **are** you **going to** wear your T-shirt?
Leah	I'**m going to** wear it to Hayleigh's party.
Isaac	Are you sure?
Leah	Yes! Why? **Is** it **going to** be a formal party?
Isaac	Yes, it is.
Leah	**Are** the girls **going to** wear dresses?
Isaac	Yes, they are ... I think! **Are** you **going to** buy a new dress?
Leah	No, I'm not! I can't borrow any more money!

Grammar notes p.138

2 Complete the chart with words from the Grammar in context.

Questions	Short answers
Am I **going to** need something to wear?	Yes, you are. / No, you aren't.
[0] Are you **going to** buy a new dress?	Yes, I am. / No, I'm [1] ____.
[2] ____ it **going to** be formal?	Yes, it [3] ____. / No, it isn't.
Are you / we / they **going to** buy new dresses?	Yes, we / you / they are. / No, we / you / they aren't.
When [4] ____ you **going to** wear your T-shirt?	I'**m going to** wear it to Hayleigh's party.

3 Match the questions with the answers.

0 Daniel, are you going to keep the receipt? c
1 Are you and your friends going to pay by credit card? ____
2 What is Sofia going to buy? ____
3 Is the store going to close early? ____
4 Is the sales clerk going to check the price? ____
5 Are we going to need more money? ____
6 Jinho! When are you going to save some money? ____

a No, we aren't. I borrowed some from my dad.
b She's going to buy a new computer game.
c ~~Yes, I am. I always put them in my wallet.~~
d No, it isn't. It's open till 10 p.m. tonight.
e Yes, she is. We need to wait a few minutes.
f No, we aren't. We have cash.
g Soon! Very soon! But can I borrow some today?

4 Use *be going to* and the words to write questions for the pictures. Then write short answers.

0 Are you going to pay (you / pay) by credit card?
No, I'm not.

1 ____________ (he / buy) the pants?
____

2 ____________ (they /use) the coupon?
____

3 ____________ (I / be) free on Tuesday evening?
____

4 ____________ (Mom / lend) us the money?
____

5 ____________ (you / save) your cash?
____

5 48 **Listen and check.**

6 Find and correct one mistake in each question.

0 ~~Am~~ you going to go shopping this weekend? Are
1 What do you and your friends going to buy on your next shopping trip? ____
2 Are your parents going to lending you any money this week? ____
3 What are you go to save your money for? ____
4 How are you going be money smart this month? ____

7 Your turn **Discuss the questions in exercise 6.**

3 Listening Skills

LO Listen to a podcast and use context to guess meaning

The Outfit Repeater

1 49 **Listen to a podcast about fashion. What is the message? Choose the correct answer.**

a Fashion doesn't need to be expensive.
b The coolest clothes are in secondhand stores.

Active Listeners
Guessing meaning from context

Active listeners try to guess the meaning of new words. We can use the words before and after a new word to help us discover its meaning.

2 50 **Read the tip. Listen to the first part of the podcast. Can you explain these words in your own language?**

1 vlogger 2 haul

3 49 **Listen to the whole podcast again. Answer the questions with a maximum of four words.**

0 What is Hannah Rupp's job?
She's a fashion vlogger.
1 What does Hannah Rupp look for in secondhand clothes stores?
______
2 What does she do when she's bored of a piece of clothing?
______
3 What is The Outfit Repeater?
______
4 When did she start The Outfit Repeater?
______
5 Who can afford great fashion?
______

4 Your turn **Do you buy secondhand things? Why? / Why not? Discuss with a partner.**

I often buy secondhand video games because you can find great bargains.

I don't. I like spending my money on new things.

Reading Skills

LO Read forum posts and understand pronoun references

Forum posts

1 51 **Read and listen to the forum posts. Match the people with their opinions about shopping.**

0 Caleb *d*
1 Paco ____
2 Beth ____
3 Keiko ____

a "I have better things to do than go shopping."
b "I enjoy it, but I need to change my shopping habits!"
c "I go shopping regularly, but I don't spend a lot of money."
~~d "I prefer shopping online to stores."~~

2 **Read again. Write the names.**

0 Who doesn't have a job? *Paco*
1 Who likes going to sales? ____
2 Who doesn't like going to stores? ____
3 Who sometimes makes bad decisions in stores? ____
4 Who is going to borrow money for something expensive? ____
5 Who does research online before buying things? ____
6 Who is saving for an event at the moment? ____
7 Who only goes shopping when it's necessary? ____

Active Readers
Understanding pronoun references

Active readers can understand who or what pronouns refer to in a text. We often use pronouns when we do not want to repeat a word or phrase.

*I love reading reviews of things before I buy **them**.*

3 **Read the tip. Find the highlighted words in the forum posts. What do they refer to?**

0 It
(a) reading reviews
b computer games
c burgers

1 mine
a Beth's friend
b Beth's bike
c Beth's life

2 some
a concert tickets
b money
c small things

3 them
a shoes
b sales
c receipts

4 Your turn **Are you most like Caleb, Paco, Beth, or Keiko? Discuss with a partner and give reasons for your answers.**

I think I'm most like Caleb because I always shop online.

Oh really? I'm most like Keiko. I love looking for bargains, and I never keep receipts!

What kind of shopper are you?

Treasure

Treasure community > Shopping

Moderator

We all do it. Most of us love it. What about you?

Caleb, *the U.K.*

I don't like going to the shopping centre because the shops are always really crowded. I buy almost everything online – from computer games to burgers. I love reading reviews of things that I want before I buy them. It's a lot of fun! I borrow my parents' credit card and then I give them the money.

Beth, *the U.S.*

I only go shopping when I need to – for clothes or presents. Shopping is OK, but I have more interesting hobbies. Right now, I'm saving for a bike like my friend's. Mine is getting old. My parents are going to lend me some money, too.

Paco, *Argentina*

I go to the mall every weekend, but not because I love shopping. I usually meet friends there. I always think "I'm not going to buy anything," but I often buy something small. I save my money every week, too. Right now, it's for some concert tickets. I don't earn any money, but I get some from my parents every week.

Keiko, *Japan*

I always feel excited when I buy something. I love bargains, so I love shopping in sales. I sometimes waste a lot of money on shoes. I take them home and I think, "Am I really going to wear those sandals?" I know it's a good idea to keep receipts and return stuff, but I don't.

Buy

Buy

Buy

Buy

Buy

Buy

International English

shopping centre (UK) = mall (US)

shop (UK) = store (US)

3 Speaking & Global Skills

LO Use functional language in a clothes store

Clothes shopping

1 52 **Read and listen. Is the customer going to buy the jacket?** ____________

Customer Excuse me, can I try on this jacket?
Sales clerk Sure! The changing rooms are right here.
Customer Great, thanks.

Later ...

Sales clerk So, how does it fit?
Customer It's a bit big. Do you have a smaller size?
Sales clerk Sorry, we only have this one left. But did you know it's in the sale? There's a 50% discount!
Customer Wow, that's a bargain! But ... it really doesn't fit. Thanks anyway.
Sales clerk Sure, no problem! Can I help you with anything else?
Customer No, I'm OK for now, thanks. I'm only going to buy things on my list today.

2 53 **Listen and repeat.**

Active Speakers
A clothes store

Active speakers use these phrases in a clothes store:

Can I try on this / these ... ?
It's / They're a bit big / small.
Do you have a smaller size / bigger size / different color?
It (really) doesn't fit / They (really) don't fit.
Thanks anyway.
No, I'm OK for now, thanks.

3 54 **Read the tip. Then complete the conversation with words from the tip. Then listen and check.**

Customer Can I [0] try on these sunglasses?
Sales clerk Of course. There's a mirror over there. How do they fit?
Customer Well, I like them, but they're [1] ____________ big.
Sales clerk They're usually $20. But there's a 50% discount on them today only.
Customer Wow, that's so cheap. But look, they really don't [2] ____________! Thanks [3] ____________.
Sales clerk Oh, that's a shame. Can I help you with anything else?
Customer No, I'm [4] ____________, thanks. I need to save my money at the moment.
Sales clerk Sure. No problem.

Global Skills
Shopping responsibly

12 RESPONSIBLE CONSUMPTION AND PRODUCTION

Fashion changes very quickly. People often buy things and only wear them a few times. Here are some ways we can shop responsibly:

- Make a list of what you're going to buy.
- Think: how many times am I going to use this?
- Don't buy something just because it's cheap!

4 **Read the Global Skills box. Then read the conversation in exercise 1 again. Answer the questions below.**

1 How does the Sales clerk try to sell the jacket to the customer?

____

2 How does the customer shop in a responsible way?

____

____

____

5 **Copy the chart into your notebook. Complete it with your own ideas about three items of clothing you want to buy.**

Item	Reason to buy	Reasons not to buy
sandals	in fashion	I'm not going to wear them often

6 **In pairs, have a conversation. Take turns to be the customer and the Sales clerk in a clothes store. Use the model below and the conversation in exercise 1.**

Customer	Sales clerk
Excuse me, can I try on this/these ... ?	Sure! The changing rooms are right here.
It's/They're a bit ... Do you have a ... ?	How does it/do they fit?
Wow, that's ... ! But ...	Sorry, we only have this/these one(s) left. But did you know ... ?
No, I'm OK for now, thanks.	Can I help you with anything else?

Watch

LO Understand a video about shopping habits

Shopping habits in the U.S.

Before you watch

1 **Look at the pictures on the right. Which type of shopping do you prefer? Why?**

A mall

An outdoor market

2 **Video** **Match the sentence halves. Then watch the video and check your answers.**

0 Do you like shopping __c__   a usually go shopping?
1 Where do you ____   b thing about going to the mall?
2 What's the best ____   ~~c for clothes?~~
3 Do you look for ____   d most of your money on?
4 What do you spend ____   e bargains when you go shopping?

While you watch

3 **Video** **Watch the video and complete the chart.**

Who …	Rob	Tripp	Amy	Vicky
0 likes shopping for clothes?			✓	
1 doesn't go to the mall?				
2 never goes to the mall alone?				
3 doesn't look for bargains?				
4 spends most of their money on clothes?				
5 spends money on camping equipment?				
6 does chores for money?				
7 reads reviews for games?				

4 **Video** **Watch again. Complete the sentences.**

0 Rob loves looking at __cameras__.
1 Amy says it's fun to spend time with ________ at the mall.
2 Vicky hates ________.
3 Rob loves finding ________ on the internet.
4 Vicky spends money going to the ________ and on meals.
5 When Vicky borrows money from Amy, she ________ returns it.
6 Amy can't afford to ________ money.

After you watch

5 **Read the Global Skills box. Interview your friends. Use the questions in exercise 2 or your own ideas. Do you have similar opinions about shopping?**

Do you like shopping?

Yes, I do. I love it!

Global Skills
Showing empathy for others

Everybody has different likes, dislikes, and perspectives. But it doesn't mean we can't be friends!

Project p.110

4 Big issues

Metro VIDEO

Documentary
The climate heroes

Ava 10 hours ago
These children are so smart! I think their invention will really help people.

13 Reply

A Video 55 **Watch or listen. What does the children's invention do?**

a It tells you when there's a problem in a forest.
b It puts out fires with water.
c It plants trees in forests.

B **Watch or listen again. Complete the sentences with one word.**

0 These children, from California in the U.S., are taking part in a _science_ competition.
1 California has a global connection to _________ because they have the same climate.
2 They want to put cameras in the _________.
3 People can see images from the cameras on the internet and look for _________.
4 The children's invention is _________ to use.
5 The children _________ the international competition.

C **Do you think the children's invention is a good idea? Add good points and bad points to the chart.**

Good points	Bad points
• free	• false alarms

Vocabulary

LO Talk about human-caused and natural problems

Human-caused and natural problems

1 56 **Match the words with the pictures. Listen, check, and repeat.**

climate change disease drought earthquake flood ~~heat wave~~ overpopulation pollution war wildfire

0 heat wave

1 ______

2 ______

3 ______

4 ______

5 ______

6 ______

7 ______

8 ______

9 ______

2 **Choose the correct options.**

Did you know?

- The longest [0] **heat wave** / **overpopulation** was in Marble Bar, Australia in 1924. It was hotter than 100°F (37.8°C) for five months.
- The Three Hundred and Thirty-Five Years' [1] **earthquake** / **war** is the longest conflict in history. It was between the British Scilly Isles and the Netherlands and lasted from 1651 until 1986.
- One of the longest [2] **diseases** / **droughts** was in Australia, from 1996 until 2010. The government paid $4.5 billion to farmers who didn't have any water.
- A [3] **wildfire** / **pollution** can travel up to 20 km/h. That's faster than a typical cyclist.
  As a result of [4] **climate change** / **floods**, ice in the Arctic is disappearing.

3 **Your turn** **Which of the problems in exercise 1 is most common in your country?**

International English
Linking

The speakers in the video are from the U.S. They often link two words so that they sound like one word. This happens when a word ends with a consonant sound and the next word begins with a vowel sound.

What is a problem, in our community, related to the climate?'

D Video 57 **Read the International English box. Watch or listen to the example from the video.**

E Video 58 **Watch or listen to the extracts from the video. Write two words in each blank.**

0 Then you have to find a global connection which is some place ______ the world ...
1 ... that ______ similar climate to us ______ similar problem.
2 ... they ______ huge problem with ______ there.
3 This enables the public to be the forest guards, to ______ forests safe.
4 ______ the teams is from Australia ...

Pronunciation p.124 Workbook p.140

13 CLIMATE ACTION

An article

1 59 **Read and listen to the article. Which problem do you think is the most serious? Why?**

Our biggest challenges (part 1)

In the future, our planet will face many challenges. But will they come from space, the Earth, or even from ourselves?

Space

On February 15, 2013, an asteroid entered the Earth's atmosphere over Russia. When it exploded, 30 km above the ground, it was traveling at about 65,000 km/h. Many glass windows broke in the explosion and about 1,000 people were injured. The largest piece of the asteroid landed in a lake. Many scientists think that another large asteroid will hit the Earth one day. It will probably land in the ocean, and it will cause floods.

The Earth

From March to May, 2010, a volcanic eruption in Iceland created an enormous cloud over Europe. It didn't cause any injuries or disease, but planes couldn't fly for more than a week. The eruption cost $7.3 billion. But that was just a normal volcano. Supervolcanoes are over 1,000 times bigger. There is one under Yellowstone Park in the U.S. It is about the same size as Mount Everest. One day, it will erupt!

Humans

By 2050, experts think there will be over 9.7 billion people on the planet. They worry that many people won't have food, water, or homes. Cities will become more crowded; traffic and pollution will get worse. More people will use more energy, and this will cause climate change, too. Is overpopulation our biggest challenge?

2 Read the article again. Choose the correct answer.

0 The asteroid ...
- a exploded on the ground.
- b hit Russia 30 km from a city.
- c landed in the ocean.
- (d) broke windows in buildings.

1 The volcano in Iceland ...
- a was a supervolcano.
- b hurt lots of people.
- c caused problems for travelers.
- d erupted for a week.

2 The article says that ...
- a experts think that cities are bad places to live.
- b people don't have the energy they need.
- c overpopulation causes environmental problems.
- d traffic creates the most pollution.

3 Read again. Complete the sentences with one word.

0 The asteroid in Russia hurt about 1,000 people.

1 A large asteroid in the ocean can create a ________________.

2 For three ________________, there was an enormous cloud over Europe.

3 The Yellowstone Park ________________ is the size of Mount Everest.

4 The ________________ of the world will be 9.7 billion in 2050.

5 ________________ is possibly the world's most serious problem.

4 Your turn **Which facts from the article surprise you the most? Discuss with a partner.**

I'm really surprised by the asteroid!

I didn't know about the one in Russia!

Grammar

LO Use *will / won't* to make predictions about the future based on opinion

will / won't (future predictions)

1 🔊60 **Read and listen to the Grammar in context. How do humans really feel about the possibility of alien life?**

Grammar in context — Present and Practice

Scientists believe we **will** find alien life in space one day. But how **will** people react to this challenge? Movies and TV shows tell us that we **won't** be very happy: we**'ll** fight wars and the aliens **will** try to destroy us! But in reality, recent surveys tell us something different. People **will** be pleased. Finally we**'ll** know that we aren't here alone!

Grammar notes p.141

2 **Complete the chart with words from the Grammar in context.**

We use *will / won't* to make predictions about the future based on opinion.

Affirmative	Negative
People ⁰ __will__ be pleased.	We ¹ ______ be very happy.
Questions	**Short answers**
Will we find alien life in space?	Yes, we will. / No, we won't.
How ² ______ people react?	

Stop

We can contract *will* with subject pronouns.
We'll (= We will) know that we aren't alone.
You'll (= You will) be happy.

3 **Look at the pictures. Complete the sentences with *'ll* or *won't* and the verbs.**

0 You __'ll like__ this movie. (like)

1 I ____________ any goals today. (score)

2 I ____________ in a big house like that one day. (live)

3 She ____________ a software developer one day. (be)

4 **Make questions about the future with the words.**

>> In 25 years ...

0 a robot / every home / will / have / ?
__Will every home have a robot?__

1 will / cash / people / use / ?
____

>> In 50 years ...

2 people / drive / cars / will / ?
____

3 on vacation in space / go / will / tourists / ?
____

>> In 100 years ...

4 live / people / on a different planet / will / ?
____

5 will / exist / diseases / ?
____

5 🔊61 **Listen and check.**

Stop

After *I think / I don't think*, use *will*, not *won't*.
*I **think** it **will** rain.* *I **don't think** it **will** rain.*

6 **Your turn** **What do you think? In pairs, use *I think / I don't think* to answer the questions in exercise 4.**

I don't think people will drive cars. Travel will be relaxing.

I disagree. I think people will drive cars, but they'll be electric.

Workbook p.141 Metro Express p.111

Environmental problems and solutions

1 Match the problems with the solutions.

Problems	Solutions
0 We are **running out** of the world's natural resources. b	**a** We need to **protect** the places where they live.
1 We **throw away** a lot of things. ___	**b** We have to **save** resources like water and electricity.
2 Animals are **becoming extinct**. ___	**c** We should: • **reduce** the number of things we buy. • **reuse** things like water bottles and bags. • **recycle** – don't put everything in the trash!

2 62 Match the highlighted words in exercise 1 with the definitions. Listen, check, and repeat.

0 become extinct : when a plant or animal doesn't exist anymore
1 ______________ : to finish or use all of something
2 ______________ : to keep something safe
3 ______________ : to use less of something and not waste it
4 ______________ : to make something less or smaller
5 ______________ : to put something in the trash
6 ______________ : to use something again
7 ______________ : to make trash into something that we can use again

3 Your turn Discuss the questions.

1 How can you save natural resources in your daily life?
2 What things do you reuse and recycle at home?
3 Which animals are in danger of becoming extinct in your country?

I think I can save water.
I can take shorter showers.

Listening Skills

14 LIFE BELOW WATER

LO Listen to a presentation about an invention that can reduce pollution

The Ocean Cleanup

1 Look at the items. Do you know how long they take to decompose? Match the items with the times.

3–4 weeks 50–100 years 450–1,000 years ~~never~~

0 never

1 ______________

2 ______________

3 ______________

2 63 Listen to the presentation. What is Boyan Slat's company trying to do?

a collect plastic in the ocean
b stop plastic going into the ocean
c recycle plastic we only use once
d make swimming safe

3 63 Listen again. Choose the correct options.

0 About 8 million **tons** / **kilograms** of plastic go into the ocean every year.
1 Every year, about **100,000** / **1 million** sea birds die from eating plastic.
2 *The Ocean Cleanup*'s plastic tube is 600 **meters** / **kilometers** long.
3 In **2018** / **2019** the tube collected plastic for the first time.
4 Boyan is going to recycle the plastic to make **a new tube** / **different products**.
5 In five **months** / **years** the project will reduce the plastic pollution in the worst part of the Pacific Ocean by **50%** / **60%**.

Boyan Slat's invention

Workbook p.140

Grammar

LO Use *be going to* to make predictions about the future based on evidence

be going to (future predictions)

1 64 **Read and listen to the Grammar in context. What problems do you think the Great Pacific Garbage Patch causes?**

Grammar in context — **Present and Practice**

Boyan's Slat's *The Ocean Cleanup* project focuses on the Great Pacific Garbage Patch – an enormous area of plastic in the Pacific Ocean. When a piece of plastic enters the Pacific, research tells us that it **is** probably **going to** reach the garbage patch. Photos of the patch's size indicate that it **isn't going to** disappear. A report from *The Ocean Cleanup* also said that it **is going to** grow bigger. Luckily, Boyan Slat is working hard to protect our planet.

Grammar notes p.142

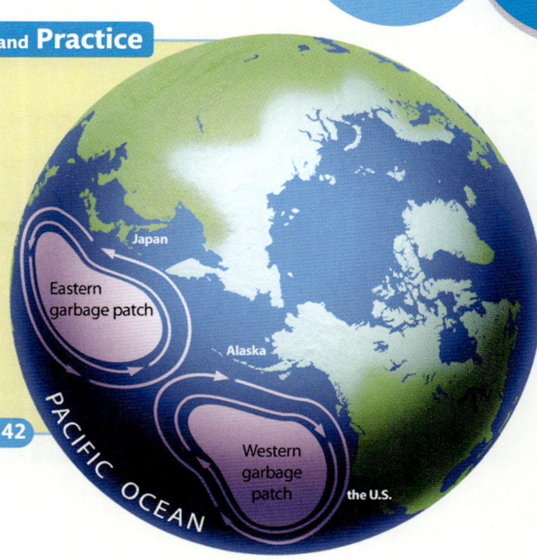

2 Complete the chart with words from the Grammar in context.

We use *be going to* to make predictions based on present evidence.	A report said that the Great Pacific Garbage patch [1] __________ bigger. The patch's size indicates that it [2] __________.

Stop

Remember we also use *be going to* to talk about plans and intentions.

*I'm **going to** meet some friends at the mall later.*

3 Look at the pictures. Complete the predictions with the correct form of *be going to*.

0 The volcano __is going to__ erupt.

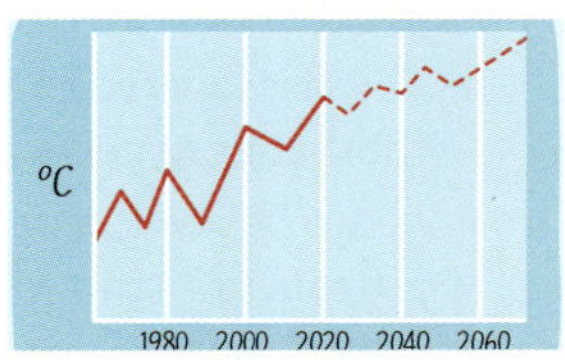

1 The temperature on Earth __________ increase.

2 These people __________ clean up the beach.

3 They __________ become extinct.

4 The traffic __________ get worse.

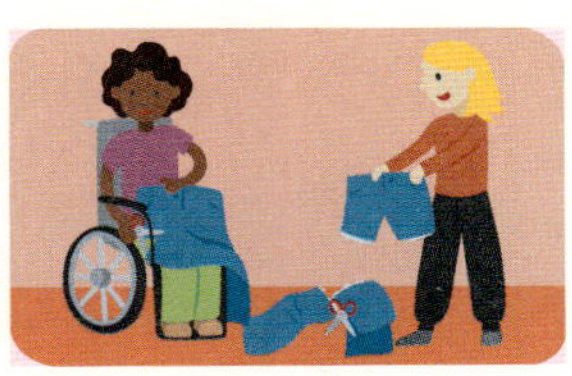

5 We __________ recycle our old clothes.

4 Read the situations. Then complete the sentences with the affirmative or negative of *be going to* and the verbs.

~~be~~ become have run out

0 Amy is recycling her sister's jeans, but her sister doesn't know.
Amy's sister __isn't going to be__ happy.

1 Robots can do a lot of boring jobs.
People __________ more time for creative activities in the future.

2 There's a drought and Jason is worried about the animals on his farm.
__________ the farm
__________ of water?

3 Zoos are working hard to protect different species of animals.
The animals __________ extinct.

5 65 **Listen and check.**

6 Choose the correct options. Use *be going to* for predictions based on present evidence, and *will* for predictions based on opinions.

0 One day, I think we **will** / **are going to** stop fighting wars.

1 Look at all this rain! There **will** / **is going to** be a flood.

2 I believe that in the future humans **will** / **are going to** live for hundreds of years.

3 Mom is collecting our old plastic bottles. **Is she going to** / **Will she** recycle them?

7 Your turn Read the facts below. With a partner, make predictions using your own ideas and *be going to*. Use the vocabulary from the unit.

1 Our planet is getting warmer.

2 The world's population is growing.

3 Countries are recycling more plastic.

4 A lot of countries are planting more trees.

Our planet is getting warmer. That means we're going to have more heat waves.

4 Listening Skills

LO Listen to a news report and take notes about important details

School climate strike

1 🔊66 **Listen to the first part of a news report. What happens during a school climate strike?**

a Students talk about the environment at school.
b Students don't go to school because they want to protest and protect the environment.
c Students walk to school to protect the environment.

2 🔊67 **Listen to the whole report. Are the sentences T (*true*) or F (*false*)?**

		T	F
0	The reporter is at a climate strike.	☑	☐
1	Ria thinks that only students will come to the event.	☐	☐
2	The plan is to speak to someone from the government.	☐	☐
3	The reporter asks Ria about the students' education.	☐	☐
4	Ria wants to recycle more trash.	☐	☐

Active Listeners
Taking notes

Active listeners think about what information they need, and take notes about the most important details.

3 🔊67 **Read the tip. Then read the notes below. What information do you need? Listen again and complete the notes.**

Location of climate strike: [0] Wellington
Number of people: [1] ______
Plan: give a [2] ______ to the government.
Future problems: more droughts, [3] ______ and floods in New Zealand
Objective: country will take more action against [4] ______.

4 ➔ Your turn **Discuss the questions.**

1 Are there school climate strikes in your country?
2 Do you think school climate strikes will make a difference around the world?

In my country, there are sometimes climate strikes in the capital city.

Reading Skills

LO Read comments and recognize opinions

Readers' comments

1 **Look quickly at the readers' comments on page 51. Match the name of the person with the topic.**

0 Pedro b
1 Alyssa ____
2 Scott ____

a space
b the Earth
c humans

Active Readers
Recognizing opinions

Active readers can recognize people's opinions. Sometimes these opinions are implicit. We can look for positive / negative adjectives, words like *but*, and modal verbs like *need to* and *can*.

2 🔊68 **Read the tip. Then read and listen to the comments. Choose the correct opinions.**

0 Pedro thinks ...
(a) volcanoes are a bigger threat than supervolcanoes.
b we need to study supervolcanoes carefully.

1 Alyssa thinks richer countries need to ...
a share their resources with poorer countries.
b reduce their use of resources.

2 Scott thinks ...
a scientists can protect the planet from asteroids.
b there is a high chance of an asteroid disaster.

3 **Read the comments again. Are the sentences T (*true*), F (*false*), or NG (*not given*)?**

		T	F	NG
0	The last supervolcano erupted thousands of years ago.	☑	☐	☐
1	Pedro believes people in his area are safe from the volcano.	☐	☐	☐
2	People in many richer countries use 90 kg of resources a day.	☐	☐	☐
3	People in richer countries need to do more to protect the environment.	☐	☐	☐
4	Things from space don't often enter our atmosphere.	☐	☐	☐

4 ➔ Your turn **In pairs, discuss the questions.**

1 Do you agree with Pedro, Alyssa, and Scott?
2 Can you think of any other solutions to the problems?

I agree with Alyssa. I think we can save resources and reuse more things!

Me too! I also agree with Pedro. We don't need to worry about things like supervolcanoes. There are more important problems!

Our biggest challenges (part 2)

Home | News | Readers' comments | Videos

Pedro, Chaitén, Chile

Interesting article, but there aren't many supervolcanoes in the world and the last one erupted in New Zealand – 27,000 years ago. This isn't going to be a global problem! It's more important to reduce the risk to populations near smaller volcanoes. I live near the Chaitén Volcano in southern Chile. When it last erupted in 2008, the government acted quickly and evacuated the area in 24 hours. But the next time it happens, will everyone escape?

Alyssa, Oregon, U.S.

Overpopulation doesn't need to be a problem. There is space for everyone on our planet. People in richer countries simply need to change their lifestyles. At the moment, a person in the U.S. uses about 90 kg of water, energy, materials, and land every day! In some poorer countries, it's only 10 kg! People in richer countries can save more energy, reuse things, and recycle more trash. When we do that, things are going to get better!

Scott, Leeds, U.K.

The asteroid in Russia caused a lot of problems, but about 100,000 kg of material enters our atmosphere from outer space every day! Scientists have the technology to protect our planet from asteroids. They also watch the largest asteroids in space carefully. They think there is only a very small chance that one will hit us in the next 100 years.

Workbook p.143 Writing Skills p.103

4 Speaking & Global Skills LO Exchange opinions

Exchange opinions

1 69 **Read and listen. Does Elias believe the story about polar bears?**

Elias Wow, this social media post says that the number of polar bears in the Arctic is growing! What do you think?
Zoe Hmm ... It's difficult to say.
Elias It's great news. It'll show that climate change isn't happening. So the polar bears are safe!
Zoe I disagree, Elias. Personally, I think that climate change is a serious problem! I mean, think about all the wildfires and floods in the news. But let's check the story. Can you find it anywhere else?
Elias Let's see ... The *New York Times* mentions it here!
Zoe Yes, but look! It says the story isn't true.
Elias Oh, right. Are you saying that it's fake news? Well ... I guess I'm not going to send this to anyone!

2 70 **Listen and repeat.**

Active Speakers
Exchanging opinions

Active speakers use expressions like *What do you think?* and *Personally, I think that ...* to ask for and give opinions. For difficult questions, we can say *It's difficult to say ...* . When things aren't clear, we use phrases like *I mean* and *Are you saying that ... ?*.

3 71 **Read the tip. Then order the words to make some of the phrases from the tip. Then listen and check.**

0 say / to / it's / difficult
It's difficult to say
1 think / I / personally, / that
______
2 that / you / saying / are /
______
3 you / do / think / what / ?
______
4 mean / I
______

Global Skills
Identifying fake news

16 PEACE, JUSTICE AND STRONG INSTITUTIONS

Not all news on social media is true! When you aren't sure about a story, follow this checklist:

1 Check news websites you can trust. Is the story there?
2 Check spelling and punctuation! Fake news posts often have spelling and punctuation mistakes.
3 If you think the story is fake, tell the sender and don't share it.

4 **Read the Global Skills box. Look at the conversation in exercise 1 again. Which points from the checklist do Elias and Zoe follow?**

____ and ____

5 **In pairs, look at the social media post. Find two mistakes with spelling and two mistakes with punctuation.**

Climet change isn't real!

Last year had one of the coldest winter's on record. This shows that climate change isn't hapening. Scientists are inventing story's because they want to make money!

6 **In pairs, have a conversation about the social media post. Use the model below and the conversation in exercise 1.**

Wow, this social media post says that ... What do you think ... ?
Hmm ... It's difficult to say.
Look, it also says that ...
I disagree. Personally, I think that ... I mean, ...
Are you saying that ... ?
Yes, the post is wrong!
Oh, right. Well, I guess ...

11 SUSTAINABLE CITIES AND COMMUNITIES

A smart city Songdo, South Korea

Before you watch

1 Look at the pictures. Describe the cities with the words and your own ideas.

clean crowded green noisy open polluted quiet

2 Answer the questions.

1 Does your city or town have parks or green spaces? Where?
2 Which parts of your city or town are crowded? When are they the most crowded?
3 How do most commuters get to work in your town or city?

While you watch

3 Video Watch the video and choose the correct options.

0 Seoul is a **smart** / **big** city.
1 Songdo is a **new** / **polluted** city.
2 Songdo has a lot of **green space** / **traffic**.
3 Computer technology helps Songdo to **protect animals** / **recycle waste**.
4 Smart cities **help** / **cause** problems such as overpopulation and climate change.

4 Video Watch again. Complete the sentences.

0 Nearly ___26___ million people live in Seoul.
1 Songdo is about ______ km from Seoul.
2 Songdo is called a ______ city because it has lots of things that protect the environment.
3 In the middle of Songdo, there's a large ______.
4 Songdo has ______ apartments.
5 The city uses ______ to make energy.
6 There is space in Songdo for new ______.
7 Families love Songdo because of the ______.

After you watch

5 Read the Global Skills box. Then discuss the questions.

1 How similar is your hometown to Seoul? Why?
2 How similar is your hometown to Songdo? Why?
3 How do you think your city will change in the future?

My hometown is very different from Seoul. It's a lot smaller!

Global Skills
Being curious about other cultures

The modern world is very connected, so it helps to be curious about other cultures. You can learn about what things are similar and different in other countries. This will give you more perspective to think about your own life.

Project p.111

B Review

Vocabulary

1 Complete the money verbs in the conversation.

Sophie Dad, can I [0]bo _r_ _r_ _o_ _w_ $30 for a new tennis racket?

Dad But you got $50 for your birthday last weekend. What did you [1]sp___ ___ ___ it on?

Sophie I went to the movies three times last week.

Dad You [2]c___ _n_ '___ aff___ ___ ___ to do that! You need to [3]s___ ___ ___ some money. I'm not going to [4]le___ ___ you any money, Sophie. Sorry.

Sophie Dad!

Dad But you can [5]ea___ ___ some money. What about cleaning the car for me?

Sophie Are you going to [6]pa___ me $30 for cleaning the car? Great!

Dad No, I'm not! I'm going to make a list of chores. And when you finish them, you can have $30. And don't [7]wa___ ___ ___ it!

2 Complete the sentences with the shopping nouns.

change counter coupon discount price receipt ~~sale~~

1 **Sophie** I love this sports store. They have a great _sale_ at the moment.

2 **Sophie** Wow. The ______ for this was $40. But now it's $20! That's a 50% ______!

3 **Sophie** I also have a ______ for 25% off. That means it's only $15!

4 **Sophie** Excuse me. Where's the ______?
Sales clerk It's over there.

5 **Sales clerk** Here's your ______, $5. And also your ______.

3 Label the pictures of human-caused and natural problems.

~~climate change~~ disease drought earthquake flood heat wave overpopulation wildfire

0 _climate change_

1 ______

2 ______

3 ______

4 ______

5 ______

6 ______

7 ______

4 Match the sentence halves.

0 Don't throw away _d_
1 We need to protect ___
2 The world is going to run out ___
3 Remember to keep and reuse ___
4 We're going to reduce ___
5 Take shorter showers and ___
6 It's easy to recycle paper, ___
7 The Tasmanian tiger ___

a your plastic bags.
b of oil and gas in 100 years.
c our natural environment.
~~d those boots. You can sell them online.~~
e glass, and metal.
f became extinct in the 1930s.
g our carbon emissions by 20%.
h save water!

Grammar

1 Complete the sentences with the affirmative (✓) or negative (✗) form of *be going to* and the verbs.

buy ~~have~~ lend take throw away use

0 Jenny ___is going to have___ a sleepover on Friday. (✓)
1 I ______ those canvas pants. I can't afford them. (✗)
2 We ______ $300 with us on vacation. (✓)
3 My parents ______ me some money for the ski trip. (✓)
4 Archie ______ that coupon. Do you want it? (✗)
5 Roberta and I ______ these glass bottles. We want to reuse them. (✗)

2 Reorder the words to make questions. Then write affirmative (✓) and negative (✗) answers.

0 any money / to / you / borrow / going / are
___Are you going to borrow any money?___
___Yes, I am.___ (✓)
1 going / the receipt / she / to / is / keep
______
______ (✓)
2 throw away / going / is / Dad / to / those bags
______
______ (✗)
3 to / they / save / are / going / their Christmas money
______
______
______ (✗)

3 Complete the predictions with *will* / *'ll* or *won't*.

I love studying in high school so I [0]___'ll go___ (go) to college. I think I [1]______ (choose) science or geography because I want to protect the environment. I [2]______ (study) history. I'm not good with dates!

I have a good feeling about today's protest against the new road. I think the local government [3]______ (listen) to us and do more to protect local wildlife. They probably [4]______ (say) anything immediately, but I think our efforts are making a difference. It [5]______ (be) great for the animals in our area.

4 Complete the predictions with the correct form of *be going to* or short answers.

Abi Is it cold today? [0]___Am___ I ___going to need___ (need) a sweater?
Fran Yes, you [1]______. It's really cold. I think it [2]______ (snow) later!

Adam Do you want to go shopping tomorrow?
Zac Yes! There's a sale at our favorite store!
Adam I know! I think we [3]______ (find) some great bargains!

Kris [4]______ the heat wave ______ (end) soon?
Amy No, it [5]______. The weather report said the weather [6]______ (get) cooler before next weekend.

Livia Watch out! You [7]______ (fall)!
Jude No, I [8]______. I know there's a hole in the sidewalk, so I [9]______ (walk) into it!

Look back: Units 3 and 4

Read the blog post. Then choose the correct answers.

Dan's blog

Clothing for our planet

I love [0]___spending___ my money on clothes. I love looking for [1]______ – and it's easy to find cheap clothes! But a lot of people buy cheap clothes and then [2]______ them away – and this is bad for the environment. The chemicals from the clothing industry cause a lot of [3]______ on our planet. And without change, things are [4]______ to get worse.
So I [5]______ do something about this. From now on, I'm going to buy all my clothes in secondhand stores. What [6]______ my friends think? I don't know, but I hope they'll do the same! What are your plans to help the planet? [7]______ join me?

	a	b	c
0	a spending	b lending	c earning
1	a bargains	b counters	c receipts
2	a reduce	b protect	c throw
3	a overpopulation	b pollution	c wildfires
4	a will	b goes	c going
5	a am going to	b will	c won't
6	a are	b will	c going
7	a Do you	b You will	c Are you going to

CLIL B p.118

5 Good job!

Metro VIDEO

Nina's vlog
Life as an athlete

Maira 1 hour ago
For athletes, I think the most important things are hard work and practice, but they also need natural ability!
42 Reply

A Video 72 **Watch or listen. What is Nina's vlog about?**

- **a** The differences between dance and sport
- **b** Doing more than one sport at the same time
- **c** The things all athletes have in common

B Watch or listen again. Are the sentences T (*true*) or F (*false*)?

0	Nina wants to be a professional dancer.	T ☑	F ☐
1	Nina started dancing when she was eight years old.	T ☐	F ☐
2	She also tried swimming and surfing.	T ☐	F ☐
3	Now she practices her dancing every day.	T ☐	F ☐
4	Nina says surfing has similarities to dancing.	T ☐	F ☐
5	All athletes practice with a teacher or coach.	T ☐	F ☐

C What does Nina need to get her dream job? Put the things below in order from 1 (= very important) to 6 (= not very important). Is this order the same for all jobs?

- **a** ___ hard work
- **b** ___ luck
- **c** ___ money
- **d** ___ motivation
- **e** ___ natural ability
- **f** ___ a teacher

Vocabulary LO Talk about the job I want to do

Jobs

What job do you want to do?

1 73 **Look at the pictures and choose the correct options. Listen, check, and repeat.**

0 (nurse) / builder
1 chef / firefighter
2 doctor / lawyer
3 fashion designer / salesperson
4 soldier / software developer
5 police officer / hairdresser

2 74 **Read the sentences. Who is speaking? Choose from the jobs you didn't use in exercise 1. Then listen, check, and repeat.**

0 "I sold six TVs today." salesperson
1 "I made over 50 pizzas today!" ______
2 'Do you often have headaches?' ______
3 "My job is to protect my country." ______
4 "I'm working on a wooden house at the moment." ______
5 "Would you like it long or short?" ______

3 **In which jobs do people …**

1 often work outside?
2 help sick people or people in danger?
3 spend a lot of time in front of a computer?
4 wear special clothes or a uniform?
5 do something creative?

4 Your turn **Which job do you want to do? Give reasons.**

I want to be a software developer because I love computers!

I want to be a fashion designer because I love clothes and art.

International English
Contractions

Nina is from the U.S. She is speaking in an informal situation, so she uses spoken contractions. Some common spoken contractions are:
'cause (because), *wanna* (want to), *I'll* (I will)
*whaddu*z (what does), *kinda* (kind of)
watcha (what do you), *dunno* (don't know)

D 75 **Read the International English box. Listen to the examples.**

E Video 76 **Watch or listen to the extracts from Nina's vlog. Complete the sentences with the long forms of the contractions that you hear.**

0 Today, I want to talk about life as an athlete and the work it takes.
1 But ______ it mean to be an athlete?
2 I also tried gymnastics ______ my friends at school did it.
3 We ______ get that movement …
4 ______ see you next time!

Workbook p.144

8 DECENT WORK AND ECONOMIC GROWTH

A magazine article

Unusual jobs

A

Lucy Clements from the U.K. loves shopping. In fact, it's her job: she's a mystery shopper! Shops pay her to pretend to be a real customer. She doesn't buy anything, but she takes notes and answers questions about her experiences. The most important thing is: she can't tell the shop assistants why she's there!

"The questions aren't hard," says Lucy. "A lot of the answers are just 'yes' or 'no.' And I can spend all my time doing my favorite thing!"

B

Hannah Chadwick's job is very unusual. "I trained to be a chef, and now I'm a food stylist," she says. "I prepare food for blogs and online articles." Hannah makes the food look delicious and then photographers take pictures. However, she uses some surprising methods! "Food stylists can't use milk," explains Hannah. "It makes everything really soft, so we use shampoo instead! We also put cardboard inside cakes so that they don't collapse! Even when it's lunchtime, we know we can't eat anything!"

C

Hip-hop artist Biggs Riggs has a special job. "I'm a singer for soldiers in different countries," he says. "These soldiers can't go home, but I can go to them!" Biggs Riggs (real name Kevin Reid) feels lucky because he can fly all over the world. But he believes his job has an important role, too: "I can't help the soldiers do their job," he explains, "but my music brings happiness to everyone!"

International English

shop assistant = sales clerk, salesperson

1 **Look at the pictures. What jobs can you see? Read the article quickly and check.**

2 **77 Read and listen to the article and answer the questions. Write A, B, or C.**

In which jobs do you ...

0 answer questions? A
1 visit different countries? ____
2 work with images? ____
3 make people feel better? ____
4 need to keep a secret? ____
5 use unusual materials? ____

3 **Read the article again. Answer the questions.**

0 How does Lucy remember her different experiences in stores?
She takes notes.
1 Which two positive things does Lucy say about her job?
______
2 What does Hannah prepare food for?
______
3 Why can't you eat her cakes?
______
4 Who does Biggs Riggs sing for?
______
5 Where does he do this?
______

4 **Your turn** **Which job from the article would you like to do? Why?**

I'd like to be a food stylist. I love cooking and taking photos.

can / *can't* (rules and permission)

1 78 **Read and listen to the Grammar in context. Ed is a young photographer, and it's the end of his first day working with Jess, a food stylist. Why isn't the food OK to eat?**

Present and Practice

Grammar in context

Ed That was a great photo shoot – your food looks great!
Jess Thanks!
Ed Um … **Can** I eat that cake? I guess you're going to throw everything away!
Jess No, you **can't**! Sorry, that's the rule!
Ed Oh. But it all looks amazing. What **can** I eat?
Jess You **can** look at it, but you **can't** eat anything! There's cardboard in the cake, brown paint on the chicken, and the burgers aren't cooked. But there's a great café down the street!

Grammar notes p.145

2 **Complete the chart with words from the Grammar in context.**

Affirmative	
I / You / He / She / It / We / You / They	[0] can look at it …
Negative	
I / You / He / She / It / We / You / They	[1] ______ eat anything.
Questions	**Short answers**
[2] ______ I / you / he / she / we / you / they eat the cake?	Yes, I / you / he / she / we / you / they **can**.
	No, I / you / he / she / we / you / they [3] ______.

3 **Choose the correct options.**

I work in the kitchen of a café on Saturdays. Work starts at 7 a.m. and I [0] **can** / **can't** be late! I can't [1] **to wear** / **wear** my own clothes – there's a uniform for all workers in the kitchen. But the waiters can [2] **choose** / **choosing** what they want to wear. It's a long day, but I [3] **can** / **can't** take two breaks – one for lunch, and a short break in the afternoon. And I can [4] **talk** / **talks** to the other kitchen workers – they're all great! I [5] **can** / **can't** eat anything while I'm working in the kitchen, but at the end of the day, I can [6] **take** / **taking** a lot of food home with me. The food is delicious, and on Saturday night, no one needs to cook at home!

4 79 **Listen and check.**

5 **Look at the rules for workers. Write questions and short answers with the words below.**

David / go home early   I / share this information
I / use social media   they / answer personal phone calls
we / eat at our desks   ~~you / wear your own clothes~~

0 Can you wear your own clothes?
No, you can't.

1 ______________________________

2 ______________________________

3 ______________________________

4 ______________________________

5 ______________________________

6 Your turn **Think of a job, but don't tell anyone. Write two things you can do and two things you can't do in this job.**

7 **Read your sentences to your partner. Can they guess the job?**

5 Vocabulary

LO Describe people's personality

Personality

1 🔊80 **Match the personality adjectives with their definitions. Then listen, check, and repeat.**

0 friendly __d__
1 polite ____
2 patient ____
3 kind ____
4 honest ____
5 careful ____
6 reliable ____
7 helpful ____

a You can wait for a long time.
b You concentrate on what you are doing.
c You always say "please".
d ~~You like to meet new people.~~
e You are always on time and do things well.
f You are generous and care about other people.
g You like to help other people.
h You always tell the truth.

2 **Read the job ads. Choose the correct options.**

Salespeople needed

The fashion store Bales is advertising for salespeople. Are you always [0] **careful** / **(polite)** when you speak to customers? Do you greet people with a [1] **friendly** / **patient** smile? Can you show you are [2] **kind** / **reliable** by arriving on time? Are you [3] **helpful** / **honest** when you are working with money? If the answers are yes, send your CV to info@bales.com

Nursery staff needed

Teeny Tinies, a busy nursery for children aged 0–4 years old, is looking for nursery workers. A typical *Teeny Tinies* worker is [4] **kind** / **reliable** to our children, and [5] **patient** / **friendly**, especially when the children want to do things their way! We are always [6] **careful** / **honest** and check that the children are safe. And we are [7] **friendly** / **helpful** – not only to the children, but when other workers need assistance, too! If you think *Teeny Tinies* is the right workplace for you, send your CV to lucille@teenytinies.com

3 🔊81 **We can add affixes to adjectives to make them negative. Complete the chart below with the adjectives in exercise 1. Then listen, check, and repeat.**

Affixes	Negative adjectives
un-	[0]unkind [1]unh________ [2]unr________ [3]unf________
dis-	[4]disho________
-less	[5]________eless
im-	[6]impa________ [7]impo________

Listening Skills

LO Listen to a podcast about jobs for teens

8 DECENT WORK AND ECONOMIC GROWTH

What jobs can teenagers do?

1 🔊82 **You are going to listen to Luis and Katelyn's podcast about jobs for teenagers in the U.S. Listen and check the topics they mention.**

0 ☑ minimum age
1 ☐ money
2 ☐ personal qualities
3 ☐ safety
4 ☐ leaving school

2 🔊82 **Listen again and answer the questions with a maximum of four words.**

0 What age can you start work in the U.S.?
__14__

1 What can't U.S. teens aged 16 do in their jobs?
____

2 Which three possible workplaces for teens does Katelyn mention?
____

3 Who does Luis want to work with?
____

4 Why do the listeners need to be careful?
____

3 **Your turn** **Think of a job a friend or family member does. How does their personality match their job? Tell a partner.**

> My brother is a police officer. He is often in very difficult situations, but he is always patient and never impolite. When people are sad or injured, he is always very kind and helpful.

Pronunciation p.125 Workbook pp.144

Grammar

LO Use (*not*) *as* ... *as* and *too* or *not enough* to make comparisons

(*not*) *as* ... *as*

1 83 **Read and listen to the Grammar in context. What is the minimum working age in the U.K.?**

Grammar in context | **Present and Practice**

In some cases, U.S. laws for children and jobs are **as strict as** laws in the U.K. For example, in both countries, children can't work before 7 a.m. or after 7 p.m. But some U.S. laws **aren't as strict as** British ones. Children in the U.S. can work for three hours on a school day, but children in the U.K. can only work for two hours. However, children aged 13 in the U.K. can work, but in the U.S., 13 is **too young**. In the U.S. children **aren't old enough** to work until they are 14.

Grammar notes p.146

2 Complete the chart with words from the Grammar in context.

as ... as (similar)	*not as ... as* (different)
My working hours are **as long as** yours	This job is**n't as interesting as** my last one.
In some cases, U.S. laws are [1] ________ laws in the U.K.	But some U.S. laws are [2] ________ British ones.

3 Complete the sentences with *as ... as* or *not as ... as* and the adjectives.

0 Julia is a better worker than the others. They aren't as careful as she is. (careful)
1 My brother works after school every day. I'm ________ my brother in the mornings. (tired)
2 This job is ________ my last job. When will I find something interesting?! (boring)
3 Juan always says please and Gabriel always says thank you. Gabriel is ________ Juan! (polite)
4 I work with very young children, but it isn't the right job for my sister. She is ________ me! (patient)
5 Today, I'm starting a new job that pays better than my last one, but my hours are ________ before. (long)

4 84 **Listen and check.**

too or *not enough*

5 Complete the chart with words from the Grammar in context.

too + adjective	*not* + adjective + *enough*
Children aged 13 in the U.K. can work, but in the U.S., 13 is [1] ________.	In the U.S., children are [2] ________ to work until they are 14.

6 Complete the sentences with *too* or *enough* and the adjectives.

careless interesting thick ~~young~~

0 The minimum age is 14, Josh. You're only 13, so you're too young.
1 I don't want to sit in an office all day. It isn't ________ for me.
2 Silvia is a nice girl, but she's a terrible hairdresser. She's ________ with the customers' hair!
3 That jacket is very thin for an outdoor job in winter. It won't be ________!

7 Look at the pictures. What are the people saying? Complete the sentences. Use *be* and *too ...* or *not ... enough*.

0 Don't carry those boxes. They 're too heavy! (heavy)

1 I'm sure you're a great software developer. But you ________ for the job. (old)

2 Late again, Violet? I'm sorry, but you ________. (unreliable)

3 I'll never be a professional basketball player. I ________. (tall)

8 85 **Listen and check.**

9 Your turn **Complete the sentences below with your own ideas. Then compare your sentences in pairs.**

1 A doctor's job is as difficult as a ...'s job.
2 A ...'s job isn't interesting enough for me.
3 I wouldn't like a job that's too ... .

I wouldn't like a job that's too dangerous.

5 Listening Skills

LO Use the topic and pictures to predict the content of a TV show

It's too dangerous for me!

1 86 **Listen to the first part of a TV show. What is it about?**

Active Listeners
Thinking before you listen

Active listeners think about the topic and look at related pictures before listening. We can use these things to predict possible key words. Key words are important nouns, verbs, or adjectives.

2 87 **Read the tip and look at the pictures. Check (✓) the key words you think you will hear. Then listen to the second part of the TV show and check your answers.**

Nouns	Verbs	Adjectives
☑ astronaut	☐ drive	☐ reliable
☐ fishermen	☐ catch	☐ boring
☐ soldier	☐ spend	☐ exciting
☐ window cleaner	☐ clean	☐ careful
☐ vacations	☐ protect	☐ careless

3 87 **Listen to the second part again. Choose the correct answers.**

0 People in the first job can't make ... .
 a friends (b) mistakes c money

1 This year, ... people wanted to be an astronaut.
 a 10,000 b 12,000 c 20,000

2 People in the second job work in some of the ... conditions.
 a hottest b coldest c worst

3 They often work ... hours without a break.
 a 12 b 16 c 24

4 The people in the third job are about ... meters above the ground.
 a 600 b 700 c 800

4 **Your turn** **Discuss the questions with a partner.**

1 Imagine you need to choose one of these jobs. Which one will you choose, and why?

2 Think of two more dangerous jobs. Why are they dangerous?

Out of these jobs, I'd like to be an astronaut. I love space!

Reading Skills

LO Read an article and understand the topic of each paragraph

An article

1 **Look at the title of the article. Answer the question. Then read the first two paragraphs of the article and check. Ignore the missing words.**

How old are the youngest child workers?

Active Readers
Understanding the topics of paragraphs

Every paragraph in an article has a topic. Active readers try to understand the main topic of every paragraph.

2 **Read the tip. Look at topics a–f carefully. Then read the article. Ignore the missing words. Match the paragraphs 1–6 with the topics a–f.**

a The negative effects of child labor ____
b How some people are helping with the problem ____
c Ali's story __1__
d The reasons for child labor ____
e General information about child labor ____
f Zarina's story ____

3 88 **Read the article. For each blank, choose the missing word. Then listen and check.**

0	(a) school	b home	c restaurant
1	a buy	b wear	c make
2	a bad	b good	c interesting
3	a sleep	b work	c school
4	a normal	b unusual	c illegal
5	a start going to	b stop	c do

4 **Read again. Answer the questions.**

0 What things can't Ali do because of his job?
He can't do homework, play sports, or see friends.

1 Which jobs for child laborers does the text mention?
______

2 What is the effect of Zarina's job on her education?
______

3 How are Ali and Zarina "luckier" than some child laborers?
______

4 What is the most common reason for child labor?
______

5 How are some organizations trying to help?
______

5 **Your turn** **How does the article make you feel about your own education? Discuss your answers in pairs.**

I feel really lucky that I can go to school.

Me too. I'm glad I don't need to go to work in dangerous conditions.

1 NO POVERTY

Too young to work: child labor

1 Ali is 14 and he lives in Jordan. His friendly smile hides the reality of his daily life. "I work in a restaurant. I work for 8 hours on a [0]__________ day and 12 hours during vacations. My working hours are too long for homework or sports. I never see my friends."

Ali works between 8 and 12 hours every day.

2 Around the world, about 152 million children from 5 to 17 have a job. Some work on farms or in mines. Others work in factories. They [1]__________ everything from clothes to cell phones.

3 Zarina, a polite girl from Uzbekistan, is 15. Every fall, she works in cotton fields and can't go to school. "One day, I want to be a doctor," she explains, "but right now my grades aren't [2]__________ enough."

4 Many child laborers aren't as lucky as Ali and Zarina. A lot of them never go to [3]__________. Some of their jobs are also bad for children's health. About 50% of child laborers work in unhealthy or dangerous conditions.

5 The problem is often money. Ali's father is too sick to work. His family needs the money from Ali's job. In other countries, child labor is [4]__________. Families expect children, especially boys, to work.

6 Many countries are trying to [5]__________ child labor. Some organizations give the children's families money. Ali is optimistic about the future. "I'd like to be a chef one day," he says. "Then I will really help my family."

Zarina collects 40 kg of cotton every day.

5 Speaking & Global Skills

LO Say what my dream job is and explain why

Talk about my dream job

1 89 **Read and listen. What is a portfolio and why does Antonio want to make one?**

Hi, I'm Antonio, and my dream is to be a fashion designer because I love color and clothes! I also want to help people to think carefully and responsibly about the clothes they buy. My favorite fashion designers are the South American ones, especially the Brazilian designer Bruno Basso, but I also love the British designers, especially Vivienne Westwood. I'll probably never be as famous as Bruno or Vivienne – but I think I'm good enough to make a difference in the fashion world! But first, I need to study fashion, so I'm going to make a portfolio with pictures of my designs. You can't take some fashion courses without one! Another reason I'd like to make a portfolio is that it will help me to find my own style. After that, I can apply for a fashion degree! Remember my name – Antonio Roberts! I'm going to be famous one day!

2 90 **Listen and repeat.**

Active Speakers
Giving reasons

Active speakers use phrases like these to explain why they want to do things:

*My dream is to ... **because** ...*

*I **also** want to ...*

*I need to ... **so** I'm going to ...*

***Another** reason (I'd like to ...) is*

3 91 **Read the tip. Complete the mini-presentation with the words below. Then listen and check.**

also another ~~because~~ so

I want to be a doctor [0] *because* I like helping people. [1] ______ reason is that I'm really interested in how the human body works. You need good grades and work experience to become a doctor, [2] ______ I'm going to study really hard. I'm [3] ______ going to do some work experience in my local hospital when I'm old enough.

Global Skills
Your place in the world

8 DECENT WORK AND ECONOMIC GROWTH

We all have the potential to make a positive difference in the world, but it's hard to know what job will help us to do this. The first step is to identify our skills and the things we enjoy. Careers advisers and online quizzes are a great way to start.

4 Read the Global Skills box. Then take the quiz below.

Find your dream job!

1 What are your best subjects at school?
- a the arts
- b the sciences
- c history & politics
- d languages

2 What's your favorite activity?
- a an afternoon in an art gallery
- b a trip to a computer store
- c watching the news
- d visiting foreign countries

3 What do you talk about with your friends?
- a fashion and music
- b gaming
- c laws and government
- d traveling around the world

4 What is most important to you?
- a beauty
- b amazing machines
- c a fair world
- d an understanding of other cultures

5 Go to page 126 to read your results. Do you agree with them?

6 Answer the questions. Use the phrases from the tip.
1. What's your dream job? Why?
2. What do you have to do to get this job?
3. What do you want to do in your future job?

7 Plan and then give a presentation about your dream job. Use the model below, your notes from exercise 6, and the presentation in exercise 1.

Identify your dream job.
↓
Give two reasons why you want to do it
↓
Explain what you have to do to get your dream job.
↓
Say what you'd like to do in your future job and why.

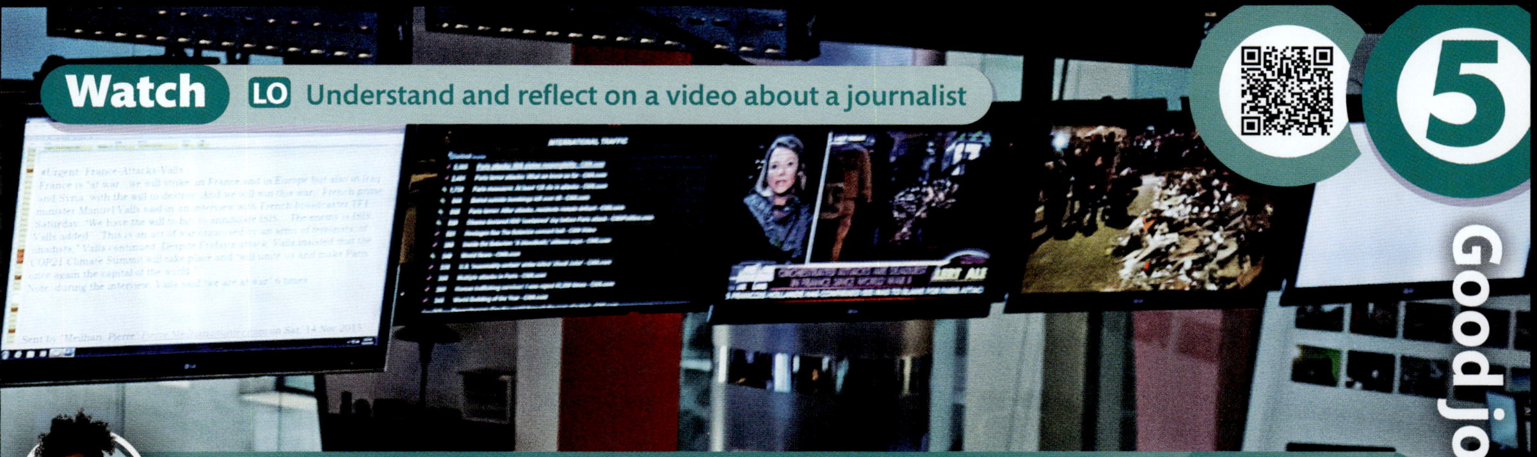

Watch

LO Understand and reflect on a video about a journalist

5 Good job!

I'm a journalist, New York City, U.S.

Before you watch

1 **Portia is a journalist in New York City. Why do you think these things are important to her?**

~~alarm clock~~ bike guitar laptop pen phone

0 *Maybe she needs an alarm clock because she gets up early.*
1 ______
2 ______
3 ______
4 ______
5 ______

While you watch

2 **Video** **Watch the video and choose the correct options.**

0 Portia starts work (**early**) / **around lunchtime**.
1 She does a lot of her work **in London** / **at home**.
2 She **drives** / **rides a bike** to her interview.
3 After her interview, Portia **reads the news online** / **writes a news article**.
4 At the end of the day, Portia **watches** / **doesn't watch** the news.

3 **Video** **Watch again. Are the sentences T (*true*) or F (*false*)?**

		T	F
0	Portia wakes up at 6:30 every morning.	☐	☑
1	She has a uniform.	☐	☐
2	She works for a large organization.	☐	☐
3	She travels all over the world.	☐	☐
4	She's going to interview a police officer.	☐	☐
5	Portia likes reading in the evening.	☐	☐
6	Portia loves her job because it's easy.	☐	☐

After you watch

Global Skills
Knowing yourself

When you're thinking about what job you'd like to do in the future, it's important to consider who you are as a person. Does your personality match your dream job?

International English

92 The letter "o" often has a short vowel sound in British English and a longer vowel sound in American English.

job 🇬🇧 /dʒɒb/ = 🇺🇸 /dʒɑb/
boss 🇬🇧 /bɒs/ = 🇺🇸 /bɔs/
lost 🇬🇧 /lɒst/ = 🇺🇸 /lɔst/

4 **Read the Global Skills box. Then answer the questions.**

1 Look at the adjectives. What personality traits do you need to be a journalist? Which do you think are most important?

cheerful confident friendly hard-working helpful honest polite smart

2 Would you be a good journalist? Why? / Why not?
3 What personality traits do you need for your dream job?

I think I need to be hard-working to be a police officer.

Yes, but you also need to be helpful and reliable.

Project p.112

6 It's a crime!

Metro VIDEO

Angela's vlog
A day in the life of a forensic science student

Ava 2 hours ago
I didn't think I liked science. But while I was listening to Angela, I decided that it's really cool! I want to help the police to solve crimes!

78 Reply

A Video 93 **Watch or listen. Angela is a forensic science student at university. Check (✓) the things the video mentions.**

0 ☑ laws for criminals
1 ☐ the police
2 ☐ something Angela really enjoys about her course
3 ☐ different crimes
4 ☐ why people commit crimes
5 ☐ talking to victims of crimes
6 ☐ investigating a crime

B Watch or listen again. Choose the correct options.

0 In her first class of the day, Angela learned about the laws for criminals who **break into houses** / **steal things**.
1 A forensic scientist investigates different crimes **in different ways** / **the same way**.
2 After lunch, Angela's next class was in a **library** / **laboratory**.
3 She spent the afternoon working on **a project** / **an experiment**.

C Answer the questions.

1 Do you think Angela's classes sound interesting? Why? / Why not?
2 Why does Angela analyze people's clothes?
3 Forensic science is one way the police get evidence about crimes. What are some other ways?

Vocabulary LO Talk about crime

Crime

1 94 **Match the crime verbs 0–7 with the definitions a–h. Listen, check, and repeat.**

0 steal something _e_
1 break into a place ____
2 catch someone ____
3 arrest someone ____
4 rob someone / somewhere ____
5 chase someone ____
6 commit a crime ____
7 investigate something ____

a to take someone to a police station and ask them questions
b to run after someone to stop them
c to do something that is illegal
d to enter somewhere and take something that is not yours
~~e to take something that is not yours~~
f to take something that is not yours from someone or somewhere
g to find information about a crime
h to find and stop someone

2 **Match the headlines with the pictures.**

0 Detectives investigate judge for corruption
1 Thieves break into school and steal 30 tablets.
2 Detectives catch phone thief from selfies
3 Police chase 240 km/h motorcycle
4 Someone commits a crime online every four seconds, says report
5 Men rob watch store
6 Police arrest man after he agrees to meet victim

A ____

B ____

C ____

D ____

E ____

F _0_

G ____

Stop

Irregular plurals

thief

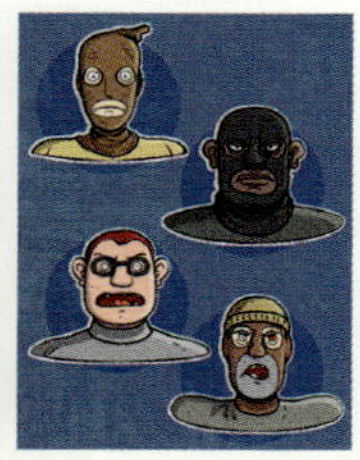
thieves

International English
Elision of /d/ and /t/

Angela is from the U.K. She doesn't always pronounce /d/ and /t/ sounds at the ends of words.
/d/ sound
*I **had** to analyze a pair of trousers ...*
/t/ sound
*The trousers **didn't** commit the crime ...*

D Video 95 **Read the International English box. Watch or listen to the examples from Angela's vlog.**

E Video 96 **Watch or listen to the extracts from Angela's vlog. Can you hear the final /d/ or /t/ sounds in the highlighted words? Choose *Y* (yes) or *N* (no)**

0 I'm Angela, and I'm a vlogger and student from England. Y ☑ N ☐
1 My first lesson of the day was about the laws we use ... Y ☐ N ☐
2 For example, burglars may be sentenced to spend some time in jail. Y ☐ N ☐
3 Finding out about the different ways people commit the crime is really interesting ... Y ☐ N ☐
4 After a tiring day at university, I walked home. Y ☐ N ☐
5 I hope you enjoyed joining me for a day at university. Y ☐ N ☐

Pronunciation p.125 Workbook p.148

A comic strip

1 97 **Read and listen to the comic strip. Does Gorski catch a criminal? Explain your answer.**

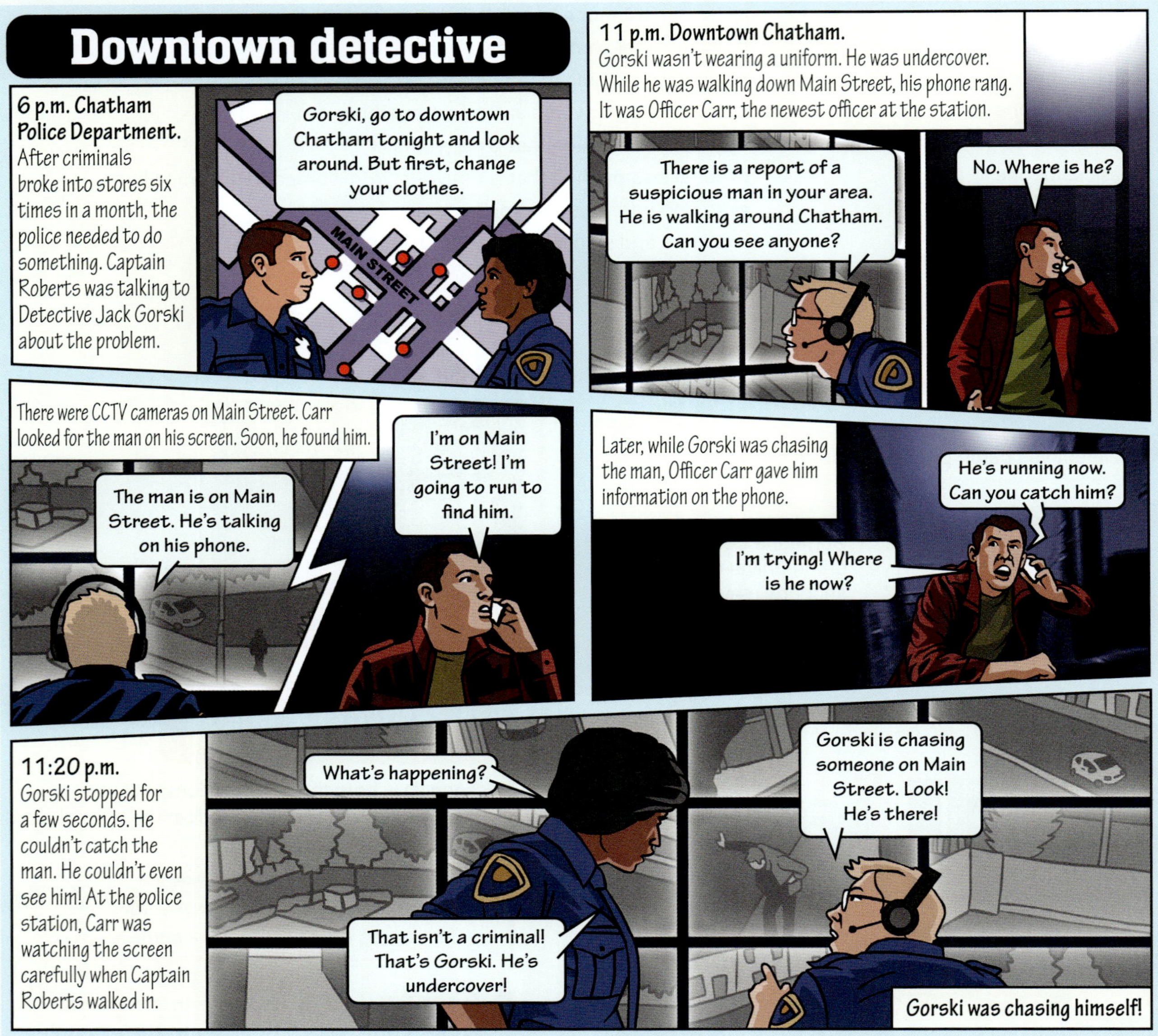

2 Read the comic strip again. Are the sentences T (*true*) or F (*false*)? Correct the false sentences.

0 Detective Gorski never wears a uniform. T ☐ F ☑
Detective Gorski doesn't wear a uniform when he's working undercover.

1 Gorski called Officer Carr. T ☐ F ☐
______

2 Carr used the CCTV cameras to find the man. T ☐ F ☐
______

3 Captain Roberts speaks to Gorski on the phone. T ☐ F ☐
______

4 Carr didn't know Gorski was undercover. T ☐ F ☐
______

3 Complete the summary with words from the story.

It was 11 p.m. and Detective Gorski was undercover in [0] downtown Chatham. Suddenly, he got a phone call from Officer Carr. There was a [1] ______ of a possible criminal in Chatham. Gorski decided to investigate and Carr used the [2] ______ cameras to help him. Gorski chased the man, but he couldn't [3] ______ him. After 20 minutes, Gorski [4] ______. He was tired. At that moment, Captain Roberts saw the man on the [5] ______. The man was Gorski, not a criminal! Officer Carr didn't know Gorski was [6] ______. And Gorski was [7] ______ himself!

4 **Your turn** **Why do you think so many comics, TV shows, and movies are about crime? Discuss with a partner.**

I think crime is very exciting, so people enjoy reading about it!

Past progressive and simple past

1 98 **Read and listen to the Grammar in context. Complete it with the words *map* or *phone*.**

Grammar in context | **Present and Practice**

Woman I **was sitting** right there **when** this guy walked in. He had a map but he needed directions. He put his [0] _map_ on my table and I showed him the way. And now my [1] ________ is missing! Did he steal my phone **while** I **was giving** directions?

Gorski Aha! This is a classic technique! He covered your [2] ________ with his map. **While** he **was leaving**, he took your phone and his [3] ________ at the same time.

Grammar notes p.149

2 Complete the chart with verbs from the Grammar in context.

Past progressive	Simple past
I [0] _was sitting_ right there	when this guy [1] ____________ in.
While he [2] ____________,	he [3] ____________ your phone …
Simple past	**Past progressive**
Did he [4] ____________ my phone	while I [5] ____________ directions?

Stop

when / while

We use *when* / *while* to talk about an action (simple past) that interrupts a longer action (past progressive). We use *when* before the simple past and *while* / *when* before the past progressive.

We can change the order of the two parts of a sentence and the meaning is the same.

It was raining when I got on the bus. =
When I got on the bus, it was raining.

3 Choose the correct verb forms. Choose one simple past verb and one past progressive verb in each sentence.

0 While I **swam** / **was swimming**, someone **took** / **was taking** my bag.
1 The sales clerks **had** / **were having** lunch when the men **robbed** / **were robbing** the store.
2 Someone **stole** / **was stealing** my dad's car while we **watched** / **were watching** the soccer game.
3 When I **arrived** / **was arriving** at school, everyone **walked** / **was walking** to the gym.

4 Complete the sentences with the simple past or past progressive form of the verbs.

0 While I _was getting on_ (get on) the bus, someone _stole_ (steal) my wallet.

1 The police ____________ (investigate) a robbery when a police dog ________ (see) the criminal.

2 A bird ________ (take) my hot dog while we ____________ (have) a cookout.

3 When the police ________ (catch) the man, he ____________ (escape) out of a window.

5 99 **Listen and check.**

6 Your turn **Complete the sentences with your own ideas. In pairs, compare your sentences.**

1 When the teacher walked into the classroom this morning, I ____________________.
2 I was doing my homework when ____________________.
3 I ____________ while I ____________________.

When the teacher walked into the classroom this morning, I was looking for my pen under my desk.

Really? What did the teacher say?

Workbook p.149 Metro Express p.113

6 Vocabulary

LO Talk about safety online

Safety online

1 100 **Complete the questions about internet safety. Listen and check.**

click on links · install antivirus software · ~~log out of websites~~ · share personal information · use different passwords

5 internet safety tips

1 Do you *log out of websites* after you finish using them?

2 Do you ______________ on your devices?

3 Do you ______________ on every website?

4 Do you think carefully before you ______________ online?

5 Do you ______________ in messages?

2 101 **Listen and repeat.**

3 **Match questions 1–5 in exercise 1 with answers a–e.**

a Yes, I do! I always use letters and numbers so no one can guess them. _____

b Yes, I never write my address or phone number online. _____

c Yes, I do. We share one device in my family! *1*

d Yes, I do on my laptop. But I don't think it's necessary on my phone. _____

e Yes, but I only do this when I know the website is safe. _____

4 Your turn **In pairs, ask and answer the questions in exercise 1.**

Do you log out of websites after you finish using them?

Yes, I do. I always log out of websites because I share a computer with my sister!

Listening Skills

LO Listen to a conversation about protecting your personal information online

16 PEACE, JUSTICE AND STRONG INSTITUTIONS

Phishing

1 102 **Listen to the conversation between two friends. Then choose the correct answer.**

Criminals send phishing emails because they want ...

a personal information about you.

b to sell software to you.

c you to send money to them.

d your email address.

2 102 **Listen again. Are the sentences T (*true*) or F (*false*)?**

Alex ...

		T	F
0	couldn't remember his password.	☐	☑
1	changed his password yesterday.	☐	☐
2	knew about phishing emails.	☐	☐
3	uses the same password for everything.	☐	☐
4	is going to get help from the police.	☐	☐

3 102 **Answer the questions. Then listen again and check.**

0 What is Alex's password? *AlexBeth2011*

1 Why did he change his password?

____

____

2 What really happened when Alex put in his old password?

____

3 Tony is going to help Alex solve the problem. What is Alex going to do next?

____

Workbook p.148

Grammar

LO Use adverbs of manner to talk about how we do things

Adverbs of manner

1 103 **Read and listen to the Grammar in context. Tony is talking about Alex's phishing email. What is his advice?**

Grammar in context — **Present and Practice**

We checked the password again and wrote it **slowly**, but it didn't work. So we looked up the problem online **quickly**. Then we answered some security questions, and it's all OK now. Think **carefully** and don't click on links in messages. With your password, thieves can steal your personal information **easily**.

Grammar notes p.150

2 Complete the chart with adverbs from the Grammar in context.

Regular adverbs	
Adjective	**Adverb**
slow	We wrote the password [0] slowly.
quick	We looked up the problem online [1] ______.
careful	Think [2] ______.
easy	With your password, thieves can steal personal information [3] ______.
Irregular adverbs	
Adjective	**Adverb**
good	I can play the guitar **well**.
late	The party finished **late**.
fast	The car was driving very **fast**.

3 Complete the sentences with the correct adjective or adverb.

0 They caught the thief quickly. (**quick** / **quickly**)
1 The woman shouted at me ______. (**loud** / **loudly**)
2 The police were really ______. (**helpful** / **helpfully**)
3 My dad can speak English, but not very ______. (**good** / **well**)
4 When I got back from school, I was feeling ______. (**hungry** / **hungrily**)
5 We waited for news ______. (**anxious** / **anxiously**)
6 The fans were singing ______. (**noisy** / **noisily**)
7 You were very ______ while you were speaking. Well done! (**confident** / **confidently**)

4 Complete the sentences with the adverb form of the adjectives.

beautiful easy fast late ~~quiet~~ terrible

0 The man was talking on a phone quietly.

1 Isabel sang ______ at the concert.

2 The thief was running ______.

3 Our team won the game ______.

4 I slept ______ last night.

5 We arrived home ______ and the front door was open.

5 104 **Listen and check.**

6 **Your turn** **Complete the sentences about you with the adverbs.**

badly quickly slowly well

1 I do my homework ______.
2 I cook ______.
3 I play tennis ______.
4 I eat ______.
5 My parents speak English ______.

7 Can your partner guess the adverbs you used in exercise 6?

You do your homework quickly.

Yes, but I also do it well!

6 Listening Skills

LO Identify the genre of listening texts

Smart crimes?

1 105 **You are going to listen to two stories about robberies. Match the pictures with the people.**

Alan Godfrey	Jim Lee	Lucy Brown	Alison Keane
C	___	___	___

2 105 **Listen again and put the images in exercise 1 in the correct order. Then explain one of the crimes to your partner.**

1 C, 2 ___, 3 ___, 4 ___

Active Listeners
Identifying the genre

Active listeners notice the type of language that they hear in recordings and can identify the genre.

3 Read the tip. Then match the genres 0–2 with the different types of language a–c.

0 an interview b
1 a story ___
2 a news report ___

a formal language, quotes, dates, and numbers
~~b questions and answers~~
c informal language and opinions

4 105 **Listen again. What genre is each recording?**

1 ___
2 ___

5 Your turn **With a partner, discuss which criminal made the biggest mistake.**

I think it was Alan Godfrey – why did he check Facebook!?

Reading Skills

LO Read a quiz and use context to guess meaning

A quiz

1 106 **Read and listen to the quiz on page 73. Match the laws 1–8 with the comments a–h.**

a "You can't enter the country with that!" 2
b "Please continue your conversation outside." ___
c "Please wait till the morning. I'm trying to sleep!" ___
d "It's a nice jacket, but people won't like it." ___
e "But I wanted to call him Stormzy!" ___
f "Be careful with that! There's a very important face on it!" ___
g "This place is a pet's paradise." ___
h "What is that terrible odor? I feel sick!" ___

Active Readers
Guessing meaning from context

Active readers use context to guess the meaning of unknown words.

2 Read the tip. Then look at the highlighted words in the quiz. Follow the steps below and try to guess the meaning of each word.

1 Look at the pictures and the words before and after.
2 Think: is the word a verb, adjective, or noun?
3 Guess the meaning of the word.
4 Check your guess in a dictionary.

3 Answer the questions with a maximum of four words.

0 How often must you walk your dog in Turin?
once a day
1 If you visit Singapore, what should you leave at home?
___
2 Who must follow the law about camouflage in Barbados?
___
3 What is unusual about durian fruit?
___
4 What do people in Denmark need to do if they want to give their baby an unusual name?
___

4 107 **Do the quiz. Are the rules T (*true*) or F (*false*)? Then listen and check.**

5 Your turn **Why do you think these countries have these laws? Discuss with a partner.**

Maybe the Italians are animal lovers.

Is that really illegal?

People love sharing stories about weird laws in different countries ... There's just one problem – they aren't always true! Can you guess which two rules are false?

1 Dogs love Turin, Italy! Why? Because in Turin it's illegal not to walk your dog every day! The city council advises three walks a day. T ☑ F ☐

2 "I was walking through the airport when someone stopped me and said, 'You can't chew gum!' That's right! It's illegal to bring gum into Singapore." T ☐ F ☐

3 Choose your clothes carefully on the small Caribbean island of Barbados. No one can wear camouflage, not even children! T ☐ F ☐

4 In the U.K., it's illegal to destroy banknotes, stamps, or anything else with a picture of the Queen of England on it. T ☐ F ☐

5 "We were eating a durian – it's a kind of fruit – on a bus in Jakarta when we realized the driver was looking at us angrily." In many countries in South East Asia, you can't take a durian into hotels or on public transportation. Why not? Because they smell really bad! T ☐ F ☐

6 You're not allowed to flush the toilet after 10 p.m. in Switzerland because people say it's too noisy. T ☐ F ☐

7 In Denmark, people choose their children's names carefully. You can only name a baby with one of the names from a government list, or you need to ask for special permission. T ☐ F ☐

8 "A police officer asked me to leave a bank while I was talking quietly on my cell phone." That's right – it's illegal to use a cell phone inside a bank in Brazil! T ☐ F ☐

6 Speaking & Global Skills

LO Tell a story

Tell a story

1 108 **Read and listen to Bill's story. Choose the correct options.**

At first, Bill thought that a woman was [1] **robbing** / **helping** a boy. In the end, the woman [2] **chased** / **saved** him.

Bill Did I tell you about the time I saw someone save a life? It all happened when I was walking home one day after school. There was a boy outside a store. A tall woman was walking toward him. First, I saw the woman look up. Next, she ran towards the boy and pushed him into the entrance of the store. I thought she was trying to steal his phone! Then, there was a terrible sound as a big bag of construction materials fell onto the sidewalk. I looked up. Some construction workers were working above us. In the end, I realized that the woman wasn't trying to rob the boy, she was saving his life!

2 109 **Listen and repeat.**

Active speakers
Telling a story

Active speakers use these phrases to tell a story:

Introducing a story:

Did I tell you about the time (when) ... ?

It all started / happened when I was / we were ...

Time expressions:

First, Then, Next, In the end,

When we use time expressions at the start of a sentence, we usually use a comma.

3 110 **Read the tip. Then complete the story with the words in the box. Then listen and check.**

first happened in the end next then ~~time~~

Did I tell you about the [0] ___time___ when an old woman attacked some robbers? It all [1] ____________ when I was shopping in Northampton, England, a few years ago. I heard a loud noise and saw some men breaking into a jewelry store. I felt really scared, but this woman appeared out of nowhere! [2] ____________, she ran toward the men. [3] ____________, she hit them with her handbag! [4] ____________, the men were terrified and they tried to escape! [5] ____________, the police arrested all the men. And the woman? Her name is Ann Timson, and she's a local hero!

Global Skills
Storytelling

We use stories to remember and to understand experiences. Knowing how to tell a story well is an important skill.

4 **Read the Global Skills box and look at the poster. Then read Bill's story again and answer the questions.**

1 What was happening before the dramatic experience?

____

2 How does Bill make the story memorable?

____

Think – Plan – Tell!

Think of an exciting or dramatic experience.

Then plan:

1 What was happening before, during, and after?

2 Senses make a story more memorable. What did you see, hear, feel, smell, or taste?

3 Write down time expressions for introducing the story and ordering the events.

Tell the story!

5 **Think of an exciting or dramatic experience. Then follow the steps in the poster and make notes.**

6 **Tell your story. Use the model below and the story in exercise 1.**

Introduce the story
↓
Describe what you saw or heard.
↓
Use time expressions to describe the events in order
↓
Describe how you felt
↓
End the story

Watch

LO Understand and reflect on a video about a famous literary character

Sherlock Holmes

Before you watch

1 **Read the Global Skills box. Look at the photo from a TV show about Sherlock Holmes. Then make notes to complete rows 1 and 2 of the chart below.**

Sherlock Holmes	
1 I know …	*He's a detective.*
2 I want to know …	
3 I learned …	

Global Skills
Using your background knowledge

Before you watch, read, or listen to something new, think about what you already know about the topic. Then decide what you want to learn.

While you watch

2 **Video** **Watch the video. What do you see?**

0 a picture of (Sherlock Holmes) / **detectives today**
1 a picture of **teacher** / **author** Arthur Conan Doyle
2 an interview with **a forensic scientist** / **a detective** talking about Sherlock Holmes
3 someone **investigating** / **committing** a crime
4 a **prison** / **house** where forensic science students practice
5 someone checking **a book** / **a door** for fingerprints

International English
Understanding different accents

Everybody speaks differently, so it's important to practice listening to different accents. Dr. Carolyn Morton has a Northern Irish accent. The way that she pronounces some consonants and vowels is different from standard American or British English pronunciation.

3 **Video** **Watch again. Are the sentences T (*true*) or F (*false*)? Correct the false sentences.**

0 Conan Doyle's stories were some of the world's first detective stories. T ☑ F ☐

1 Conan Doyle studied to join the police. T ☐ F ☐

2 Conan Doyle read about real crimes to get ideas for his Sherlock Holmes stories. T ☐ F ☐

3 Today, evidence of crimes includes mud on shoes, fibers from clothing, or broken glass. T ☐ F ☐

4 Sherlock Holmes used fingerprints to catch criminals before any other detectives. T ☐ F ☐

5 Detectives need to work very quickly to solve crimes. T ☐ F ☐

After you watch

4 **Complete row 3 of the chart in exercise 1. Then compare your answers with a partner.**

What did you learn?

I learned that Sir Arthur Conan Doyle used real science in his stories, and that the police started using his ideas to catch criminals!

Project p.113

C Review

Vocabulary

1 Complete the sentences with jobs words. Then match them with the pictures.

0 I'm interested in clothes. I want to be a f<u>ashion</u> d<u>esigner</u>. ____
1 My aunt is a f__________. Her job is dangerous, but she loves helping people. ____
2 A h__________ helps people with their physical appearance. ____
3 My sister loves cooking. She wants to be a c__________. ____
4 My dad works in a hospital. He's a n__________. ____
5 My cousin is a s__________. He sells windows. ____

2 Choose the correct personality adjectives.

0 Toby is <u>reliable</u>. He's never late and works hard.
a unkind (b) reliable c unhelpful
1 I like your brother. He's really __________.
a impolite b friendly c careful
2 Your food will arrive soon. Don't be so __________!
a kind b dishonest c impatient
3 Thanks for your help. It was really __________ of you.
a kind b careless c polite
4 Isabel is often late. She's __________.
a unreliable b honest c helpful

3 Complete the story with the crime verbs.

arrested broke into chased didn't catch ~~robbed~~ stole

Thieves in Delaware [0] <u>robbed</u> a jewelry store last night. They [1] __________ the store at 1 a.m., and they [2] __________ some expensive watches. A security guard [3] __________ them, but they escaped on motorcycles so he [4] __________ them. Police [5] __________ one of the thieves this morning, but they're still looking for two more.

4 Correct the mistakes in the phrases for safety online.

0 On public computers, you should always log out of ~~information~~. w<u>ebsites</u>
1 You should think before you click on ~~passwords~~ in emails. l__________
2 I want to keep my personal information safe, so I use about six different ~~links~~. p__________
3 You should be careful about how you share personal ~~software~~. i__________
4 Remember to install antivirus ~~websites~~ to protect your computer. s__________

Grammar

1 Complete the job rules. Use *can* and *can't*.

I'm a hairdresser. I have my own salon and I love it. I [0] <u>can</u> control everything in it, and I [1] ______ make my own decisions. But I [2] ______ always do what I want. I [3] ______ get up late on a workday. And I [4] ______ choose how I cut a customer's hair. I need to listen to what they want. The customer is always right!

2 Read the situations and write sentences. Use *as … as* or *not as … as*.

0 My best friend Jules is 15. I am 15.
<u>Jules is as old as me.</u>
(Jules / old / me)
1 Joao always says please. But David never says it.
____
(David / polite / Joao)
2 Today it's really hot, but yesterday it was hotter!
____
(today / hot / yesterday)
3 Your antivirus software is OK. But mine is better.
____
____
(your antivirus software / good / mine)
4 I'm 1.65 m. My mom is 1.65 m, too.
____
(I / tall / my mom)
5 English is difficult, and math is difficult too!
____
(English / difficult / math)

3 **Complete the sentences. Use *too …* or *not … enough*.**

0 I can't follow her! She's cycling and she's ____too fast____! (fast)

1 José isn't on the team because he ____________________. (good) He should practice more.

2 We don't want to buy anything. Everything is ____________________. (expensive)

3 I can't carry this bag. I'm ____________________! (strong)

4 **Write sentences. Use the simple past and past progressive form of the verbs and *when* / *while*.**

0 we / chasing / the robbers when Detective Jones / fall / over
We were chasing the robbers when Detective Jones fell over.

1 Mason / play / soccer when he / hurt / his leg
____

2 someone / steal / my bike while I / study / in the library
____

3 the builder / work / on the house when she / drop / some glass
____

4 while Noah / walk / to school, he / lose / his phone
____

5 the police officers / catch / the robber while he / try / to escape
____

5 **Complete the sentences with the adjectives in the box and their adverb forms.**

careful easy fast good noisy ~~quiet~~

0 Aubrey speaks __quietly__. She has a __quiet__ voice.

1 Be __________. You need to cut this paper __________.

2 You speak Spanish really __________. You're __________ at languages.

3 Joseph sings __________. He's very __________ in the shower!

4 The race was __________ for us. We won __________.

5 This is a __________ motorcycle. It goes very __________.

Look back: Units 5 and 6

Read the story. Then choose the correct answers.

Detective Jenny Jones [0] __was sitting__ in her car and reading her work emails. It was a cold, dark afternoon. It wasn't as cold [1] ______________ the previous day, but she didn't like winter weather. She was starting to think about her summer vacation when she heard a message on the radio: "Attention! … Robbery … jewelry store … Fifth Avenue."

"Time to [2] ______________ another crime," Jones thought. She [3] ______________ her email and started the car. When she arrived at the store, she stopped the car [4] ______________ and got out. She could see two [5] ______________ inside the store, looking carefully for clues.

"[6] ______________ I come in?" she asked them.

"Of course ma'am!" one of them said. "But there aren't any fingerprints. This is going to be difficult."

"Look," said Jones, and pointed to a T-shirt on a CCTV camera.

"One of the robbers covered it with a T-shirt but forgot about it," she said, smiling.

"It'll be full of evidence!" said the other officer.

"Yes," said Jones. "That was [7] ______________ of them!"

	a	b	c
0	a sitting	b was sitting	c were sitting
1	a as	b than	c more
2	a arrest	b investigate	c break into
3	a clicked on	b installed	c logged out of
4	a quicker	b quickly	c quick
5	a lawyers	b software developers	c police officers
6	a can	b can't	c don't
7	a impolite	b reliable	c careless

CLIL C p.120

7 Bucket list

Metro VIDEO

Steve's vlog
Exploring the island of East Java

Maira 14 minutes ago
East Java is really beautiful. I've never seen a waterfall in real life. Steve is very lucky!

42 Reply

A Video 111 **Watch or listen. Check (✓) the geographic locations Steve mentions in his vlog.**

0 ☑ waterfall	2 ☐ volcano	4 ☐ beach	6 ☐ ocean
1 ☐ river	3 ☐ mountain	5 ☐ lake	7 ☐ forest

B **Watch or listen again. Are the sentences T (*true*) or F (*false*)?**

0	You can only see the Tumpak Sewu waterfall from the top.	T ☐	F ☑
1	Steve goes on a boat ride.	T ☐	F ☐
2	Visitors can ride up Bromo for a view from the top.	T ☐	F ☐
3	At the bottom of Bromo there's a lake.	T ☐	F ☐
4	On Mount Ijen, Steve watched the sun come up.	T ☐	F ☐
5	Steve visited two waterfalls on East Java.	T ☐	F ☐

C **Answer the questions.**

1 Which location in the video would you most like to visit? Why?
2 Do you watch travel videos like the ones that Steve makes? Why? / Why not?
3 Would you like to be a travel vlogger? Why? / Why not?

Vocabulary **LO** Talk about exciting experiences

Experiences

1 112 **Match the experiences with the pictures. Listen, check, and repeat.**

0 G appear on TV
1 ___ camp under the stars
2 ___ decorate my bedroom
3 ___ dye my hair a different color
4 ___ go backpacking
5 ___ go snorkeling
6 ___ interview my favorite YouTuber
7 ___ make a viral dance video
8 ___ perform with a live band
9 ___ race across a desert
10 ___ sail around the world
11 ___ write my own novel

2 Complete the intentions and predictions with the correct experiences from exercise 1.

0 I love water and boats. One day, I'm going to sail around the world.
1 I'm training to become an actor. I'm going to ______________ very soon!
2 I want to change my style. I'm going to ______________!
3 My friends and I want to travel the world, but we don't want to spend a lot of money. So we're going to ______________.
4 It's a warm night with no clouds in the sky. So we're going to ______________!
5 I want to change the color of these walls. I'm going to ______________!

3 Your turn **Choose three experiences from exercise 1 for your bucket list. Write adjectives to describe them in your notebook. Then explain your choices to your partner.**

International English
t between vowels

Steve is from the U.S. He often pronounces a *t* sound as a very soft *d* when it is between two vowel sounds.

beautiful *waterfall* *visited*

D 113 **Read the International English box. Listen to the examples.**

E Video 114 **Watch or listen to the extracts from the video. Do you hear a *t* sound or a *d* sound in the highlighted words?**

0 I want to share with you ...
t ☑ *d* ☐
1 ... all the way down to the bottom ...
t ☐ *d* ☐
2 Very near, there is an active volcano ...
t ☐ *d* ☐
3 A few days later ...
t ☐ *d* ☐
4 I saw a beautiful sunrise from the top.
t ☐ *d* ☐
5 This is a huge wall of water in the forest.
t ☐ *d* ☐

Workbook p.152

Social media posts

1 **Look at the title of the social media post and the images. Complete the summary with one word.**

Ashley's post is about how to have fun without much ________.

2 **115** **Read and listen to the social media posts. Write the letters of the correct ideas.**

0 Which bucket list ideas cost money? A, B

1 Which bucket list ideas use the internet? ______

2 Which bucket list idea reuses different things? ______

3 Which bucket list ideas did Ashley do with other people? ______

3 **Are the sentences T (*true*), F (*false*), or NG (*not given*)? Choose the correct answer.**

0 Ashley dyed her hair many times before last weekend. T ☐ F ☑ NG ☐

1 Someone taught Ashley to decorate before she changed her bedroom. T ☐ F ☐ NG ☐

2 Ashley camped in the backyard with some friends. T ☐ F ☐ NG ☐

3 Ashley is a fantastic dancer. T ☐ F ☐ NG ☐

4 A lot of people have read Ashley's blog. T ☐ F ☐ NG ☐

4 **Your turn** **What activities do you do when you don't have much money to spend? Tell a partner.**

I hang out in the park with my friends.
In the summer, we go swimming in the lake.

Budget bucket list!

114 Posts **578** Followers **197** Following

Ashley

How big is your budget: do you have a lot of money, or only a little? I can show you how to have fun on a small budget!

#budget #bucketlist #fun

Follow Message Contact

A

Have you ever dyed your hair a different color? I did it for the first time last weekend! But I didn't go to a hairdresser. I did it myself at home! It only cost me $4! What do you think?

1 day ago Reply

B

I've never learned to decorate anything, but ignorance has never stopped me! I recently decorated my bedroom myself! I used some old paint and my sister's old shelves, and bought some fairy lights. I'm really happy with it and it only cost $15!

1 day ago Reply

C

Have you ever camped under the stars? I have, and it's one of the most amazing and beautiful things I've done. My friends and I wanted to go camping, but as usual, we didn't have much money. But camping in your friend's backyard costs nothing – and the stars? They come for free!

1 day ago Reply

D

I've never been good at dancing, but I love to dance! And last week my friends and I made a dance video. We put it on YouTube, and a lot of our friends have commented on it. Now we hope it goes viral!

1 day ago Reply

E

I've always wanted to write a novel, but I'm not sure I can do it. For now, I've started a blog about my budget bucket list – and you can read it here! ashleycope@blogspot.com

1 day ago Reply

Present perfect (experiences): affirmative and negative

1 116 **Read and listen to the Grammar in context. Who is going to decorate their bedroom?** ______

Present and Practice

Grammar in context

Chloe Look at Ashley's post about her bedroom. She**'s decorated** it!
Ben It looks great! She said she **hasn't decorated** anything before.
Chloe I know! She's really good at it though. I**'ve never decorated** anything!
Ben I**'ve done** it a few times. My bedroom walls **have had** three different colors on them! Do it, Chloe. You'll love it!
Chloe OK! Will you help me?
Ben Sure!

Grammar notes p.153

2 Complete the chart with words from the Grammar in context.

Affirmative
She / He [0]*'s decorated* ______ it.
I / You / They / We [1] ______ it a few times.
My bedroom walls [2] ______ three different colors on them!
Negative
She / He [3] ______ anything before.
I / You / They / We [4] ______ anything!

3 Choose the correct options.

0 I **'s** / **('ve)** never dyed my hair.
1 He **hasn't** / **haven't** written a novel.
2 You **'s** / **'ve** appeared on TV three times!
3 I haven't **made** / **never made** a video.
4 My mom **has** / **have** sailed around the world.
5 We **haven't** / **'ve** never been backpacking.

Stop

Past participles of regular verbs are the same as the simple past *-ed* forms.

Past participles of irregular verbs aren't always the same as the simple past. See the Irregular verbs list at the back of the book.

4 Look at Brian's list of things he has and hasn't done on his bucket list. Complete the sentences with the past participles of the irregular verbs.

Bucket list

0 I've *thought* (think) about dyeing my hair, but I haven't *done* (do) it!
1 I've ______ (write) half a novel.
2 I've ______ (eat) food from around the world.
3 I've ______ (make) my own movie.
4 I've ______ (read) Frankenstein.
5 I haven't ______ (go) to Africa.

5 117 **Listen and check.**

6 Complete the sentences with the past participle form of the correct verb in parentheses.

Are you an adrenaline addict?

Or do you prefer to stay at home?

Check the sentences that are true for you to find out!

0 ☐ I've *climbed* a mountain. (**climb** / **dye**)
1 ☐ I've ______ a whole novel in one day. (**read** / **visit**)
2 ☐ I've ______ parkour. (**do** / **take**)
3 ☐ I've ______ an entire series on Netflix in one day. (**sail** / **watch**)
4 ☐ I've ______ a desert. (**decorate** / **visit**)
5 ☐ I've ______ a whole day in my pajamas. (**enjoy** / **sail**)
6 ☐ I've ______ my hair. (**dye** / **sleep**)
7 ☐ I've never ______ being outside in bad weather. (**like** / **read**)
8 ☐ I've ______ under the stars. (**find** / **sleep**)
9 ☐ I've always ______ coming home after a vacation. (**love** / **visit**)
10 ☐ I've ______ on the ocean. (**like** / **sail**)
11 ☐ I've ______ my bedroom. (**decorate** / **watch**)

7 Your turn **Do the quiz in exercise 6. Go to page 126 to read your results. In pairs, compare your answers.**

I've climbed a mountain, and I've visited a desert.

Me too! But I've also watched a lot of Netflix in my pajamas.

Phrasal verbs (movement)

1 118 **Match the phrasal verbs with the pictures. Listen, check, and repeat.**

get back   get off   get on   ~~go away~~
go out   stay in   take off

0 go away

1 ________

2 ________

3 ________

4 ________

5 ________

6 ________

2 How do you say the phrasal verbs in exercise 1 in your language?

3 Replace the highlighted phrases with the correct form of the phrasal verbs from exercise 1.

0 They're going to go on vacation for the weekend. go away
1 The plane left at 11 p.m. last night. ________
2 She entered the wrong bus! ________
3 Are you going to go to an event this evening? ________
4 It's late and Sofia hasn't come home. ________
5 If it rains tomorrow, I'll be inside all day. ________
6 Excuse me, this is my stop. I have to leave the bus. ________

4 Your turn **In pairs, discuss the experiences.**

Tell your partner about a time you ...
1 got back really late from a party.
2 got on the wrong bus.
3 got off a train or bus at the wrong place.

Listening Skills

LO Listen to an audio diary about a vacation

A trip to NYC

1 119 **Listen to Juliana's audio diary about her vacation. Put the images in the correct order.**

A ____

B 1

C ____

D ____

2 119 **Listen again. Are the sentences T (*true*) or F (*false*)?**

0 Juliana's flight to New York was in the evening. T ☐ F ☑
1 She was tired when she arrived at her hotel. T ☐ F ☐
2 On her first day, she visited a science museum. T ☐ F ☐
3 She forgot to bring something important with her from the hotel. T ☐ F ☐
4 On the bus tour, she learned about TV shows and movies in New York. T ☐ F ☐
5 She didn't want to go home. T ☐ F ☐

3 119 **Listen again. Complete the sentences with one word.**

0 Juliana didn't sleep on the plane.
1 Juliana stayed in the hotel while her ________ explored the city.
2 The family got on the wrong ________.
3 After the bus tour, Juliana went to the ________.
4 On their ________ night, the family went out for dinner.

Pronunciation p.125 Workbook p.152

Present perfect (experiences): questions

1 120 **Read and listen to the Grammar in context. Choose the correct answer.**

Antonio **has** / **hasn't** seen Mario's videos about Africa.

Grammar in context **Present and Practice**

Antonio Hi Juliana! How was your trip to New York?
Juliana Great! I'm going to make a travel video about it.
Antonio Oh, I like travel vlogs! **Have** you ever **heard** of Mario Rigby?
Juliana No, I **haven't**. Who is he?
Antonio He's a travel vlogger. His best videos are about Africa. He'**s walked** across the whole continent!
Juliana I want to do something as amazing as that! **Has** he ever **visited** any other continents?
Antonio Yes, he **has**! He'**s cycled** across Canada, too!

Grammar notes p.154

2 **Complete the charts with words from the Grammar in context.**

Questions	
[0]Have you / we / they ever **Has** he / she ever	[1]________ of Mario Rigby? [2]________ any other continents?
Short answers	
Yes, I / you / we / they **have**. Yes, he / she [3]________.	No, I / you / we / they [4]________. No, he / she **hasn't**.

Stop

We use *been* and *gone* as the past participles of *go*.
been: I went and came back.
gone: I went and I am there now.

3 **Complete the questions.**

0 Has your mom ever been (go) to the U.S.?
Yes, she has.

1 ________ you ever ________ (get) off a train at the wrong station?
____

2 ________ your teacher ever ________ (sing) in class?
____

3 ________ you ever ________ (write) a blog?
____

4 ________ you ever ________ (sail) on the ocean?
____

4 121 **Listen and check. Then write true answers.**

5 **Complete the questions 1–7 with the correct form of the verbs. Then write two more questions.**

act do go meet ride ~~sing~~ take watch

Have you ever ...

0 sung on stage?
1 ________ a horse?
2 ________ a picture of a celebrity?
3 ________ in a school play?
4 ________ a bungee jump?
5 ________ a sports star?
6 ________ a concert or a sports game in a big stadium?
7 ________ rafting?
8 ________________________?
9 ________________________?

6 **Your turn** **In pairs, discuss the questions in exercise 5. Then compare answers in groups.**

Have you ever sung on stage?

Yes, I have! In a school concert.

Workbook p.154 Metro Express p.114

7 Listening Skills

LO Listen to an interview and identify linking words

Around the world by train

1 122 **Listen to an interview with Aaron Young. How many countries does he mention?**

Cloud train, Salta, Argentina

2 122 **Listen again. Answer the questions with a maximum of four words.**

0 Where did Aaron begin his trip?
In San Francisco.

1 What did he see on his train trip in Italy?
______

2 What three forms of transportation does he mention?
______

3 How did Aaron feel on the cloud train from Salta?
______

4 Who took him home?
______

Active Listeners
Identifying linking words

Active listeners listen for different types of linking words: *and / also* for addition, *but* for contrast, *because* for reasons and *so* for results.
Linking words help us to predict what will come next.

3 122 **Read the tip. Then read the sentence halves from the interview and try to remember how they finish. Listen and check.**

0 "I wanted to remember everything, **so** ..."
I moved slowly.

1 "In India some trains are very uncomfortable, **but** ..."
______

2 "Sometimes I flew on planes, and in Africa I **also** ..."
______

3 "I did this **because** ... "
______

4 Your turn **Imagine you are traveling around the world. Which forms of transportation would you like to use and why? Tell a partner.**

I'd like to travel by plane because it's quick!.

Oh really? I'd like to travel by train because you see more!

Reading Skills

LO Read an article and recognize examples

An article

1 Read the article quickly. Which is the main idea?

a Be in control of your life.
b Put down your phone more often.
c Stop going out.

Active Readers
Recognizing examples

Active readers look for examples. This helps us to understand the main points of a text.

2 123 **Read the tip. Then read and listen to the article again. Put the highlighted activities in the correct part of the chart.**

FOMO	JOMO
checking your phone	*I only go out occasionally*

3 Read again. Choose the correct answer.

0 When you have FOMO you ...
 (a) want to do what other people are doing.
 b don't want to see your friends.
 c worry about your homework.
 d can't find your phone.

1 About 25% of teenagers ...
 a have experienced JOMO.
 b don't know what FOMO is.
 c have had FOMO.
 d have never missed a party.

2 Grace discovered that she ...
 a wanted to organize other people's lives.
 b didn't want to spend time with people.
 c needed to organize her own life better.
 d wasn't happy with her novel.

3 Dr. Taylor says that ...
 a we'll go to more boring parties in the future.
 b we won't worry about the parties we missed.
 c we won't have time for hobbies.
 d we'll spend more time watching TV.

4 Your turn **Do you get FOMO or JOMO? Give examples.**

I think I get FOMO. I look at my friends' photos on social media and I want to do the same things!

Well, I get JOMO! I'm happiest when I'm at home in my pajamas watching TV!

3 GOOD HEALTH AND WELL-BEING

Missing out?

All your friends have gone to a party. You can't go because you have homework, but you can't stop checking your phone. Have you ever been in this situation? Then perhaps you have FOMO – Fear of Missing Out.

"Sometimes I see a picture of some friends online," explains Lucas, 16. "They're doing something amazing, like surfing or snorkeling. It makes me unhappy. My friends are having fun and I'm not!"

About 25% of teenagers say that they get this feeling, but there's another, far better feeling: JOMO – the joy of missing out!

Grace, 18, has learned to feel JOMO. "In the past, I never stayed in. But I wasn't in control of my life, and other people were organizing it for me! When I finally understood this, I made changes. Now, I only go out occasionally, and I spend more time on my interests. I'm writing my own novel, and I've never felt happier!"

Dr. Stella Taylor, a psychologist, says social media makes FOMO worse. "It makes other people's lives look interesting and our own lives feel boring," she says.

So how can we learn to feel JOMO?

"Remember that you are in control of your life," says Dr. Taylor. "When you're older, you won't remember all those boring parties. You'll think about the time you wasted! With JOMO, you'll have more time for hobbies you enjoy, and you'll feel much happier!"

Right! It's time to put down your phone and find your pajamas. How about some TV?

7 Speaking & Global Skills

LO Ask about general experiences and details

An interview about experiences

1 124 **Read and listen. What was good and bad about Mr. Fry's experience?**

Robert	Mr. Fry, you teach us music, but we know you play a lot of sports, too. Have you ever participated in a big sports event?
Mr. Fry	Yes, I have!
Robert	What did you do?
Mr. Fry	I sailed across the Atlantic Ocean about 15 years ago.
Robert	That's amazing. How long did the journey take?
Mr. Fry	It took about four weeks.
Robert	And did you feel scared or worried sometimes?
Mr. Fry	Well, we were in a terrible storm. We were very scared, but then we reminded each other that people go on these trips all the time!
Robert	And your family? Did you miss them?
Mr. Fry	Yes, I missed them a lot. But I thought of the future and seeing them again soon. It was difficult, but it's an experience that I'll never forget.

2 125 **Listen and repeat.**

Active Speakers
Asking about general experiences and details

Active speakers ask general questions about experiences in the present perfect.
Have you ever taken part in a big sports event?
They ask about details in the simple past.
What did you do? / How long did the trip take?

3 126 **Read the tip. Complete the questions in the conversation with the present perfect or past simple and the words. Then listen and check.**

Beth	0 Have you ever appeared (you / ever / appear) on TV?
Ian	Yes, I have.
Beth	What show 1 ________ (you / be) on?
Ian	I was on a quiz show.
Beth	Wow! 2 ________ (be) fun?
Ian	Yes, it was. I felt nervous before the show, but I imagined myself as the winner. That made me feel better.
Beth	3 ________ (you / win) anything?
Ian	No, I didn't. I lost in the first round!

Global Skills
Emotional well-being

3 GOOD HEALTH AND WELL-BEING

We all experience difficult situations, so it's a good idea to learn some techniques that can make us feel better.

4 Read the Global Skills box and look at the poster. Which pieces of advice did Mr. Fry follow during his race across the Atlantic?

____ and ____

Emotional well-being

1 You're away from the people you love for a few weeks – Before you leave, pack photos of them, and arrange video calls. Remind yourself the separation isn't for long.

2 Something goes wrong, for example you've gotten off a train in the wrong place – Slow down and notice if you feel stressed or angry. Take ten deep breaths. Don't be afraid to ask for help.

3 You're doing a difficult or scary activity – Imagine yourself completing the activity successfully. Tell yourself that the organizers know what they're doing. It's scary, but you will be OK.

4 You've got FOMO – Remember there is always JOMO, too! Keep a journal and write down three good things about your day before you go to sleep.

5 With a partner, choose an activity from the bucket list activities on page 79 or choose another idea. Think of problems that can happen during this activity and possible solutions.

Activity	Problem	Solution
perform with a live band	forget the words	invent some words!

6 In pairs, roleplay an interview about the activity you chose in exercise 5. Use the model below and the conversation in exercise 1.

Have you ever ... ? → Yes, I have.

What happened? / What did you ... ? → I ran / walked / climbed / traveled to ...

How did you feel? → I was very scared / worried / excited, but then ...

That's great / amazing / fantastic!

The trip of a lifetime! Carretera Austral, South America

Before you watch

1 **Imagine you are going on a trip of a lifetime. Which of the things below would you like to do? Order them from best (1) to worst (6).**

a ____ go backpacking around the world
b ____ cycle across a foreign country
c ____ sail around the world
d ____ go snorkeling
e ____ go surfing
f ____ visit famous monuments around the world

2 **Look at the photo and the map below. What can you learn about this trip of a lifetime?**

While you watch

3 **Video** **Watch the video with the sound off. Check (✓) the things you see.**

0 ☑ a beach
1 ☐ famous monuments
2 ☐ a live concert
3 ☐ a water sport
4 ☐ an airport
5 ☐ a plane taking off
6 ☐ a lake
7 ☐ a glacier
8 ☐ mountains
9 ☐ a desert
10 ☐ getting back home

4 **Video** **Watch again. Complete the sentences.**

0 Sarah started her trip in the southern-most city on _Earth_.
1 The Carretera Austral is a ________ km road.
2 Sarah says Patagonia is a ________ place if you like remote areas.
3 Sarah enjoyed the scenery and thought the ________ were amazing.
4 Sarah's incredible journey finished in the ________ of Chile.

Active Viewers
Filler words

People often use filler words like "um" or "erm" when they are thinking of what to say. When you watch a video, ignore these words and focus on the main points.

5 **Video** **Read the tip. Watch the video again. Circle the filler words that Sarah uses.**

0 (erm) 1 sort of 2 well 3 kind of 4 like 5 you know 6 yeah 7 I guess

6 **What filler words do people use in your language? Make a list with a partner.**

After you watch

7 **Would you like to go on a trip like Sarah's? What are the good and bad points? Discuss in a group.**

Project p.114

8 Creativity

Metro VIDEO

Documentary
Sophie's costume

Ava 3 hours ago
Sophie made a really smart costume that taught her a lot of new skills.
I admire her because she worked so hard on it!

45 Reply

A Video 127 **Watch or listen. Why does Sophie enjoy cosplay? Check (✓) the correct reasons.**

0 ☑ She likes dressing up.
1 ☐ She likes learning new skills.
2 ☐ You learn to get things right the first time.
3 ☐ She always wins costume contests.
4 ☐ She meets a lot of people with the same interests.

B **Watch or listen again. Answer the questions.**

0 How long did it take Sophie to make her costume?
It took two weeks.
1 What material did she learn to draw on?
____
2 What did she forget to do at Comic-Con?
____
3 What contest did she enter at Gamescom?
____
4 What is Sophie's new favorite word?
____

C **Answer the questions.**

1 Would you like to visit a convention like Comic-Con or Gamescom? Why? / Why not?
2 Do you think you need to be good at art to do cosplay?
3 Imagine you are making a costume for yourself. What is the costume like?

Vocabulary **LO** Describe works of art

Creativity: adjectives

1 128 **Match the adjectives with the descriptions. Listen, check, and repeat.**

ancient ~~brand new~~ delicate enjoyable enormous old-fashioned original recycled smart strange successful tiny

0 completely new brand new
1 made with skill and intelligence ________
2 new and interesting ________
3 very big ________
4 not modern ________
5 unusual, surprising ________
6 easily broken or damaged ________
7 very small ________
8 thousands of years old ________
9 giving a nice experience ________
10 when a material is used again ________
11 achieving what you wanted ________

2 **Complete the descriptions. Use the correct words in parentheses.**

A What do you see in this picture? A duck or a rabbit? It's a [0] smart illusion that first appeared in a German magazine in the late 19th century. Images like these can be [1] ________ activities - ask your friends who sees the same thing as you? (**smart** / **enjoyable** / **recycled**)

B This is an [2] ________ idea from West Africa. People make toy cars from [3] ________ cans and sell them by the road. This photo shows them on sale in Madagascar. (**enormous** / **original** / **recycled**)

C This [4] ________ object is an example of "steam punk." It looks like a pair of [5] ________ glasses, but actually it's [6] ________. (**brand new** / **old-fashioned** / **strange** / **successful**)

D This painting is by the street artist Banksy. It's [7] ________ - about five meters tall! Banksy has always tried to keep his true identity a secret. So far, he's been [8] ________! (**enormous** / **successful** / **tiny**)

E This vase comes from Greece. It's [9] ________ - about 2,500 years old. It is very [10] ________, so the archeologists had to be very careful when they found it. (**ancient** / **delicate** / **tiny**)

3 **Your turn** **Discuss the questions with a partner.**

1 What is your favorite piece of art from exercise 2? Why do you like it?
2 Do you like making things? Why? / Why not? What creative activities do you do?

International English
Understanding different accents

Sophie is from Germany. When she speaks in English, she probably pronounces some consonant and vowel sounds differently from you. Everyone has an accent, and it's important to practice listening to as many different ones as possible.

D **Video** 129 **Read the International English box. Then read the sentences from *Sophie's costume* aloud and watch or listen to Sophie saying them.**

1 So the reason why I didn't make a video in such a long time is ... this!
2 But then it also teaches you about all these things that you would never even think about.
3 People wanted to talk to me and take pictures with me.
4 Yeah! It was awesome. That's my new favorite word.

E **In pairs, discuss the questions.**

1 How is Sophie's accent different from yours?
2 How easy is Sophie to understand? Why?
3 Are there any English sounds that you find difficult to pronounce?

Workbook p.156

8 Reading Skills

LO Read an article about unusual art

An article

1 **Read the article quickly and match the pictures with the parts of the article, A–C.**

A ___ B ___ C ___

But is it art?

In the past, "art" meant a painting, a drawing, or a sculpture which people could see in a gallery or in a wealthy home. These days, people are creating non-traditional art in unusual places. The question is: "Is it really art?"

A Ben Wilson is an artist who lies on the sidewalk to paint tiny pictures. But why? When people drop old gum in the street, we find it disgusting. Ben takes the gum and makes it into something delicate and beautiful. It's creative – but is it art?

B This little animal looks cute, but did you know, it's made from rice? Jolanda Stokkermans is a Belgian mother of two who makes food art. At first, Jolanda wanted to create recipes which were quick to prepare for busy families, but soon her project was more about art than saving time. She started posting her images on Instagram, which became very popular. Today, Jolanda has 14,000 followers!

Jolanda uses vegetables and different sauces to make her creations. It's an original idea – but is it art?

C Ai-Da is an artist who recently held her first exhibition in Oxford, England. The exhibition showed a series of beautiful drawings and paintings. However, there's something very unusual about their creator: she's a robot! Ai-Da, whose pictures show famous scientists, can do more than reproduce images. She has also learned to create beautiful abstract art. Each of her paintings and drawings is unique. Ai-Da is changing people's ideas about robots and what they can achieve. But are her paintings and drawings art?

1

2

3

2 130 **Read and listen to the article again. Complete the sentences with the names of the artists.**

0 Ben Wilson makes art from dirty things.
1 You can eat ________________'s art.
2 ________________'s art is the work of a machine.
3 ________________'s abilities have made people think differently.
4 ________________ makes art using recycled materials.
5 ________________ wanted a more organized life.

3 **Answer the questions.**

0 Why does Ben Wilson work lying down?
He paints old gum on the sidewalk.
1 What does Ben Wilson's art look like?
____
2 How does Jolanda Stokkermans combine art and cooking?
____
3 Why did Jolanda start her food project?
____
4 Where did Ai-Da first show her work to the public?
____
5 Who does Ai-Da paint pictures of?
____

4 Your turn **Are gum paintings, food pictures, and robot drawings really art? Explain your answer.**

Personally, I think they're art because they are all something that people can look at.

It's difficult to say. They're images. But two of the items in the text are food!

Grammar

LO Use relative pronouns to describe people, places, things, and possessions

Relative pronouns: *who*, *that*, *which*, and *whose*

1 131 **Read and listen to the Grammar in context. What is *Little People*?**

a an artist
b an artwork
c an art project

Grammar in context | **Present and Practice**

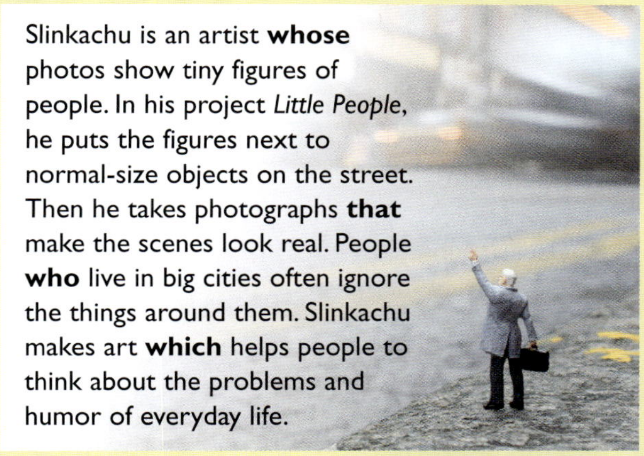

Slinkachu is an artist **whose** photos show tiny figures of people. In his project *Little People*, he puts the figures next to normal-size objects on the street. Then he takes photographs **that** make the scenes look real. People **who** live in big cities often ignore the things around them. Slinkachu makes art **which** helps people to think about the problems and humor of everyday life.

Grammar notes p.157

2 Complete the chart with words from the Grammar in context.

who (people)
People live in big cities. They often ignore the things around them. People [0]who live in big cities often ignore the things around them.
whose **(possessions)**
Slinkachu is an artist. His photos show tiny figures of people.
Slinkachu is an artist [1]_______ photos show tiny figures of people.
that **(people, places and things)**
… he takes photographs. They make the scenes look real.
… he takes photographs [2]_______ make the scenes look real.
which **(things)**
Slinkachu makes art. It helps people to think about …
Slinkachu makes art [3]_______ helps people to think about …

Stop

We can use *that* instead of *who* and *which*.

*Michelangelo was a famous artist **who** was born in Italy. = Michelangelo was a famous artist **that** was born in Italy.*

*Impressionism is an art genre **which** focuses on light. = Impressionism is an art genre **that** focuses on light.*

3 Choose the correct options.

0 Picasso was a Spanish artist **which** / **(who)** lived in France.
1 A self-portrait is a painting **that** / **whose** shows the artist.
2 Michelangelo was an artist **whose** / **who** sculptures and paintings are very famous.
3 A drawing is a picture **which** / **who** you make with a pencil.

4 132 **Listen and check.**

5 Complete the text with *who*, *whose*, or *which*.

Edgar Müller is a German painter [0] who is famous for his street art. Müller, [1]_______ fascination with art began in childhood, paints amazing images of things [2]_______ seem real. Actually, they're smart 3-D illusions [3]_______ look real from certain angles. This picture shows people [4]_______ are walking along the edge of a street in Geldern, Germany.

6 Complete the sentences with a relative clause. Use *who*, *whose*, or *which*.

0 She is an artist. Her sculptures are famous.
She is an artist whose sculptures are famous.
1 Alex is my friend. He draws portraits.
Alex is my friend ____________________.
2 Cubism is an old-fashioned style of art. My dad loves it.
Cubism is an old-fashioned style of art ____________________.
3 Marc Chagall was a Russian-born artist. His paintings told stories of his life.
Marc Chagall was an artist ____________________.
4 This is the art campaign. I was telling you about it.
This is the art campaign ____________________.

7 In which sentences in exercise 6 can you use *that*?

8 Your turn **Describe famous people and things using relative pronouns. Can your partner guess what you are describing?**

It's a big statue that you can see in New York.

Is it the Statue of Liberty?

8 Vocabulary

LO Talk about creative activities

Creativity: verbs

1 133 **Complete the creative activities in the sentences. Which activities can you see in the photos? Listen and check.**

What do *you* want to do when *you're* older?

build compose create ~~design~~ direct

0 I want to *design* and make my own furniture.
1 My brother works in construction. I'm going to help him to ________ houses.
2 I love programming. One day, I'm going to ________ a new computer game.
3 I can play the piano and read music. I want to ________ music for movies.
4 I think I'll ________ a movie one day. I make a lot of videos with my friends.

discover invent paint set up sew

5 I'd like to ________ a new form of transportation.
6 My dream is to ________ a new business with my friends. Maybe we can open a coffee shop!
7 I'd like to do something amazing one day, like ________ a cure for cancer.
8 I'm going to ________ fingernails in a beauty salon.
9 I'd like to be a fashion designer and ________ clothes on a machine.

2 134 **Listen and repeat.**

3 Your turn **Which of the activities in exercise 1 would you like to do when you're older? Tell a partner and give reasons for your answers.**

I'd like to set up my own company one day.

Listening Skills

LO Listen to a quiz about creative people

Creative people

1 Do the quiz. Compare your answers in pairs.

1 Who designed the Sydney Opera House?
Jørn Utzon / Oscar Niemeyer

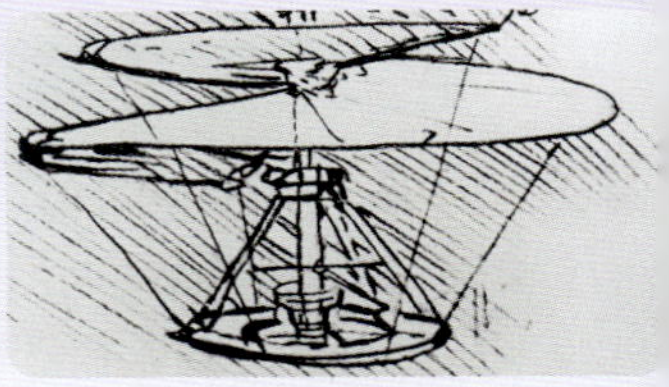

2 Who built the first helicopter?
Igor Sikorsky / Leonardo da Vinci

3 Who discovered radioactivity?
Albert Einstein / Marie Curie

4 Who invented the World Wide Web (WWW)?
Steve Jobs / Tim Berners-Lee

5 Who composed music after he went deaf?
Beethoven / Mozart

6 Who created *The Lord of the Rings* series?
George R. R. Martin / J. R. R. Tolkien

2 135 **Listen and check.**

3 135 **Listen again. Are the sentences T (*true*) or F (*false*)? Correct the false sentences.**

1 Niemeyer designed buildings in Brasília. T ☐ F ☐
2 Sikorsky designed the first parachute. T ☐ F ☐
3 Einstein won one Nobel Prize. T ☐ F ☐
4 Berners-Lee made a lot of money from the World Wide Web. T ☐ F ☐
5 Wolfgang Amadeus Mozart was a German composer. T ☐ F ☐
6 George R. R. Martin's novels became the TV series *Game of Thrones*. T ☐ F ☐

Workbook p.156

Grammar

LO Use subject and object questions to ask about people and events

Subject and object questions

1 136 **Read and listen to the Grammar in context. Luke and Milo are visiting the Rijks museum in Amsterdam, the Netherlands. What is strange about the eyes in the portrait?**

____

Grammar in context — Present and Practice

Milo **What did** you **want** to show me?
Luke I wanted to show you this portrait. I love it.
Milo Yeah, it's great. **Who drew** it?
Luke Rembrandt drew it!
Milo **Who did** he **draw** in the portrait?
Luke He drew himself: Rembrandt! But have you noticed his eyes when you move away from the portrait?
Milo No! **What happens**?
Luke Something strange happens! Look, his eyes follow you!
Milo Wow! You're right. Everywhere I stand, he's looking at me!

Grammar notes p.158

2 **Complete the chart with words from the Grammar in context.**

Subject questions	Object questions
⁰Who drew it? Rembrandt drew it!	¹__________ you want to show me? I wanted to show you this portrait.
²__________ happens? Something strange happens!	³__________ he draw in the portrait? He drew himself: Rembrandt!

3 **Look at the questions and answers. Choose the correct options.**

0 **Who designed** / **Who did design** the Cathedral of Brasilia?
Oscar Niemeyer designed it.

1 **What did Sikorsky design** / **What Sikorsky designed** ?
He designed **the first helicopter that could fly**.

2 **What did happen** / **What happened** to Beethoven in his 20s?
A problem with his ears started.

3 **Who did write** / **Who wrote** the opera *The Marriage of Figaro*?
Wolfgang Amadeus Mozart wrote it.

4 **Who did Steve Jobs** / **Who Steve Jobs** set up Apple with?
He set up Apple with **Steve Wozniak**.

4 137 **Listen and check.**

5 **Do the quiz. What can you remember? Write the questions and answers. Then ask and answer in pairs.**

Memory test

0 design / Jørn Utzon / did / what / ?
What did Jørn Utzon design?
He designed the Sydney Opera House.

1 discovered / Who / relativity / ?
____
____

2 Marie Curie / did / What / discover / ?
____
____

3 painted / Who / the Mona Lisa / ?
____
____

4 What / Slinkachu / does / make / ?
____
____

5 pictures on chewing gum / Who / paints / ?
____
____

6 **Your turn** **Write five more quiz questions about things you have learned in Metro. Use subject or object questions. Then in groups, ask and answer them.**

Who started the Ocean Cleanup project?

Boyan Slat started it.

What does a forensic scientist do?

A forensic scientist investigates crimes.

Pronunciation p.125 Workbook p.158 Metro Express p.115

8 Listening Skills

LO Listen to radio recordings to find specific information

Promoting art

1 138 **Listen to three short recordings from the radio. Which exhibition is the photo from: A, B, or C?**

2 138 **Listen again. Match the exhibition (A, B, or C) with the headlines. There are two extra headlines you don't need.**

0 Incredibly small art made from old materials __B__
1 A world of light and color through the eyes of an artist ____
2 Enormous sculptures made from pencils ____
3 A journey into the past through art ____
4 The everyday life of an artist in an ancient city ____

Active Listeners
Listening for specific information

Active listeners think about what type of information they need, for example, a time, date, or prices.

3 Read the tip. Then look at the sentences in exercise 4 and decide what type of information you need for the blanks: a time, a date, or a price.

4 138 **Listen again and complete the sentences.**

0 The Pompeii exhibition starts on Monday August __28__.
1 The Dalton Ghetti exhibition is open every day from ________ to 5 p.m.
2 Entrance to the Monet exhibition is ________ for local residents.

5 Your turn **In pairs, discuss which of the things in the recordings you would like to see. Give reasons for your answers.**

I'd like to see the ... because ...

I'm more interested in the ... because ...

Reading Skills

LO Read an article and recognize paraphrasing

A teen magazine article

1 139 **Read and listen to the article. What did Hannah and Guillaume design?**

____

____

____

Active Readers
Recognizing paraphrasing

Questions and texts will often say the same thing but use different words. This is called paraphrasing. Active readers can recognize paraphrasing in texts.

2 Read the tip. Use words from the text to complete the second sentence so that it has the same meaning as the first sentence.

At the age of 13, Hannah Herbst discovered that science was very enjoyable.
= Hannah Herbst first discovered __________ science when she was 13.

3 Read the article again and choose the correct answers.

0 Her pen pal needed help because ...
a she was unhappy in her community.
(b) her local area needed reliable energy.
c she didn't have the energy to write letters anymore.

1 Designing and making Beacon
a costs a lot.
b doesn't cost much.
c is difficult.

2 Before SensorWake, Guilllaume Rolland
a woke up in a bad mood every morning.
b didn't have an alarm clock.
c slept in his parents' garage.

3 The SensorWake clock can ...
a smell things.
b show you images of food.
c produce different smells.

4 Thanks to Sensorwake, Guillaume has
a built a lot of clocks.
b made a lot of money.
c set up more businesses.

4 Find examples of paraphrasing in the correct answers from exercise 3 and the text.

5 Your turn **Which invention do you think is smarter? Why?**

I think Hannah Herbst's machine is smarter. It uses energy from the ocean, so it won't create pollution!

Teen creators

Evidence shows that teenage brains are the most creative! Today, we meet two young people who invented incredible things while they were still at school.

Hannah Herbst first discovered a love for science and engineering when she was 13. At a science camp, she learned to build robots and solve engineering problems. That same year, she received a letter from her Ethiopian pen pal, whose community had some problems: they didn't have a reliable source of energy. Immediately, Hannah decided to help her friend. She designed a smart machine which uses energy from the ocean and costs only $12 to make. The machine is called Beacon and provides enough energy for lighting, clean water, and other essential things.

18-year-old French student Guillaume Rolland hated his alarm clock, which woke him up every morning with a loud noise. Guillaume wanted to wake up in a better mood, so he decided to do something about it!

Guillaume started working in his parents' garage, and he developed an original idea. Soon he had an alarm clock that wakes you up with a smell: lemon, apples, chocolate, or even grass! He then set up a company which builds and sells the clocks. The popular clock is called SensorWake, and it has made Guillaume a successful businessman.

These two teenagers show that any problem – big or small – can start a creative process. And inside a teenage brain, who knows what will happen?

Workbook p.159 Writing Skills p.107

8 Speaking & Global Skills

LO Talk about art we like or dislike and make comparisor

Likes, dislikes, and comparisons

1 140 **Read and listen to the comments about the song. Check (✓) the correct boxes in the table.**

	... likes it	... doesn't like it.
Kaitlyn	☑	☐
Ana	☐	☐
Eduardo	☐	☐

Kaitlyn What does everyone think of Billie Eilish's song?

Ana I really like it! It reminds me of the songs from her first album. And it sounds a bit like music from the 70s!

Kaitlyn Me, too, I love it! The part I like best is the second half of the song when the music gets faster.

Eduardo It isn't really my kind of thing. I'm not a fan of Billie Eilish's music. It isn't original enough, and it's too boring!

Ana You can't say her music is boring! I'm really into it! And this is the best song on the album!

Eduardo Sorry! It's just not for me!

2 141 **Listen and repeat.**

Active Speakers
Likes, dislikes, and comparisons

Active speakers use these phrases to talk about their likes and dislikes, or to make comparisons.

Likes

I love it! *I really like ...* *I'm really into ...*
The part I like best is ...

Dislikes

It isn't really my kind of thing. *I'm not a fan of ...*
It's too ... *It isn't ... enough* *It's just not for me.*

Comparisons

It reminds me of ... *It looks / sounds (a bit) like ...*

3 142 **Read the tip. Complete the comments below with expressions from the tip. Then listen and check.**

0 ___It sounds___ a bit like ___Lewis Capaldi___.
1 ________________ of paintings by the Spanish artist Dalí.
2 ________________ modern for me.
3 It isn't detailed ________________.
4 ________________ jazz music. I never listen to it.
5 I don't like it. ________________ for me!

Global Skills
Critical thinking

Looking at or listening to a form of art or a new invention encourages us to think critically. We automatically like or dislike it, and often compare it to other things. However, it's important to think about why we react in these different ways.

4 **Read the Global Skills box. Answer the questions.**

0 What does Ana compare Billie Eilish's song to?
She compares it to the songs from her first album and music from the 70s.

1 Why doesn't Eduardo like Billie Eilish's music?
____

2 Why does Kaitlyn prefer the second half of the song?
____

3 How does Ana compare it to the other songs on the album?
____

5 **Work in groups of four. Choose a piece of art, for example, a painting or a sculpture. You can also choose a new invention, or a favorite song or a movie.**

6 **In your group, brainstorm positive and negative opinions of the piece of art you chose in exercise 5, and things you can compare it to.**

Guillaume Rolland's SensorWake clock

Positive: smart, original, waking up to a pleasant smell is better than a loud noise
Negative: complicated, not necessary
Comparisons: a light alarm clock

7 **Have a conversation about your chosen piece of art that shows different opinions and comparisons. Use the model below and your ideas from exercise 6.**

What do you think of ... ? → I really like it! It looks / sounds a bit like ...
→ It isn't really my kind of thing. It's too ...
→ What?! I'm really into it!
→ I'm sorry. It reminds me of ... It's just not for me!

Graffiti Life, London, U.K.

Before you watch

1 Match the pictures A–C with the descriptions 1–3.

0 street art – an enormous painting on a building or wall __B__
1 a street artist at work ____
2 graffiti – words and pictures painted on a wall or a public place, by a lot of different people ____

A 

B 

C 

While you watch

Active Viewers
Predicting the content of a video

Sometimes a video begins with a short sequence of images or scenes from the main part of the video. This is called a preview. You can use a preview to predict what you will see and learn about in a video.

2 Video Read the tip. Then watch the preview and check (✓) the things you see. What do you think the video will be about?

0 ☑ a policeman photographing graffiti
1 ☐ a policeman arresting a street artist
2 ☐ tourists photographing street art
3 ☐ street art in a museum
4 ☐ people learning how to paint
5 ☐ people planning and making an enormous painting

3 Video Watch the video. Choose the best words to complete each sentence.

0 Today, street art is **popular** / **a big problem** in cities.
1 Graffiti Life **cleans up** / **makes** street art.
2 Graffiti Life also **teaches painting** / **buys street art**.

4 Video Watch again. Complete the sentences.

advertising art gallery London personality street art team work ~~vandalism~~ warehouse

0 In the past, most people thought that graffiti was __vandalism__.
1 Nowadays, ____________ sells for a lot of money.
2 A city street can now be a type of ____________.
3 ____________ is a great place to see street art.
4 Graffiti Life sometimes makes graffiti for ____________.
5 A company may send its employees to Graffiti Life to learn about ____________.
6 Young adults work on their art in a ____________.
7 Painting may help you discover a new part of your ____________.

After you watch

5 Work in groups. Answer the questions.

1 Would you like your class to have a Graffiti Life workshop? Why? / Why not?
2 Do you think more street art would improve your town or city? Why? / Why not?
3 Is there graffiti or street art in your town or city that you would like to remove? Why? / Why not?

I'd like my class to have a Graffiti Life workshop because art activities are fun for everyone. Also the workshop brings people together as a team. I think that's great for classroom work.

Project p.115

D Review

Vocabulary

1 Complete the verbs in the sentences.

0 Amy has d_y_ _e_ _d_ her hair green!
1 Have you ever d____ ____ ____ ____ ____ ____ ____ ____ your bedroom? I've painted mine blue!
2 I've never s____ ____ ____ ____ ____ around the world. I've never been on a boat!
3 Lucas has w____ ____ ____ ____ ____ ____ his own novel.
4 My little brother has m____ ____ ____ a viral dance video!
5 Bruno has i____ ____ ____ ____ ____ ____ ____ ____ ____ ____ his favorite YouTuber! He asked a lot of questions!
6 I've never r____ ____ ____ ____ across a desert. I'm terrible at running.
7 We've c____ ____ ____ ____ ____ under the stars a lot this summer. The sky at night is so beautiful!

2 Match the phrasal verbs with the pictures.

0 _C_ go away	3 ____ take off
1 ____ stay in	4 ____ go out
2 ____ get back	5 ____ get off

3 Complete the texts with creativity adjectives.

~~ancient~~ delicate strange

This is an [0] _ancient_ wall painting from the tomb of Nebamun in Thebes, Egypt. When they removed it from the tomb, it broke around the edges because it's very [1] ____________. The painting shows men with horses and two-wheeled "chariots." The [2] ____________ letters are "hieroglyphs", a writing system used in Egypt 2,000–4,000 years ago.

smart enormous tiny

In 2016, Solar Impulse 2 became the first solar-powered plane to fly around the world. It has [3] ____________ wings of 72 m, only a little smaller than the wings of an Airbus A380! Its [4] ____________ technology uses 17,000 [5] ____________ solar cells to power four engines.

4 Complete the sentences with the simple past form of the creativity verbs.

build compose ~~discover~~ invent paint set up

0 Isaac Newton _discovered_ gravity in the 1680s, after he watched an apple fall from a tree.
1 The ancient Egyptians ____________ the Great Pyramid at Giza 4,500 years ago.
2 Mozart ____________ his first piece of music when he was only five years old.
3 The Wright Brothers ____________ the airplane in 1903.
4 Picasso ____________ and drew over 13,500 pictures.
5 The international community ____________ the United Nations in 1945.

Grammar

1 Reorder the words to make sentences.

0 Ryan / appeared / has / on TV / never
Ryan has never appeared on TV.

1 her bedroom / has / decorated / Lucy
____

2 never / backpacking / been / I've
____

3 in / we've / snorkeling / the Mediterranean Sea / been
____
____

4 the world / my uncle / sailed / around / has
____

5 their hair / dyed / they / haven't
____

2 Write questions and short answers with the information in the chart.

	write / a blog	dye / hair	read / this book	eat / sushi	try / surfing	meet / before
0 I			✗			
1 you				✓		
2 he		✓				
3 she	✗					
4 we						✗
5 they					✓	

0 Have I ever read this book?
No, you haven't.

1 ______________________________?
_______, I _______.

2 ______________________________?
_______, he _______.

3 ______________________________?
_______, she _______.

4 ______________________________?
_______, we _______.

5 ______________________________?
_______, they _______.

3 Make relative clauses using *who* for people, *that* for things, *whose* for possessions, and a–e.

0 An artist is someone who c
1 Billie Eilish is a singer _______ ____
2 Stone is a material _______ ____
3 Picasso was an artist _______ ____
4 An honest person is someone _______ ____

a song *No Time to Die* is in a James Bond movie.
b paintings are very famous.
~~c paints pictures.~~
d always tells the truth.
e is very hard.

4 Read about the invention of the car. Write subject or object questions for each answer.

Karl Benz and his wife, Bertha, set up Benz & Co. in 1883. In 1885, Karl designed and made the world's first car. His invention, the Motorwagen, only had three wheels. Benz & Co. made its first four-wheeled car in 1894.

0 Who set up Benz & Co.?
Karl and Bertha Benz.

1 What ______________________________?
They set up Benz & Co.

2 What ______________________________?
He designed and made the first car.

3 Who ______________________________?
Karl Benz invented the first car.

4 How many wheels ______________________________?
Three.

5 What ______________________________?
Its first four-wheeled car.

Look back: Units 7 and 8

Read the text about Ben Fogle. Then choose the correct answers.

Have you [0] ever heard of Ben Fogle? He's a British television personality, explorer, and writer. Fogle has been very [1] _______ in his working life, and he has [2] _______ missed an opportunity to do something exciting. He's [3] _______ on TV, he's climbed Mount Everest, and he's traveled the world to [4] _______ new cultures and customs. When Fogle returns home, he writes books about his adventures, but [5] _______ happens when he isn't working? He is married, has two children, [6] _______ names are Ludo and Iona, and lives a normal family life.

	a	b	c
0	a never	b ever	c sometimes
1	a ancient	b tiny	c successful
2	a never	b ever	c always
3	a written	b appeared	c made
4	a discover	b set up	c compose
5	a what did	b what does	c what
6	a who	b whose	c that

CLIL D p.122

1 A vacation postcard

LO Write a postcard

Writing Skills

1 Read the instructions. What can you do with the *sendmypostcard* app?

Instructions for using the *sendmypostcard* app.

1. Take a photo.
2. Write your postcard and the address.
3. Press SEND.
4. We print your postcard and send it to the address!

INSTALL

Reviews ★★★★☆

2 Read the postcard. Complete the chart.

Hi Julia,

I'm on vacation in Japan! We're visiting my grandparents and my cousins.

This is a picture of Harajuku. It's a district in Tokyo with the most amazing fashion stores for teenagers. My cousins and I are here now – we love shopping! People here like wearing costumes of their favorite cartoon character. They look great!

Harajuku has the best Japanese pancakes, too. I'm eating one now. It has fruit and cream in it. Usually I don't like trying new food, but I love these.

Jaa mata! (That's "See you!" in Japanese.)

Masayo x

Where is Masayo?	0 Tokyo, Japan
Why?	1 ______
Why is Harajuku popular with young people?	2 ______
What is Masayo doing?	3 ______

Active Writers
Using contractions

Active writers use contractions in informal writing, e.g., a postcard or an email to a friend.

The verb *be*:

I am on vacation. → *I'm on vacation.*

That is "See you!" → *That's "See you!"*

Negatives

I do not like → *I don't like*

3 Read the tip. Rewrite the sentences. Use contractions where possible.

0 We are not visiting any museums today because they are closed.
We aren't visiting any museums today because they're closed.

1 My sister does not like sunbathing because she thinks it is boring.
______

2 My brother cannot swim because he is scared of water.
______

3 We are disappointed with our hotel rooms because they do not have nice views.
______

4 Imagine you are on vacation. Copy and complete the chart in exercise 2 for you. Change the highlighted information.

5 Write your postcard for the app.

- Use your chart in exercise 4.
- Use the postcard in exercise 2 as a model.
- Use contractions.
- Print and include a picture.

A product review

LO Write a review of a product

1 **A lot of people write reviews of products. What do you think are the main reasons for this? Check (✓) the sentences below. Then check your answers below.**

1 ☐ They want to give positive feedback.
2 ☐ They want to complain.
3 ☐ They want to help other people to choose the right product.
4 ☐ They want everyone to know their opinions.
5 ☐ They want to share their experiences.

According to the review website Trustpilot, the main three reasons for writing reviews are:
1 to help others
2 to share experiences
3 to thank a company for a great product or service

Women's Clothes > Sweaters

Gray cotton sweater
$18.99
Select size ▾
ORDER

Reviews: 201

KEMI_P ★★★★☆
I bought this gray cotton sweater in a size medium, and it fits perfectly. The cotton is so soft and comfortable to wear, and the quality is great. The company makes its products so well. I thought the price was good value, too. The only problem was the delivery: it took three weeks for my sweater to arrive! But apart from that I'm a happy customer. Everything on this website, from the clothes to the shoes, is so amazing and I would like to order from it again soon.

2 **Read the review. Complete the chart.**

Material	0 cotton
Color	1 ________
Size	2 ________
Quality	3 ________
Price	4 ________
Delivery time	5 ________

Active Writers
so and *such*

Active writers use the adverbs *so* and *such* to emphasize adjectives and nouns.

so **+ adjectives / adverbs**
Adjectives:
*These pants are **really cool**.* → *These pants are **so cool**.*
Adverbs:
*The line is moving **very slowly**.* → *The line is moving **so slowly**.*
such **+ adjective + noun**
*This is **a very big clothes store**.* → *This is **such a big** clothes store.*

3 **Read the tip. Rewrite the sentences with *so* and *such*.**

0 These are very expensive jeans.
These are such expensive jeans.
1 My phone was very cheap.
____
2 Wow! My new laptop works really fast!
____
3 That is a really cool jacket.
____
4 This store has very lazy sales clerks!
____

4 **You are going to write a review of a new product. It can be a real product that you own or an imaginary one. You can use an idea from the box or an idea of your own. Copy and complete the chart in exercise 2 for you.**

clothes or shoes   a gadget   furniture   sports equipment

5 **Write your review of the product.**

- Use your chart in exercise 4.
- Use the review in exercise 2 as a model.
- Use *so* and *such*.

3 A thank-you note

LO Write a thank-you note

1 **Read the note. What is the main reason Avery is writing to her grandparents?**

2 **Read the note again and answer the questions.**

0 What did Avery get from her grandparents?
She got a card and some money.

1 Why did they give it to her?
____

2 What is she going to do on Saturday morning?
____
____

3 How did she celebrate?
____
____

4 How is she going to celebrate on Saturday?
____

Active Writers
Responding and thanking

Active writers use phrases for responding to cards and letters and to say thank you for gifts.

Responding to cards and letters

I got your ...
It was so nice to receive your ...
Thank you for the ...

Saying thank you for gifts

Thank you so much!
I love my new ... I can ...
Thank you again for the ...
It was so nice of you.

3 **Read the tip. Complete the sentences with the phrases from the Active Writers.**

0 Hi Uncle Jack! *Thank you* for my new laptop.
1 I love my new boots. ________ wear them to my birthday party!
2 Thank you for my birthday money.
It ________________.
3 ________ your letter yesterday. It was so nice to receive it!
4 I was really happy to receive your present. Thank ________________!
5 Thank you again ________ books. I can't wait to start reading them!

4 **Imagine you received a gift from a relative. Complete the chart.**

What did you get?	
Who was it from?	
Why did you get it?	
What are you going to do with it?	

5 **Write a thank-you note to your relative.**

- Use your chart in exercise 4.
- Use Avery's thank-you note as a model.
- Use the phrases for responding and saying thank you.
- Include a picture.

Hi Grandma and Grandpa!

I got your birthday card and money yesterday. Thank you so much!

I saw an amazing jacket at the mall last month, and I earned over $30 by doing chores for Mom and Dad. With this money, I can now afford the jacket and a new pair of sneakers, too! I'm going to get them on Saturday morning. I'm really excited!

My birthday was awesome. I went to an amusement park with three friends, and we ate out in the evening. I'm also going to have a small party at home on Saturday.

Thank you again for the money. It was so nice of you.

I hope you are both well. See you soon!

Love,
Avery

An opinion essay

LO Write an opinion essay

1 Read Brandon's essay. Write the correct numbers.

a Paragraphs ____ and ____ make suggestions to help with the problem.

b Paragraph __1__ describes the problem.

c Paragraph ____ is the conclusion to the essay.

An opinion essay: Arriving at school

1 Every morning, over 500 students arrive at our school. A lot of students arrive in their parents' cars. Personally, I think that cars make the school entrance dangerous. The way I see it, we can do two things to protect students.

2 First, we need to tell students it's better to walk or take the bus. It's healthier to walk, and cars cause a lot of pollution.

3 Second, some students need to come to school by car, but I feel their parents can park their cars at the end of the street.

4 To sum up, cars make the school entrance dangerous. However, students can walk to school, and parents can park away from the school entrance. In my opinion, these two things are going to make our school a safer place.

by Brandon Jackson

2 Read the essay again. Answer the questions.

0 Which group of students does Brandon think are the problem?
Students in their parents' cars.

1 Why is walking to school better than driving?
____

2 What is the writer's second suggestion?
____

3 Which is the worst place that some parents park?
____

4 What phrase does Brandon use to start his conclusion?
____

Active Writers
Giving opinions

Active writers express their opinions with a variety of phrases.

In my ____________ *...* *The way* ____________ *it ...*
____________ *feel ...* ____________, *I think ...*

3 Read the tip. Then read the text again and complete the four phrases.

4 Order the words to complete the sentences.

a **feel / everyone / I / can**
There's a lot of litter on the beach. I feel everyone can clean up before they leave.

b **need / Personally, / think / more / we / I**
The buses to school are very crowded.
____________________ places for students to sit.

c **students / our / The / it, / see / I / way**
Our school needs to think more about the environment.
____________________ need more places to recycle paper.

d **to / we / need / opinion, / my / In**
There aren't many sports clubs in our area.
____________________ encourage young people to do healthy activities.

5 Plan an essay about a local problem. Use an idea in exercise 4 or one of your own.

Describe the problem.	
What are your suggestions to change the situation?	

6 Write an essay about your local problem.

- Use your plan in exercise 5.
- Use Brandon's essay as a model.
- Include a variety of phrases to express your opinion.

5 A profile of a friend

LO Write a profile of a friend

Writing Skills

1 Read Gabrielle's description quickly. Which sentence is true?

Gabrielle and Faith ...

a are the same height.
b have similar hair.
c have very similar personalities.

My friend

This is Faith. She's my best friend. We met in elementary school. We go to the same high school, and we also live in the same apartment building. We hang out every weekend, and her parents are good friends of my mom and dad.

People sometimes think Faith and I are sisters. She isn't as tall as me, but we both have long, curly, dark hair. Faith has beautiful green eyes, and mine are brown. She isn't interested in fashion, and she usually wears old blue jeans and a T-shirt.

Faith is a really kind, friendly person. I often get impatient and angry when things take a long time or I can't do what I want, but she is always patient. Faith is also a great student. She loves science and she wants to be a doctor.

Gabrielle Thompson, Chicago, U.S.

Active Writers
Using paragraphs

Active writers organize their ideas into paragraphs. Each paragraph contains a different idea, and this makes it easier to understand.

2 Read the tip. Match the ideas in the box with the paragraphs in Gabrielle's description of Faith.

~~how she knows Faith~~ personality and ambitions physical appearance

Paragraph 1: how she knows Faith
Paragraph 2: ____________
Paragraph 3: ____________

3 Read the description again. Complete the chart.

Person	0 Faith – Gabrielle's best friend
Physical appearance	She has long, curly hair and 1 ____________ green 2 ____________. She wears 3 ____________ and T-shirts.
Personality and ambitions	Faith is kind, 4 ____________, and 5 ____________. She enjoys 6 ____________ at school. In the future, she plans to become a 7 ____________.

4 Answer the questions.

0 How did Gabrielle meet Faith?
They met in elementary school.

1 Where do the girls live?
____

2 What do Gabrielle and Faith do on weekends?
____

3 How do the girls look similar?
____

4 How are their personalities different?
____

5 Copy and complete the chart in exercise 3 for someone you know.

6 Write your description.

- Use the structure in exercise 2 to organize your ideas into paragraphs and the answers in exercise 4.
- Use the description of Faith as a model.
- Include a picture of the person.

A narrative

LO Write a narrative

1 **Read the six parts of Scarlett's story. Order the events from 1–6.**

A ___

Next, a new page opened in my browser. **Surprisingly**, it was a picture of a bomb. I wasn't sure what it meant.

B ___

Usually, I ignore ads like this, but this time, I clicked on the link and downloaded a file.

C ___

I talked with my parents. They were worried about it, too, so we investigated the problem online.

D 1

I was looking at my messages on my laptop one day when an ad for a free game appeared in a pop-up window!

E ___

Suddenly, the bomb exploded and my screen went black! I was really worried about my computer.

F ___

Finally, we took my laptop to a computer store. Luckily, they were able to clean my computer. **Thankfully**, I never saw the bomb again. The internet can be a dangerous place. Now I always use antivirus software, and I never click on links in ads!

2 **Answer the questions.**

0 What was Scarlett doing when the ad appeared?
She was looking at her messages.

1 Where did Scarlett and her parents look for advice?
______

2 Where did Scarlett and her parents take the laptop?
______

3 What does Scarlett do differently now?
______
______

Active Writers
Using adverbs

Active writers use adverbs at the beginning of sentences to add interest to a text.

finally suddenly surprisingly thankfully unfortunately usually worryingly

They always put a comma after the adverb.

***Finally**, she arrived home.*

3 **Read the tip. Choose the correct options.**

It was a rainy afternoon, and Adam was waiting for the bus. [0]**Usually / Surprisingly**, it was on time, but that afternoon it was late. [1]**Suddenly / Worryingly**, the bus appeared. [2]**Surprisingly / Thankfully**, it was traveling very fast. As the bus got closer, Adam noticed that it was nearly empty, but it got faster and faster, and didn't stop! Adam was cold, wet, and tired. But [3]**finally / unfortunately**, the next bus was in an hour, so he started walking. [4]**Finally / Surprisingly**, he got back home. But as he walked through the door, his mom shouted, "Adam! Listen to this on the radio, it's your bus!" "This afternoon the number 39 bus to Hampton was involved in a bank robbery. Three bank robbers forced the driver to help them escape."

"Wow!" said Adam. "Is the driver OK?"

[5]**Usually / Thankfully**, he's fine,' said Adam's mom.

"Well I'm very wet!" said Adam. "But that's great news!"

4 **In pairs, use the prompts to tell a crime story. Use each of the adverbs from the tip box once.**

Rachel was traveling on a very crowded bus. Unfortunately, there wasn't anywhere to sit.

A Rachel – travel on a very crowded bus – nowhere to sit
B two young boys – push past her while they get off the bus
C Rachel – realize wallet not in bag!
D Rachel explain to the bus driver – bus driver very helpful
E the police – use CCTV to find the boys

5 **Write a short crime story.**

- You can write Rachel's story from exercise 4, or you can write the bus driver's description of events from exercise 3. Or, you can use your own ideas.
- Use the past progressive and simple past.
- Use five of the adverbs from the tip box.

7 An informal message

LO Write an informal message

1 **Read the messages. Put the points in the correct order.**

Alex ...

thanks Ted for the invitation ____

says he think he can attend the party ____

congratulates Ted on his trip ____

receives a message about a party __1__

Ted

I'm home again!
Please come to the Cottage Restaurant on Saturday, September 25th at 8 p.m. to help me celebrate!
Hope to see you there!
Ted

Hey Ted!
Congrats on sailing around the world. When did you get back? You're such an amazing superstar! **TBH** I always knew you could do it! I've decided to be more like you and go away more often! Thanks for the **invite** to your celebration party on the 25th. I never miss an opportunity to wear my party shirt! (**JK**!) I've messaged the restaurant to check that I can have the night off, but I'm sure I'll be there, **no problem**.
Speak soon!
Alex

2 **Read the second message again. Are the sentences T (*true*) or F (*false*)?**

		T	F
0	Ted is going to sail around the world.	☐	☑
1	Alex was sure that Ted could sail around the world.	☐	☐
2	Alex doesn't travel as often as Ted.	☐	☐
3	Alex doesn't have anything to wear to the party.	☐	☐
4	Alex doesn't think he will be free on the 25th.	☐	☐

Active Writers
Informal messages

Active writers use shortened words, expressions, and acronyms in online messages.

Shortened words

congrats → *congratulations*
invite → *invitation*

Shortened expressions

promise → *I promise you.*
no problem → *There isn't a problem.*
speak soon → *I'll speak to you soon.*
see you there → *I'll see you there.*

Acronyms

DM me → *Direct message me*
IMO → *In my opinion*
ASAP → *As soon as possible*
TBH → *To be honest*
JK → *Just kidding*
IDK → *I don't know*

3 **Read the tip. Then read the sentences below and add the correct words, expressions, and acronyms.**

0 __Congrats__ on winning the race!
1 The geography homework is so difficult. ____________ how to do it!
2 I'm sorry I didn't finish the report yesterday. I'll do it ____________.
3 ____________. Don't worry about the money. You can give it to me next week.
4 Dad is dancing in the kitchen. He's too terrible to watch! ____________ 😂!
5 Did you get the ____________ to Taylor's party?
6 OK, I need to do some homework. ____________. Bye!
7 I contacted the YouTuber about an interview. But ____________ I don't think he'll be interested.

4 **Read the message below. With a partner, follow the points and discuss how you can respond to the message with the words, expressions, and acronyms from the tip box.**

- Congratulate Sophie on her job.
- Give your opinion of her job. It can be funny!
- Tell her you aren't worried about the money.
- End the message by saying you hope you'll see her soon.

Hi,
How are you? I haven't forgotten the money I owe you, and I'm so sorry that I haven't given back the money. The good news is, I've found a job! Unfortunately, it's not great – I wear a hot dog costume outside a restaurant and invite customers inside. TBH, I'm not sure how long I will do it! But I'll give back the money soon, promise! I'll DM you when they pay me.
Speak soon,
Sophie

5 **Write a message.**

- Use the points from exercise 4 and the words, expressions, and acronyms in the tip box.
- Use the message in exercise 1 as a model.

A biography

LO Write a biography

1 **Read the biography. (Ignore the five highlighted mistakes.) What important prize did Einstein win?**

Albert Einstein

Albert Einstein were a German scientist whose formula "$E=mc^2$" made him one of the most important figures in modern history. But what else ⁁ we know about him?

Einstein was born in 1879 in Ulm, Germany, and he has grown up in Munich. He was an intelligent child who loved the math, physics, and music: he loved play the violin all day.

In 1894, Einstein went to college in Bern, Switzerland, to study physics. He was married twice, and he had three children. While he was working in an office in Bern, he created "$E=mc^2$", which became one of his most important theories. In 1913, he moved to the University of Berlin and wrote his famous "general theory of relativity". He won the Nobel Prize for Physics in 1923.

In 1932, Einstein moved to the U.S. and lived there for the rest of his life. He died in 1955, but his incredible theories are still very popular. His life and work inspire young scientists today and will continue to inspire scientists of the future.

Silvia Ribeira, Florianopolis

2 **Read the biography again and answer the questions.**

0 What is Einstein best known for?
His $E = mc^2$ formula.

1 When and where was he born?
____

2 What were his three favorite school subjects?
____

3 Did he get married or have children?
____
____

4 What happened to him in 1923?
____

5 Where was he living when he died?
____

Active Writers
Checking your work

Active writers check their grammar. Here are five common mistakes:

a subject-verb agreement
b question forms
c confusion of simple past and present perfect
d using *the* when it isn't necessary
e use of gerund or infinitive forms

3 **Read the tip. Correct the highlighted mistakes in the first paragraph of the biography.**

a Einstein were a German scientist → Einstein was a German scientist
b what else we know → ________________
c has grown up → ________________
d the math → ________________
e he loved play → ________________

4 **Read the task and plan a biography.**

Task: You are going to write a biography of a creative person. They can be living or dead.

1 Look at the people below. Are they an inspiration to you? Do you want to do a job that is similar?

Beyoncé Knowles Billie Eilish Frida Kahlo
John Lennon Leonardo da Vinci Marie Curie
Maya Angelou Oscar Niemeyer Steve Jobs
Tim Berners-Lee

2 Choose one of the people above or any other creative person who you would like to write about.
3 Go online and find out about his / her life.
4 Answer the questions in exercise 2 about the person.
5 Find a few pictures of him / her.

5 **Write your biography.**

- Use your notes from exercise 4.
- Use Silvia's biography as a model.
- Check your grammar and correct it.

Metro Express

← Student Book p.15 p.17

1 The highlighted verbs are in the wrong sentences. Write new sentences about the vacation activities.

On vacation, ...

0 I like taking on the beach every day.
I like sunbathing on the beach every day.

1 We love eating gifts.
______

2 My brother hates going museums.
______

3 My mom loves trying in a hotel.
______

4 My parents like visiting out.
______

5 My dad doesn't like buying sightseeing.
______

6 I don't like sunbathing photos.
______

7 I hate staying new food.
______

2 Break the code and write the letters.

The writer / **The writer's brother** likes animals with eight legs!

M	y		b	r	o	t	h	e	r		i	s																					.
|	}		!	?	<	'	&	$	?		(	@		"	?	*	[	}		*	!	<	~	'		@	>	(	£	$	?	@	

					'																	!
!	~	'		(		|		@	"	*	?	$	£		<	%		'	&	$	|	

Key

A	B	C	D	E	F	G	H	I	J	K	L	M	N	O	P	Q	R	S	T	U	V	W	X	Y	Z
*	!	"	£	$	%	^	&	(	)	+	=	|	\	<	>	/	?	@	'	~	#	{	]	}	[

Project

Make a video advertisement

1 **What are the similarities and differences between your town and Miami? In your group, make a list using information from the *Miami, Florida* video on page 21 and your own ideas.**

2 **Research and plan a video ad for your town.**

1 Make a list of the most popular places and activities for tourists in your town.

2 Choose the places and activities you want to include in your video.

3 **Write a first draft.**

1 On a large piece of paper, sketch the scenes in your video. Then divide the presentation between the students in the group.

2 Write a draft of the presenter's words for your section.

3 Decide when and where to film the video.

4 **Check and redraft.**

1 Swap your draft with a partner. Give feedback.

2 Listen to feedback about your work. Then write a second draft.

5 **Compile.**

1 Film your ad. The presenters can be in the video, or you can add their words afterwards.

2 Add music to your ad.

6 **Share.**

1 Share your video ad with the class.

2 Which ad do you like? Why?

7 **Reflect.**

I'm proud of ______

For next time, I want to improve ______

← Student Book p.21

WOW! Metro Express

← Student Book p.25 | p.27

1 What can you see in the photos? Write the material.

cotton leather ~~metal~~ plastic wood wool

0 metal

1 ________

2 ________

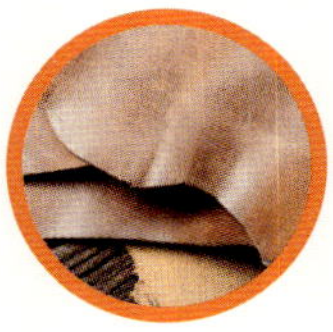
3 ________

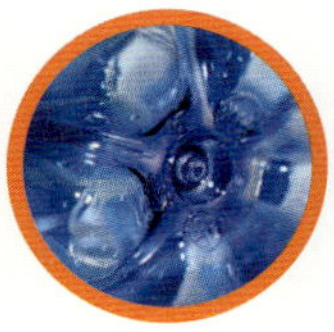
4 ________

5 ________

2 Solve the riddles. What are the materials?

0 When it's clean you can see through it. When it's dirty, you can't. glass

1 You can use this thick material to make boxes to carry heavy things. But when it gets wet, it goes soft and breaks! ________

2 This can be hard or soft, thin or thick, and heavy or light. It's everywhere, but it's 100% synthetic! ________

3 This thick material is great for bags, but not for clothes like T-shirts! ________

4 This natural material comes from animals. It's soft, but very strong, and people use it to make bags and shoes. ________

Project

Make a digital slideshow

1 The *Surfers against sewage* video on page 31 talks about the different types of litter on beaches. What are the most common types of litter where you live? Tell your group.

2 Research and plan a digital slideshow about your litter.

1 Take photos of all the litter you produce in one day before you throw it away.
2 Share your photos with your group. Who produces the most and least litter? What are the most common types of litter?
3 Discuss how your group can produce less litter.

3 Write a first draft.

1 Decide how you are going to present each person's collection of litter and the possible solutions to this. Then divide the work between the students in the group.
2 Write a draft of the presenter's words for your section.
3 Decide which photos to include and the design for your slideshow.

4 Check and redraft.

1 Swap your draft with a partner. Give feedback.
2 Listen to feedback about your work. Then write a second draft.

5 Compile.

1 Make your slideshow. Record the presenters.
2 Add music to your slideshow.

6 Share.

1 Share your slideshow with the class.
2 Which slideshows do you like? Why?

7 Reflect.

I'm proud of ________________________________

____

For next time, I want to improve

____

← Student Book p.31

Metro Express

← Student Book p.37 p.39

1 Complete the money verbs in the crossword.

						0B				
				2L		O				
		3		1		R	N			4
		W				R				
5S						O				V
						6W				

2 Complete the puzzle with the shopping words.

There are a lot of [0]sales right now. These sneakers are a [1]b_______ ! Look at the [2]p_______ : they're only $15! And I have a [3]c_______ for 20% off. At the [4]c_______ , I'm going to give the salesperson $15. He's going to give me a [5]r_______ and how much [6]c_______ ?

0 s	a	l	e	s		
1						
2						
3						
4						
5						
6						

What is Lorna saying? Use the letters on the colored squares to complete the sentence.

I				v						v	
			y		m				y	!	

Project

Create a video survey

1 **In the *Shopping habits* video on page 43, the teenagers talk about things they like spending their money on. What is the last nice thing you bought for yourself? Where did you buy it? Tell your group.**

2 **Plan a video survey about your friends' shopping habits.**

1 In your group, think about what you would like to know about your friends' shopping habits. Choose some topics below or use your own ideas.
- online vs stores
- secondhand vs new
- save vs spend
- clothes vs films, video games, and music

2 Divide the topics between the students in the group.

3 **Write a first draft.**

1 Write a draft of questions you can ask about your topic.
2 Think of five people that you can speak to for your survey.
3 Decide when and where to film your video.

4 **Check and redraft.**

1 Swap your work with a partner. Give feedback.
2 Listen to feedback about your work. Write a second draft.

5 **Compile.**

1 Film your section of the video.
2 Compile the different sections of the video to create a complete survey.
3 Add any music, pictures, headings, or sound effects.

6 **Share.**

1 Share your video survey with the class.
2 Which videos do you like? Why?

7 **Reflect.**

I'm proud of _______________

____

____

For next time, I want to improve

____

____

← Student Book p.43

WOW! Metro Express

← Student Book p.47 p.49

1 Find eight human-caused and natural problems in the puzzle. (↑, ↓, ↗, ↘, →, ←)

X	N	O	E	O	W	E	P	W	M
R	Y	V	V	Q	P	G	O	G	O
W	V	E	A	C	T	N	L	S	M
W	P	R	W	T	Q	A	L	R	F
T	Y	P	T	W	E	H	U	T	H
H	E	O	A	I	N	C	T	H	M
G	M	P	E	L	Z	E	I	S	S
U	H	U	H	D	K	T	O	H	U
O	D	L	U	F	M	A	N	J	D
R	G	A	J	I	G	M	Y	O	A
D	U	T	B	R	L	I	O	U	T
L	T	I	B	E	T	L	M	P	P
A	D	O	S	J	F	C	U	C	G
X	Y	N	E	S	A	E	S	I	D

2 Unscramble the words and complete the posters.

vase cuered ereus creptto ~~eclyere~~

Project

Make a map

1 What do you remember about Songdo in the video *A smart city* on page 53? Discuss these things:

1 green spaces, ocean, lakes
2 places to live
3 education
4 reducing pollution
5 recycling trash
6 transportation

2 Plan a map of your ideal city.

1 In your group, brainstorm all the things you would like to have in your ideal city. Use exercise 1 to help you.
2 On a large sheet of paper, plan a map of your city, and think about its size, layout, and location.

3 Make a first draft.

1 Divide the different sections of the map between the students in the group.
2 Draw your map, make drawings, and look for photos to illustrate your section.
3 Write a draft of a paragraph about what is in your section of the map.

4 Check and redraft.

1 Swap your draft with a partner. Give feedback.
2 Listen to feedback about your work. Then do a second draft.

5 Compile.

1 Compile the sections to make a complete map. Use a large piece of paper or a design app on a computer.
2 Add headings.
3 Label the photos.

6 Share.

1 Share your map with the class.
2 Which maps do you like? Why?

7 Reflect.

I'm proud of ______________________

For next time, I want to improve ______________________

← Student Book p.53

Metro Express

← Student Book p.59 p.61

1 Find eight more jobs in the grid. You can move (↑, ↓, →, ←). Use every square.

0 nurse
1 ______
2 ______
3 ______
4 ______
5 ______
6 ______
7 ______
8 ______

N	U	S	P	E	E	O	H	A	R
S	R	E	S	R	C	F	F	I	E
E	C	L	O	N	I	L	I	R	S
E	H	A	T	W	P	O	C	D	S
F	R	S	F	A	E	I	E	R	E
F	E	N	O	R	R	D	R	D	L
A	I	G	S	E	O	L	R	E	I
S	S	E	D	D	S	R	E	P	U
H	I	O	N	E	V	E	L	O	B

2 Follow the colors in the word maze to find the correct person.

This person ...

0	always tells the truth	honest	kind
1	is happy to wait	careful	patient
2	says please and thank you	polite	reliable
3	often loses things	unfriendly	careless

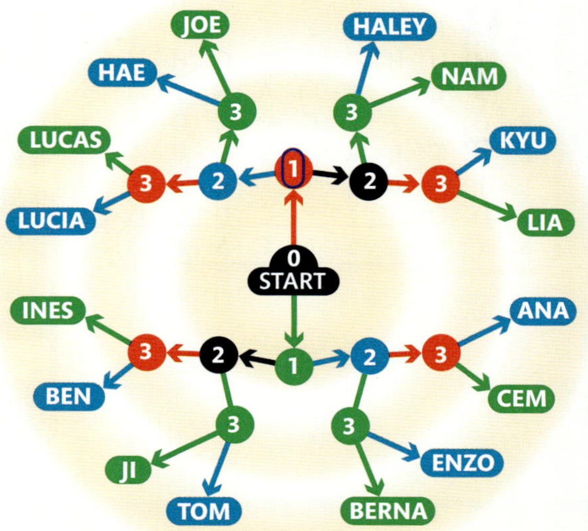

Who is it? ______

Project

Create a profile with photos

1 What do you remember about the *I'm a journalist* video on page 65? Discuss the following questions about Portia's job in your group.

1 working hours?
2 time spent alone / with others?
3 personal qualities
4 best and worst parts

2 Research someone whose job you would like to do.

1 In your group, choose a person who does an interesting job. It can be someone you find on the internet, or someone you know.
2 Divide the questions in exercise 1 between the students in the group. Use the questions to research online or do an interview with this person.

3 Write a first draft.

1 Share the information from your research with the students in the group.
2 Write a paragraph about the person and their job for your section.
3 Find photos or drawings to illustrate the profile.

4 Check and redraft.

1 Swap your work with a partner. Give feedback.
2 Listen to feedback about your work. Then write a second draft.

5 Compile.

1 Compile the sections to make a complete profile. Use a large piece of paper or a design app on a computer.
2 Add headings.
3 Label the photos.

6 Share.

1 Share your profiles with the class.
2 Which profiles do you like? Why?

7 Reflect.

I'm proud of ______

For next time, I want to improve ______

← Student Book p.65

WOW! Metro Express

← Student Book p.69 | p.71

1 **Look at the picture for thirty seconds. Then cover it and answer questions 1–5.**

0 How many people were committing crimes? four

1 What was the dog stealing? ___________

2 Who was chasing the dog? ___________

3 Was the police officer arresting a man or a woman? ___________

4 What was the name of the store? ___________

5 What color was the car that the man was breaking into? ___________

2 **Complete the advice on the poster. Then choose *always* or *never*.**

click information install links ~~out~~ passwords share software use ~~websites~~

Stay Safe Online

0 **(Always) / Never** log out of websites after you finish using them.

1 **Always / Never** ___________ personal ___________ with people you don't know.

2 **Always / Never** ___________ on ___________ in unusual emails.

3 **Always / Never** ___________ antivirus ___________ on your computers.

4 **Always / Never** ___________ different ___________ for websites.

Project

Create a true crime podcast

1 **The *Sherlock Holmes* on page 75 video describes how the brilliant detective solves many different types of crime. What kind of crimes do you think are the most difficult to solve?**

2 **Research and plan a true crime podcast.**

1 Choose one of the following crimes:
- **a** The Antwerp Diamond Heist
- **b** The Gunpowder Plot
- **c** The theft of the *Mona Lisa*
- **d** The Coughing Major

2 Research the crime online. Divide the following questions between the students in your group: Who committed the crime? What happened? When did it happen? Where did it happen? How did it happen?

3 **Write a first draft.**

1 Share the information from your research with the students in the group.
The podcast will be in the form of an interview with some crime experts.

2 Write questions and answers for your section.

4 **Check and redraft.**

1 Swap your work with a partner. Give feedback.

2 Listen to feedback about your work. Then write a second draft.

5 **Record.**

1 Decide who will be the crime experts and who will be the interviewers.

2 Record the interview for your podcast.

6 **Share.**

1 Share your podcast with the class.

2 Which podcasts do you like? Why?

7 **Reflect.**

I'm proud of ___________

For next time, I want to improve ___________

← Student Book p.75

Metro Express

Student Book p.81 p.83

1 Find the experiences.

0

1

2

3

4

5

6

7

2 Complete the phrasal verbs with the correct words. Then answer the questions.

~~away~~ back in off on out

We went [0] ___away___ last summer. We visited relatives in Canada. We got [1] ____________ the plane at 9 a.m., but there was a problem. It took [2] ____________ at 11:30, and the flight was 6 hours and 30 minutes!

How long were they on the plane? [3] ____________

Yesterday, I went [4] ____________ in my favorite green dress with my friends. "Do you like my new hair color?" I asked them, but no one said anything. When I got [5] ____________ home I looked in the mirror. My hair matched my clothes! Tonight, I'm staying [6] ____________!

What color was Rosie's hair? [7] ____________

Project

Make a class presentation

1 **The *Trip of a lifetime!* video on page 87 tells us about Sarah Darby's trip across Patagonia. Tell your group about a friend or family member who has been on an exciting trip.**

2 **Research and plan a presentation about an exciting trip.**

1. In your group, choose one of the people you mentioned in exercise 1 to interview.
2. Interview the person and make notes. Ask them ...
   - where they went and how they traveled.
   - about the activities on their trip.
   - about the best and worst parts of the trip.
   - if you can use photos from their trip in your presentation.

3 **Write a first draft.**

1. Divide the information from the interview between the students in the group.
2. Write a draft of your section of the presentation.
3. Choose photos for your section of the presentation.

4 **Check and redraft.**

1. Swap your work with a partner. Give feedback.
2. Listen to feedback about your work. Then write a second draft.

5 **Compile.**

1. Compile the sections to make a complete presentation. Use a large piece of paper or a design app on a computer to do this.
2. Add headings, pictures, and maps.
3. Label the pictures and maps.

6 **Share.**

1. Give your presentation to the class.
2. Which presentations do you like? Why?

7 **Reflect.**

I'm proud of ____________________

____

____

For next time, I want to improve

____

____

____

Student Book p.87

Metro Express

← Student Book p.91 p.93

1 Find eight more adjectives. Complete the puzzle and find the hidden word.

FASH	TI	RECY	INAL	~~ENOR~~	CLED
CATE	NGE	OLD-	IENT	STRA	ANC
~~MOUS~~	DELI	ORIG	ION	NY	ED

The hidden word is ___________.

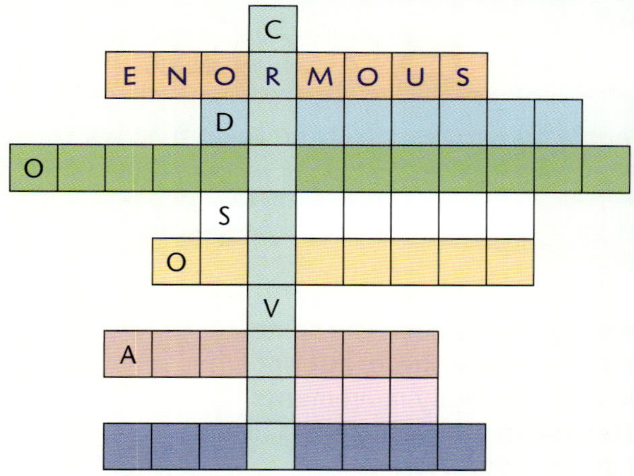

2 Find seven more creativity verbs. Complete the questions.

When did ...?

0 the French ___build___ the Eiffel Tower?

1 The Beatles ___________ *Yesterday*?

2 Bell ___________ the telephone?

3 Sikorsky ___________ the first helicopter that could fly?

4 Satoshi Tajiri ___________ Pokémon?

n	~~b~~	d	i	~~d~~	p	c	e	s	o
c	e	e	t	s	v	i	a	r	~~i~~
t	e	o	~~l~~	n	e	~~u~~	m	g	n

3 Answer the questions in exercise 2. You have one minute!

1876 1889 1939 1965 1995

0 1889 3 1939
1 1965 4 1995
2 1876

Project

Create a digital guided tour

1 Which graffiti do you like best in the *Graffiti Life* video? Why? Look at the images from the video on page 97 and discuss in your group.

2 Research and plan a guided tour of an area with graffiti.

1 In your group, think of areas with a lot of graffiti. These can be places in your town or city, somewhere you have visited, or one of these famous places:
- Hosier Lane, Melbourne, Australia
- Etnias, Rio de Janeiro, Brazil
- Lennon Wall, Prague, Czech Republic
- Tuttomund, Pisa, Italy

2 Choose one area for a guided tour and research it.

3 Make sure you know how to record your phone / computer screen with audio and use streetview on an online map.

3 Make a first draft.

1 Think about what the narrators will say during the tour and divide it between the students in your group.

2 Write a first draft of the narrator's words.

3 Think about what images you will need to show for your section of the guided tour.

4 Check and redraft.

1 Swap your work with a partner. Give feedback.

2 Listen to feedback about your work. Then write a second draft.

5 Compile.

1 Film your section of the video.

2 Edit the video.

6 Share.

1 Share your tour with the class.

2 Which tours do you like? Why?

7 Reflect.

I'm proud of ___________

For next time, I want to improve ___________

← Student Book p.97

Non-verbal communication

People love communicating. To do this, we speak and write with languages.

We also move our faces and bodies to communicate without language – for example, when we smile, wave, shake a person's hand, or point. This is called "non-verbal communication."

Some gestures have the same meaning everywhere, but not all! Face and body movements often mean different things in different countries.

A

B
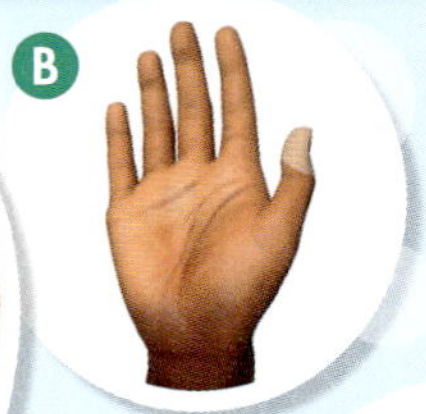

C

D

Face

When we talk, we move our eyes and mouth – for example, to smile or frown. Our faces give the best idea of how we're feeling – for example, scared, interested, or surprised.

How is this person feeling?

E
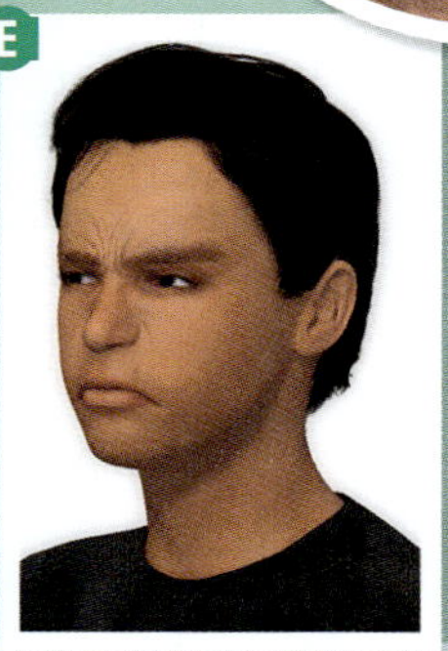

Did you know?

Non-verbal communication is different from sign language. Sign language has an alphabet and words.

These people are communicating with sign language. The woman is signing "excited."

Eyes

F

In many countries, it's most common to look people in the eye when we're talking to them. This means "I'm listening" or "I'm interested."

Not everybody likes using eye contact! In Asian countries, it isn't polite.

Head

In most countries, we nod our head to mean "yes" and shake it to mean "no."

In Greece and Turkey, people do the opposite! They nod to mean "no" and shake their heads to mean "yes"!

G

H

Hands and arms

I

In countries like Spain and Italy, people move their hands and arms a lot while they're speaking. In Asian countries, people don't do this.

In European and American countries, people point with their finger. This is rude in most Asian countries.

In the Philippines, people point with their mouths!

J
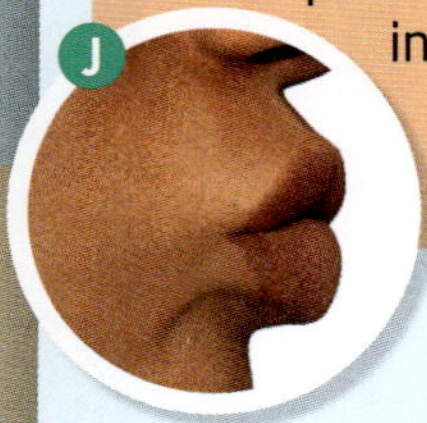

Did you know?

The high-five comes from the U.S.

Sports players used high-fives to say "Good job!" to team members. These days, it means "hello" and "goodbye" as well.

Reading

1 In one minute ... **Think of all the different types of information you can give with your body without speaking.**

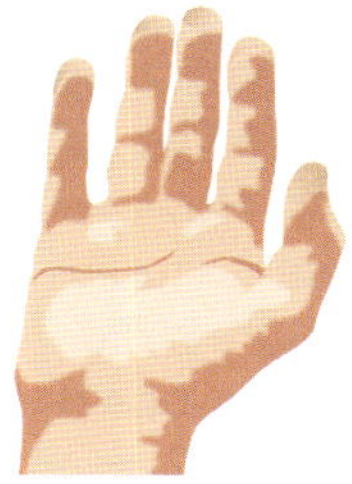

stop

three

2 143 **Read and listen to the article and choose the correct meaning of *rude*.**

a not interesting
b not polite
c not fun

3 **Match the pictures A–J in the article with the words 0–9.**

0 __E__ frowning
1 ____ hand and arm movements
2 ____ nodding head
3 ____ pointing with a finger
4 ____ pointing with the mouth
5 ____ shaking hands
6 ____ shaking head
7 ____ smiling
8 ____ staring
9 ____ waving

4 **Complete the sentences with the correct words from the box.**

~~humans~~ smiling the hands writing your face

0 __Humans__ enjoy all forms of communication.
1 ________ is a form of verbal communication.
2 ________ is a form of non-verbal communication.
3 ________ shows another person how you are feeling.
4 ________ are an important and necessary part of sign language.

5 **Read the article again. Are the sentences T (*true*) or F (*false*)? Correct the false sentences.**

According to the text, ...

0 non-verbal communication sometimes has different meanings in different cultures. T ☑ F ☐
1 eye contact is rude in some countries. T ☐ F ☐
______
2 people nod to mean "yes" in Greece. T ☐ F ☐
______
3 hand and arm movements are common in Asian countries. T ☐ F ☐
______
______
4 people in Europe point with their mouth. T ☐ F ☐
______
5 the high-five has more than one meaning. T ☐ F ☐
______

6 **Discuss the questions.**

1 What are the similarities and differences between non-verbal communication, sign language, and regular languages?
2 What non-verbal communication mentioned in the text do you use?
3 What other non-verbal communication do you use? When?

EXTRA Research project

1 **You are going to make a leaflet about non-verbal communication in your country. Think about how you can say the following:**

- Hello (greeting) / Goodbye.
- Good job!
- Come here. / Go away.
- Look over there / here.
- Can I ask a question?

2 **Copy and complete the chart. Use your answers in exercise 1 and your own ideas.**

Gesture or face movement	What it means
wave hand	hello and goodbye

3 **Make a leaflet for visitors to your country. Use your ideas in exercise 2. Remember to:**

- include pictures of the gestures or expressions.
- explain the meanings carefully for the visitors.

Off-balance!

Every day, we typically take about 4,000 steps and spend four hours on our feet. The brain sends complex signals to different parts of our body, and this helps us to balance in an upright position. Some experts believe we developed this skill 15 million years ago, when we were still living in trees! However, human balance is in danger. Recent studies show that more and more of us are suffering from serious falls. Are we going to lose the ability to stand and walk on two feet?

This news is surprising, but its cause is possibly a bigger surprise: the reason is 21st century life! From childhood, we spend long periods sitting down. Our lives are more comfortable than in the past, but we are losing some essential skills. The best way to protect these skills is to practice them. But what is the best way to practice balancing? Sports can help, but we need to choose the right ones.

These days, indoor exercise is common, for example, running on a running machine, or cycling on an exercise bike. Although these activities are great physical exercise, they don't really practice our ability to balance. Outdoor sports, such as jogging, mountain biking, tennis, or soccer make us move our eyes and heads quickly to see where we are going. We need to balance to do these sports, so they are the best way to exercise.

Outdoor sports are great for practicing balance.

We can't afford to throw away this precious skill, but protecting it isn't expensive. Instead of wasting money on going to the gym, we can play more outdoor sports. That way, we'll reduce our risk of falling and save money. On balance, it definitely makes sense!

Did you know? The phrase "on balance" means when "we consider all factors."

Reading

1 **In one minute ...** **Brainstorm all the ways humans are different from other animals. What different skills do we have?**

2 **Match the highlighted words from the article with the pictures.**

0 upright

1 ________

2 ________

3 **144** **Read and listen to the article. Complete the chart with the words in the box.**

~~balance~~ falls modern life outdoor sport

Skill	0 balance
Problem	1 ________
Cause	2 ________
Solution	3 ________

4 **Read the article again. Choose the correct options.**

0 **Not many** / **Most** of us walk 4,000 steps every day.

1 Messages from the brain to **different parts of the body** / **our feet** help us to stand up.

2 Falls **are becoming more common** / **aren't a serious problem**.

3 The problem starts **when we learn to stand up** / **before adulthood**.

4 The right practice can **damage** / **protect** your balance.

5 **Indoor** / **Outdoor** sports are better for practicing balance.

5 **Answer the questions.**

0 How long does a typical person stand up every day?
A typical person stands up for four hours.

1 According to some scientists, when did we learn to balance on two feet?
____

2 What is the problem with 21st century life?
____

3 Why don't indoor sports like running on running machines or cycling on exercise bikes practice balance?
____

4 Which sports in the text are ideal for practicing balance?
____
____

6 **Work in a group to answer the questions.**

1 What parts of the body do we use to stand up? Give reasons for your answers. Then check the answers at the bottom of the page!

2 Test your balance! Stand on one leg with your eyes closed for at least thirty seconds. Can you do it? Who has the best balance in the group?

EXTRA Research project

1 **Think of a sport you enjoy doing. Brainstorm the different ways that it is good for the body and the skills it practices.**

2 **Prepare a presentation about your chosen sport. Think about the following things:**

- the parts of the body that it exercises.
- the skills and abilities you need to do the sport well.
- the ways it helps the body.
- where you can do it.

3 **Find photos, illustrations, charts, etc., that can help describe your sport well.**

4 **Give your presentation to the class. Be prepared to answer questions afterwards!**

We use our brain, eyes, inner ear, leg muscles, stomach and back muscles, and feet.

The problem with money

A

Imagine a world with no money.

You want some new sneakers, and you want to swap some computer games for them. You need to find someone who

a has some sneakers they don't want,
and
b wants some computer games.

Not so simple! In a world with money, you can use money to obtain things easily. This is why we started using coins 5,000 years ago. Money makes life simpler! Or does it?

The first coins were made in west Asia 5,000 years ago.

B

Today's coins and banknotes have complicated illustrations and patterns. The first coins - from west Asia - showed pictures of plants. Today, illustrations of wildlife, kings, queens, and famous politicians often appear on money. Many civilizations made coins from gold, silver, and bronze. About 2,000 years ago, the Chinese were making them with white leather from deer! Today, countries use cheaper metals to produce coins. Paper money first appeared in China in the 11th century. Now, many countries use plastic banknotes. It is stronger than paper, so it lasts longer.

The Chinese made bills from the skin of white deer.

Australian banknotes are plastic.

C

The complicated designs on money are necessary. Too often, dishonest people produce counterfeit money. In 2014, the U.K. government estimated that 3% of £1 coins were fakes (not real). Money laundering is another serious problem: someone steals money and uses it to buy other products. Or someone steals things and then sells them to make money! Police all over the world regularly investigate these problems.

Counterfeit money is a serious problem.

D

A digital currency isn't from any country. This form of money doesn't have banknotes or coins – it only exists online! Bitcoin, the first digital currency, appeared in 2009. You can use it in some stores. But will digital currencies prevent crime? Sadly not. Criminals are too smart and often use digital currencies for money laundering. Money makes our lives simpler – but it causes problems, too!

This currency only exists online.

Reading

1 In one minute ... **Think of your country's money and all the illustrations that appear on it.**

2 145 **Read and listen to the article. Match the headings below with the paragraphs A–D.**

0 Money crimes C
1 Why do we have money? ____
2 The future? ____
3 The design of money ____

3 **Complete the sentences with the words.**

banknote   bronze   coin   ~~counterfeit~~   currency

0 Counterfeit money looks real, but it isn't real.
1 ____________ is similar to gold and silver because it is a precious metal.
2 A ____________ is a form of money made from metal.
3 A ____________ is a system of money that a country uses. For example, in the U.S., it is the dollar.
4 A ____________ is also called paper money.

4 **Read the article again and choose the correct answers.**

0 In a world with no money, ...
  (a) it's more difficult to get the things you want.
  b everything is free.
  c sneakers don't exist.
  d everything is worse than 5,000 years ago.

1 Today, ...
  a we make all our money in west Asia.
  b we use plants to produce money.
  c money has a complicated design.
  d kings, queens, and politicians take all our money.

2 In the 11th century, ...
  a no one could afford any gold, silver, or bronze.
  b the Chinese swapped deer for money.
  c people used cheaper metals to make money.
  d the first banknotes appeared.

3 The designs on coins and banknotes ...
  a make it harder to produce counterfeit money.
  b are the result of money laundering.
  c make it impossible to steal things.
  d show pictures of police officers investigating crimes.

4 In 2009 ...
  a stores started selling digital currencies.
  b people started using a digital currency for the first time.
  c criminals created Bitcoin.
  d Bitcoin banknotes and coins first appeared.

5 **Answer the questions.**

0 What types of people are most common on bills and coins?
Kings, queens, and famous politicians.

1 What materials for money does the text mention?
____
____

2 Why isn't paper as good as plastic for banknotes?
____

3 In 2014, how did counterfeit money affect the British currency?
____
____

4 How are digital currencies different from traditional currencies?
____
____

5 What form of crime now happens with digital currencies?
____

6 **Discuss the questions.**

1 Is counterfeit money a problem in your country?
2 Are the notes in your country plastic or paper, or both?
3 Do you think digital currencies are the future of money?

EXTRA Research project

1 **You are going to design a bill of your own currency. Look at this bill from the U.S. Notice the different features.**

2 **Copy and complete the chart with your own ideas.**

Name of your currency	
Material (e.g., plastic, paper, leather, etc.)	
Pictures, e.g., a famous person, a place, etc.	
Different colors	
Ways you can prevent counterfeit money	

3 **Design your bill.**

4 **Present your bill to the class. Give information about the following things:**

- the name of the currency and why you chose it.
- the pictures on the bill and their meaning.
- why you chose the colors.
- how much it is worth.

D CLIL: History

The Sutton Hoo treasures

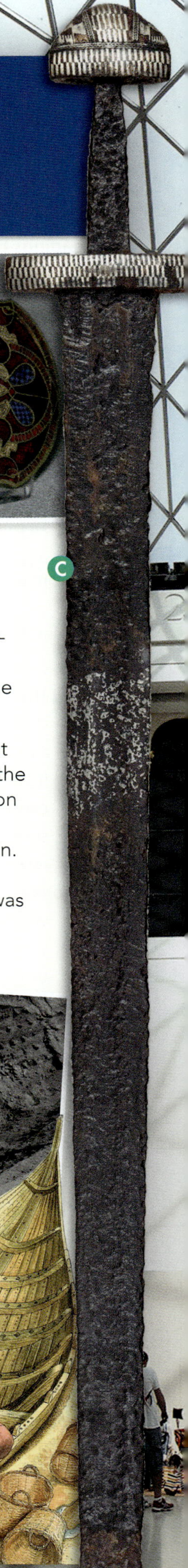

Have you ever heard of an era in European history called the Dark Ages? This negative-sounding name refers to the time after the end of the Roman Empire, from the 5th to 10th centuries. In Britain, the Anglo Saxon people from Northern Europe arrived and the period became known for its frequent wars. But in the late 1930s, a discovery in eastern England made historians think differently.

In 1938, a woman called Edith Pretty organized the excavation of 18 small hills on her land, which was called Sutton Hoo. The local museum sent an archaeologist called Basil Brown to set up the excavation. Brown had no formal education in archaeology, but he had a strong understanding of the region's land.

Brown hoped to discover something very exciting, but he found far more than anyone expected. Under the largest hill was the delicate imprint of an early 7th century burial ship. The ship was a final resting place for an important person, maybe even an Anglo Saxon king.

After thousands of years, the 27-meter-long ship no longer existed. However, there was a ruined burial chamber, **which** contained treasure for the dead person to take into the next life.

By now, a team of archaeologists from the British Museum were working with Brown on the site, **and** they discovered beautifully-designed jewelry and weapons. They also found a bronze helmet, **which** is perhaps the most famous artifact from the excavation.

Edith Pretty generously donated the ancient ship's contents to the British Museum, and the public can view them there today. The Sutton Hoo treasures are considered some of the greatest archaeological discoveries in Britain. Historians have also given the Dark Ages a different name – the Early Middle Ages. It was a time of war and change – but also one of incredible creativity.

Reading

1 In one minute ... **Make a list of your country's most important historical places and artifacts. How many can you think of?**

2 **Match the words with the pictures A–E. What do you think the article will be about?**

burial ~~helmet~~ jewelry site weapon

A helmet
B ________
C ________
D ________
E ________

3 146 **Read and listen to the article and check your answers to exercise 2.**

4 **Read again and complete each sentence with one word from the article.**

0 The name Dark Ages refers to the period after the Roman Empire.
1 Edith Pretty owned an area of ________ called Sutton Hoo.
2 Basil Brown was an ________ who set up Edith Pretty's excavation.
3 An imprint of a ________ was under the ground.
4 The Sutton Hoo contents are some of the most important ________ in British history.
5 ________ now prefer to use the term the Early Middle Ages to describe the 5th to 10th centuries.

5 **Answer the questions.**

0 Where did the Anglo Saxon people come from?
They came from Northern Europe.
1 Why were the Dark Ages a difficult era in European history?
____
2 Why was Basil Brown the ideal archaeologist for the excavation at Sutton Hoo?
____
3 When did the Anglo Saxons build the burial ship?
____
4 How long was the ship?
____
5 Where can you see the Sutton Hoo treasures today?
____

6 **Discuss the questions.**

1 What do the Sutton Hoo treasures tell you about the person who lay in the ship?
2 The excavation of the burial chamber also uncovered clothes, shoes, coins, and items for eating and drinking. Why were they there, do you think?
3 Read this sentence from the text again. How did the discovery change their beliefs about the Dark Ages?
"But in the late 1930s, a discovery in eastern England made historians think differently."

EXTRA Research project

1 **You are going to give a presentation on an important historical discovery in your country.**

Choose a discovery and research the following things:

- What is the artifact or place?
- What is its purpose?
- When and where was it discovered?
- Who discovered it?
- How did they discover it?
- What does it tell us about the past?
- What does it tell you about the person / people who created it?
- Where can you see it today?

2 **Find photos and illustrations of the discovery. Mount them on a large sheet of paper and label them clearly.**

You can also use your computer to display your photos and illustrations as part of your presentation.

3 **Give your presentation to the class. Invite questions afterwards.**

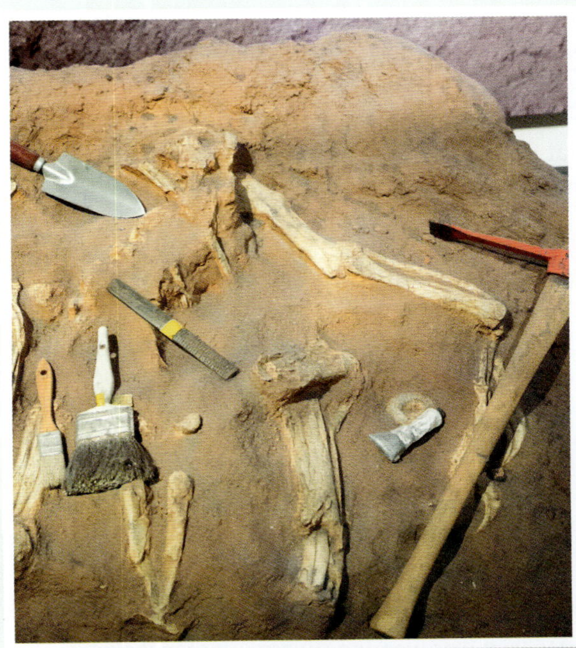

P Pronunciation

Unit 1 The silent *e* Student Book p.13

1 147 **Read the pronunciation chart. Listen and repeat.**

An *e* on the end of a word can tell you if a vowel sound is long or short.	
+*e*: long vowel sound	No *e*: short vowel sound
case	cat

2 148 **Look at the words below. Check (✓) the correct boxes in the chart. Then listen and check.**

	Long vowel sound	Short vowel sound
0 put		✓
1 gift		
2 take		
3 chips		
4 sunbathe		
5 ride		

3 149 **Listen and repeat the sentences. Focus on the long and short vowel sounds in the highlighted words.**

1 I **like** to **ride** my **bike**.
2 We **escaped** to a **lake** to **chat** and **relax**.
3 **Mom gave** us **hot dogs** and **cakes** for a **snack**.

Unit 2 /w/ Student Book p.23

1 150 **Read the pronunciation chart. Listen and repeat.**

The /w/ sound can be difficult to pronounce. Make sure you don't say a /v/ sound.		
with warm	windy worried	wood wool

2 151 **Listen to the words. Check (✓) the sound that you hear at the start of the word. Then listen and repeat.**

	/w/	/v/
0	✓	
1		
2		
3		
4		

3 152 **Listen to the sentences. Then listen and repeat.**

1 The women are waiting by the window.
2 I want to win a water bottle.
3 William was wearing a warm woolen jacket.
4 It was a windy winter last year.
5 Would you like to go for a walk in the woods?

Unit 3 /ʃ/ and /tʃ/ Student Book p.38

1 153 **Read the pronunciation chart. Listen and repeat.**

The sounds /ʃ/ and /tʃ/ are similar.	
/ʃ/	/tʃ/
ca**sh**	**ch**ange
exhibi**t**ion	bea**ch**
shopping	na**t**ural
anima**t**ion	**ch**at
share	**ch**eerful

2 154 **Choose the sound in the underlined letters. Then listen and check.**

0 exhibition (/ʃ/) /tʃ/
1 children /ʃ/ /tʃ/
2 ocean /ʃ/ /tʃ/
3 sugar /ʃ/ /tʃ/
4 ketchup /ʃ/ /tʃ/
5 picture /ʃ/ /tʃ/

3 155 **Listen and repeat the sentences.**

1 **Charlie chose** some **delicious fish** and **chips**.
2 The **exhibition shows pictures** of **traditional beach** scenes.
3 **She** was **cheerful** when she **chatted** about the science **fiction animation**.

Unit 4 Consonant clusters
Student Book p.45

1 156 **Read the pronunciation chart. Listen and repeat.**

It is sometimes hard to hear and pronounce two consonant sounds together at the beginning or in the middle of words.
place **sp**ecial car**db**oard pla**st**ic

2 157 **Listen and repeat.**

1 ssssssscared ssscared scared
2 sssssssspend ssspend spend
3 sssssssstudent ssstudent student

3 158 **Listen and repeat.**

1 c -- limate c - limate climate
2 f -- lood f - lood flood
3 th -- row th - row throw
4 p -- rotect p - rotect protect
5 d -- rought d - rought drought

4 159 **Listen and repeat.**

1 wild - fire wildfire
2 earth - quake earthquake
3 ex - tinct extinct

Pronunciation

Unit 5 /p/ and /b/ Student Book p.60

1 160 **Read the pronunciation chart. Listen and repeat.**

The sounds /p/ and /b/ are similar. The /p/ sound is explosive and you breathe out when you say it. The /b/ sound is softer and you hum when you say it.	
/p/	/b/
police officer patient	bargain borrow

2 161 **Listen and choose the words you hear.**

0 (pen) / Ben
1 pair / bear
2 pig / big
3 pack / back

3 Say different words from exercise 2. Your partner points to the correct word.

4 162 **Complete the words with *p* or *b*. Then listen and repeat the sentences.**

0 P olice officers ___ut ___ad ___eople in ___rison.
1 My ___rother does ___arkour on ___ublic ___uildings.
2 The ___olite ___uilder ___ut his ___ags in the ___athroom.

Unit 6 Pronunciation of *ea*

Student Book p.67

1 163 **Read the pronunciation chart. Listen and repeat.**

We can pronounce the letters *ea* in the following ways: /i/, /eɪ/ and /ɛ/. The vowel sounds /i/ and /eɪ/ are long, and /ɛ/ is a short vowel sound.		
/i/	/eɪ/	/ɛ/
steal	break	head

2 164 **Listen to the words. Are the *ea* sounds long or short? Then listen and repeat.**

	long	short
0 meal	✓	
1 leather		
2 breakfast		
3 great		
4 leave		
5 bread		

3 165 **Listen and repeat the sentences.**

1 Did he **steal** your **headphones**?
2 I have **bread**, **beans**, and **meat** in my bag.
3 **Heavy sweaters** aren't **great** for **heat** waves.

Unit 7 Stress in phrasal verbs

Student Book p.82

1 166 **Read the pronunciation chart. Listen and repeat.**

In phrasal verbs, we stress both parts of the verb.
The plane is **taking off** in ten minutes. What time did you **get back** last night?

2 167 **Complete the questions with the words. Listen, check, and repeat.**

away back ~~in~~ out

0 What do you do when you stay __in__ on a weekend?
1 How often do you go ______ on vacation?
2 Who do you go ______ with?
3 What time do you get ______ from school?

3 In pairs, ask and answer the questions in exercise 2. Use the phrasal verbs in your answers.

Unit 8 Stress in questions

Student Book p.93

1 168 **Read the pronunciation chart. Listen and repeat.**

In subject questions, the stress is on the main verb.	In object questions, the stress is on the question word and the main verb.
Who built this house?	When did you paint this?

2 169 **Listen and underline the words with stress in the questions. Listen again and repeat.**

0 Who invented the telephone? Alexander Graham Bell.
1 When did he invent it? In 1876.
2 Who designed the Burj Khalifa - the tallest building in the world? Adrian Smith.
3 When did he design it? In the early 2000s.

3 170 **Underline the words with stress in the questions. Listen, check, and repeat.**

0 Where do you buy your clothes? Who pays for them?
1 Who gives you money? How much do you get? What do you spend it on?
2 What happened last weekend? Where did you go?
3 What do you do after school? Who do you hang out with?

4 In pairs, ask and answer the questions in exercise 3.

P Phonetic symbols

Consonants

p	as in	**pen** /pɛn/
b	as in	**bad** /bæd/
t	as in	**tea** /ti/
ţ	as in	**better** /ˈbɛţər/
d	as in	**did** /dɪd/
k	as in	**cat** /kæt/
g	as in	**get** /gɛt/
tʃ	as in	**chain** /tʃeɪn/
dʒ	as in	**jam** /dʒæm/
f	as in	**fall** /fɔl/
v	as in	**van** /væn/
θ	as in	**thin** /θɪn/
ð	as in	**this** /ðɪs/
s	as in	**see** /si/
z	as in	**zoo** /zu/
ʃ	as in	**shoe** /ʃu/
ʒ	as in	**vision** /ˈvɪʒn/
h	as in	**hat** /hæt/
m	as in	**man** /mæn/
n	as in	**now** /naʊ/
ŋ	as in	**sing** /sɪŋ/
l	as in	**leg** /lɛg/
r	as in	**red** /rɛd/
j	as in	**yes** /yɛs/
w	as in	**wet** /wɛt/

Vowels and diphthongs

i	as in	**see** /si/
ɪ	as in	**sit** /sɪt/
ɛ	as in	**bed** /bɛd/
æ	as in	**cat** /kæt/
ɑ	as in	**father** /ˈfɑðər/
ɔ	as in	**saw** /sɔ/
ʊ	as in	**put** /pʊt/
u	as in	**too** /tu/
ʌ	as in	**cup** /kʌp/
ə	as in	**about** /əˈbaʊt/
eɪ	as in	**say** /seɪ/
oʊ	as in	**go** /goʊ/
aɪ	as in	**my** /maɪ/
ɔɪ	as in	**boy** /bɔɪ/
aʊ	as in	**now** /naʊ/
ɑr	as in	**car** /kɑr/
ɛr	as in	**hair** /hɛr/
ər	as in	**fur** /fər/
ɪr	as in	**near** /nɪr/
ɔr	as in	**north** /nɔrθ/
ʊr	as in	**pure** /pyʊr/

ˈ primary stress /ˈbɛţər/

ˌ secondary stress /ˌɪnfərˈmeɪʃn/

Quiz answers

Page 35, Super saver or big spender quiz
Are your sentences mostly As, equal As and Bs, or mostly Bs? Read your results below.
Mostly As? You're a super saver! You're very generous, too. But don't pay for other people's bad habits!
Equal As and Bs? You're sensible with money and you're generous, too. But when you see something you really like, you buy it!
Mostly Bs? You're a big spender! But friends can't help you every time you need money. It's time to stop spending - and start saving!

Page 64, Find your dream job quiz
Are your answers mostly As, Bs, Cs, or Ds? Read your results below.
Mostly As? You're an artist of the future! Your mission is to create happiness for others by making art, clothes, or music.
Mostly Bs? You're an engineer, or a software developer, or perhaps a doctor! You like systems and the way things work.
Mostly Cs? Are you our next president? Or maybe you're a future historian. You want to make the world a better place!
Mostly Ds? In a few years' time, you'll be far from here. You'll speak different languages and explore a lot of countries.

Page 81, Experiences quiz
Are your sentences mostly green, mostly orange, or a mix of green and orange? Read your results below.
Mostly green? You're never at home. You get all your energy and happiness from doing exciting things. Now, sit down for ten seconds and relax!
Mostly orange? Your home is your best friend. And you've discovered the world from your sofa! But exciting things are outside your front door!
Equal green and orange? You know how to have fun, and you're full of adventure. But you also know when to stop and relax. There are equal pleasures at home and in the outside world!

Second Edition

Metro 2

Workbook

Contents

1 On vacation

Vocabulary

← Student Book p.13 | p.16

Vacation activities

1 ★ Complete the sentences with the correct words.

0 I ... next to the pool when it's hot.
(a) sunbathe b buy

1 I like to ... museums in different cities.
a take b visit

2 We ... in a hotel every summer.
a stay b try

3 Do you always ... to the beach on hot days?
a go b eat

4 I ... gifts for my family and friends in the hotel store.
a visit b buy

5 I often ... hiking in the mountains.
a stay b go

6 How often do you ... new food?
a take b try

7 I like to ... sightseeing and learn about new places.
a go b visit

8 I ... photos of my family on my phone.
a try b take

9 On vacation, we ... out in a different restaurant every night.
a eat b go

2 ★★ Complete the words and phrases in the website.

Six things to do in Sydney, Australia

0 ___Go___ ___sightseeing___ and see famous places, including the Harbour Bridge and the Opera House.

1 ________ ________ at the city's many malls and markets.

2 ________ ________ in the beautiful Blue Mountains – only two hours from the city.

Visit The Rocks on the harbor, and 3 ________ ________ in one of its many restaurants with delicious food from all over the world.

4 ________ on the city's famous Bondi Beach.

5 ________ ________, including the Balmain Watch House, with its photos of Sydney's history.

LO Talk about vacation activities

✓ This is easy ☺ OK ☺ hard ☺ for me.

Feelings

3 ★ How do the people feel? Choose the best adjectives.

	a	b
0	a nervous	(b) happy
1	a proud	b disappointed
2	a scared	b bored
3	a interested	b bored
4	a proud	b disappointed
5	a angry	b surprised

4 ★★ Complete the conversations with the correct prepositions.

0 "Why is your mom angry ___with___ your brother?"
"Because he lost his phone on the beach."

1 "I really enjoyed our meal!"
"Me, too! And I was surprised ________ the price. It was really cheap!"

2 "I'm disappointed ________ the hotel."
"I know. The rooms are small, and the food is terrible!"

3 "Are you going on the boat trip tomorrow?"
"Yes, but I'm nervous ________ it. I don't like water!"

4 "This is your third museum in one day!"
"Yes! I'm interested ________ history!"

5 "I'm bored ________ the hotel food."
"Me, too! Let's eat out tonight."

6 "You take a lot of photos on vacation!"
"Yes, I know. I'm crazy ________ photography!"

LO Talk about my feelings

✓ This is easy ☺ OK ☺ hard ☺ for me.

Grammar

← Student Book p.15

like / love / hate + -ing

Affirmative and negative

Subject + **like(s)** / **love(s)** / **hate(s)** + **-ing** form
Subject + **don't** / **doesn't** + **like** + **-ing** form

I / You / We / They	love / like / don't like / hate	**sunbathing.**
He / She / It	loves / likes / doesn't like / hates	

We can use **love**, **like**, **don't like**, and **hate** + the -**ing** form of a verb to talk about activities and our opinion of them.

Do you **like** trying new food?
I **love** watching movies.
My sister **doesn't like** studying.

Questions

Do / **Does** + subject + **like** + **-ing** form

Do	you / we / they	like	**sunbathing?**
Does	he / she / it		

Stop

Remember: some verbs change their spelling when we add -**ing**.
swim → My brother likes **swimm**ing.
write → They love **writ**ing stories.

1 ★★ **Read the conversation and write the *-ing* forms of the verbs.**

Amy Where do you like [0] __going__ (go) on vacation?
Ben I like hot places near the ocean. And I love [1] ______ (sunbathe).
Amy Do you go sightseeing?
Ben Sometimes. I like [2] ______ (walk) around new places, and [3] ______ (take) photos, but I don't like [4] ______ (visit) museums.
Amy And do you like [5] ______ (try) new food?
Ben Oh yes! I love it! I really like [6] ______ (eat) out on vacation.

2 ★★ **Look at the chart and write sentences. Use *love, (don't) like,* and *hate.***

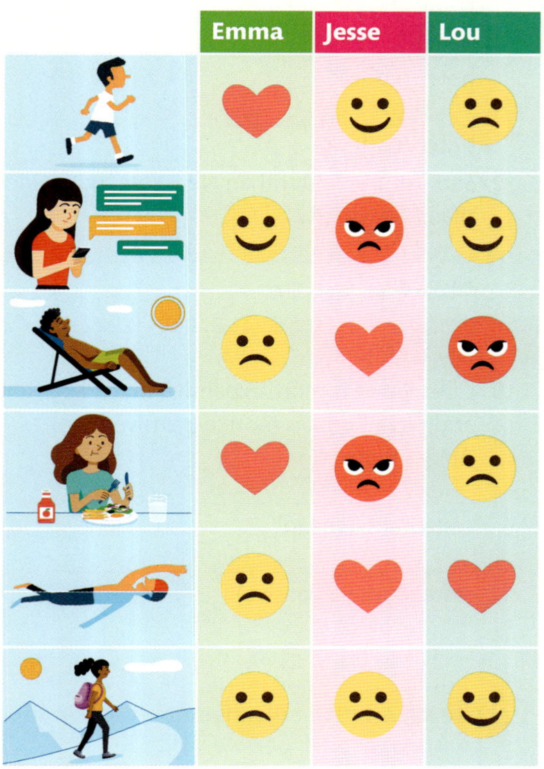

0 Emma __doesn't like sunbathing__. (sunbathe)
1 Jesse and Lou ______. (swim)
2 Jesse ______. (eat out)
3 Emma ______. (run)
4 Emma and Lou ______. (chat)
5 Emma and Jesse ______ hiking. (go)

3 ★★ **Put the words in the correct order to make questions.**

0 you / visiting / museums / do / like
__Do you like visiting museums?__
1 like / going / do / hiking / they
______
2 like / new / sister / does / your / food / trying
______
3 you / to / do / going / beach / the / like
______
4 a / your / like / in / dad / hotel / does / staying
______
5 photos / you / taking / do / like
______

LO Use *like + -ing* to talk about activities you like and don't like
✓ **This is easy** 😀 **OK** 🙂 **hard** 😐 **for me.**

1 Grammar

← Student Book p.17

Superlative adjectives

Short adjectives	
the + **-est**	**the** + ~~y~~ + **-iest**
proud ⟶ **the** proud**est**	happy ⟶ **the** happ**iest**
the + **-st**	**the** + double consonant + **-est**
nice ⟶ **the** nice**st**	wet ⟶ **the** wet**test**
Long adjectives	
the most + adjective	
disappointed ⟶ **the most disappointed**	
Irregular adjectives	
good ⟶ **the best**	
bad ⟶ **the worst**	

We use superlative adjectives when we compare three or more things.

London and Sydney are great, but New York is **the most exciting city** in the world.

We add **-est** to most short adjectives (adjectives with one or sometimes two syllables). They change their spelling in the same ways as comparative adjectives.

Trains are the eas**iest** way to travel.

August is the wet**test** month of the year.

To make the superlative form of long adjectives (two or more syllables), we use **the most** + adjective. We do not add **-est** to the adjective.

I think sightseeing is the **most interesting** vacation activity. (NOT ~~I think sightseeing is the most interestingest vacation activity.~~)

A few adjectives, including **good** and **bad**, have irregular superlative forms.

It's **the best** hotel in this city.

This is **the worst** restaurant I know.

4 ★★ Complete the vacation facts with the superlative form of the adjectives in the box.

big expensive good ~~long~~ popular small

Singapore Airlines' flight from Singapore to Newark in the U.S. is [0] ___the longest___ airplane trip in the world. It lasts 18.5 hours and has a distance of 9,534 miles.

Lover's Deep Luxury Submarine in St. Lucia is [1] ______________ hotel in the world. A room there costs $150,000 a night!

With its white sand and clear blue water, many people are crazy about Whitehaven Beach in Australia. They say it's [2] ______________ beach in the world.

Are you interested in art? Visit the Louvre, [3] ______________ museum in the world. Every year, it receives more than nine million visitors!

Do you like eating out? Try Kuappi in Finland – it's [4] ______________ restaurant in the world. Inside there is room for only two customers!

Bonanza Gift Shop in Las Vegas, U.S., is [5] ______________ gift store in the world. With over 3,700 m² of shopping space, customers are never disappointed!

5 ★★ Write superlative sentences using the information in the first sentence and the adjectives in parentheses.

0 Paris is smaller than London, but bigger than Berlin.
___London is the biggest___ city. (big)
___Berlin is the smallest___ city. (small)

1 Hotel Sol is a better hotel than Hotel Aqua, but Hotel Playa is better than Hotel Sol.
______________ hotel. (good)
______________ hotel. (bad)

2 São Paulo is hotter than New York, but colder than Mexico City.
______________ city. (hot)
______________ city. (cold)

3 Chez Pierre is more expensive than Pizza Roma, and Pizza Roma is more expensive than Andy's Burgers.
______________ restaurant. (cheap)
______________ restaurant. (expensive)

LO Use superlative adjectives to describe and compare places, people, and things

✓ This is **easy** ☺ **OK** ☺ **hard** ☺ for me.

Reading Skills

← Student Book p.18

1

A chat forum

1 ★ 171 **Read and listen to the chat forum quickly. Complete the sentences with the correct name.**

0 Ethan likes walking in the countryside.
1 ________ visits places to learn about their past.
2 ________ loves reading in the sunshine.

What's your perfect vacation?

♥ 7

Caitlin, Brighton, England

I love staying in hotels, especially hotels by the sea. I'm not crazy about going sightseeing. I like sunbathing with a good book. My favorite place to stay is on the Costa Brava in north-eastern Spain. It's an area with great beaches, fantastic weather, and some of the most delicious food in Spain! We're eating out tonight, and I'm having paella, a famous local dish. I can't wait!

21

David, Belo Horizonte, Brazil

As a child I went on beach vacations with my parents. But I got bored of sitting on the beach all day. I love visiting cities. I'm really interested in their culture and history. A few months ago, I spent a week in Osaka, Japan. I visited a very special museum there – it's all about a popular Japanese snack: noodles! I also explored the city, and took hundreds of photos. My best ones were of the beautiful Osaka Castle.

♥ 6

Ethan, Delaware, U.S.

I'm not interested in cities, and I also hate sunbathing. I love going hiking. Last year, I had the most amazing hiking vacation of my life in the Great Smoky Mountains National Park in the U.S. I took photos of wild animals, including one of the most famous residents there: the black bear! I wasn't surprised by the fact that the park is the most popular in the U.S. It was a beautiful place.

2 ★★ **Read the text again and highlight any words which you find difficult. Use a bilingual dictionary to check the meaning of each word.**

3 ★★ **Read the text. Are the sentences T (*true*), F (*false*), or NG (*not given*)? Choose the correct answer.**

		T	F	NG
0	Caitlin likes going sightseeing in Spain.	☐	☑	☐
1	Caitlin always has paella when she eats out.	☐	☐	☐
2	David didn't like sitting on the beach when he was younger.	☐	☐	☐
3	In Japan, he visited a museum of food.	☐	☐	☐
4	Ethan's vacation was two years ago.	☐	☐	☐
5	He wasn't nervous about the bears.	☐	☐	☐

4 ★★ **Read the questions carefully. Then look for key words in the chat forum that help you answer the questions. Answer the questions with full sentences.**

0 Where are Caitlin's favorite hotels?
They're by the sea.
1 What are her plans for this evening?
____
2 What does David like about cities?
____
____
3 Which photos is he proudest of?
____
____
4 What does Ethan think about cities?
____
____
5 What fact tells us that a lot of people visit the Great Smoky Mountains?
____
____

LO Read a forum and scan it for key words
✓ This is easy ☺ OK ☺ hard ☺ for me.

2 Material world

Vocabulary

← Student Book p.23 p.26

Materials: nouns

1 ★ Label the picture with the words below.

canvas cotton glass leather metal rubber stone ~~wood~~

2 ★★ Complete Ella's blog post about the things she bought on her shopping trip. Use the words in the box.

cardboard ~~cotton~~ leather paper plastic wool

Home Blog About Log In

Retro is cool!

I went shopping today with my cousin, but we didn't go to our usual stores. We went to a retro market, and we found some amazing things. I found a really cool [0] cotton T-shirt, in my favorite color, red. I also bought a hat. It's perfect for cold winter days because it's made of [1] ________. Then I found some awesome sneakers. They aren't canvas. They're [2] ________, and they look great. We didn't only buy clothes and shoes. The market also had a lot of books, and I bought four! One of the books is very old, and the [3] ________ is very thin, but the story looks really interesting. The market didn't have any [4] ________ bags, but they gave me a [5] ________ box to carry everything home in!

LO Talk about different materials

This is easy ☺ OK ☺ hard ☺ for me.

Materials: adjectives

3 ★★ Complete the materials adjectives in the sentences.

0 My sister's hair is d*ark* brown.
1 I'm carrying a h________ bag full of books!
2 You can't wear that T-shirt. It's d________!
3 I painted my walls p________ blue, the same color as the sky.
4 The house's walls are t________ and very strong.
5 Wood is a n________ material.
6 Stone is a h________ material.
7 I like to wear something l________ on a summer's day.

4 ★★ Complete the dialogues with the correct materials adjectives.

0 "I slept really well last night. My bed was really *soft* and comfortable."
"Really? I didn't. My bed was very ________!"
1 "Excuse me. This glass is ________."
"Oh, I'm sorry. Here's a ________ one."
2 "Why are you wearing that ________ T-shirt? It's cold today!"
"It's OK. I have a ________ sweater in my bag."
3 "This dress is nice, but I don't like ________ material."
"I agree. I like ________ materials, like cotton, for example."

LO Describe different materials

This is easy ☺ OK ☺ hard ☺ for me.

Grammar

← Student Book p.25

would like

Affirmative

Subject + **'d** / **would** + **like** + noun
Subject + **'d** / **would** + **like** + **to** + infinitive

Subject		
I You He She It We You They	**'d / would like**	a snack. to go.

Questions

Would + subject + **like** + noun?
Would + subject + **like** + **to** + infinitive?

	Subject		
Would	I you he she it we you they	**like**	a snack? to go?

We use **would like** to talk and ask questions about things we want to do in the future.

I'd like to build my own house.
Would you **like** to travel the world?

We also use **would like** to make offers and invitations.

"**Would** you **like** a snack?" "Yes, I would."
"**Would** you **like** to go to the movies?" "No, I wouldn't. I want to stay home."

When we add a verb after **would like**, we use the infinitive with **to**.

Would you **like to visit** this museum?
(NOT ~~Would you like visiting this museum?~~)

Short answers

Yes, subject + **would**.
No, subject + **wouldn't**.

Affirmative			Negative		
Yes,	I you he she it we you they	**would.**	**No,**	I you he she it we you they	**wouldn't.**

1 ★ **Choose the correct sentences, questions, and short answers.**

0 (a) Would you like a drink?
   b Would you liking a drink?
1 a I'd like build a wooden house.
   b I'd like to build a wooden house.
2 a Yes, she would like.
   b Yes, she would.
3 a He'd like a new jacket.
   b He like a new jacket.
4 a Would they like going to the beach?
   b Would they like to go to the beach?
5 a No, they wouldn't.
   b No, they don't would.
6 a We'd like having a snack.
   b We'd like to have a snack.

2 ★★ **Look at the pictures. Write questions and short answers using the words in parentheses.**

0 *Would you like to go hiking?* ____________ (you / go hiking)
____
1 ______________________________ (you / try my drink)
____
2 ______________________________ (he / be famous)
____
3 ______________________________ (you / a sweater)
____

LO **Use *would like* to talk about things people want**
✓ This is easy 😀 OK 🙂 hard 😐 for me.

2 Grammar

← Student Book p.27

Indefinite pronouns: words with *some*, *any*, *no*, and *every*

	Some	Any	No	Every
People	some**one** / some**body**	any**one** / any**body**	no **one** / no**body**	every**one** / every**body**
Things	some**thing**	any**thing**	no**thing**	every**thing**
Places	some**where**	any**where**	no**where**	every**where**

We use indefinite pronouns instead of nouns to talk about people, things, and places without saying exactly who or what they are.

We usually use indefinite pronouns with **some-** in affirmative sentences.

I'm going **somewhere** exciting this weekend.

We usually use indefinite pronouns with **any-** in questions.

Are you doing **anything** tomorrow?

We can form negative sentences in two ways:

- indefinite pronoun with **any-** + negative verb

  There isn't **anyone** here.

- indefinite pronoun with **no-** + affirmative verb

  There's **no one** here.

  (NOT ~~There isn't no one here.~~)

We usually use indefinite pronouns with **every-** to talk about all people, all things, or all places.

I love **everything** in this store!

We use singular verbs after indefinite pronouns.

Everyone is going to the party.

3 ★ Choose the correct endings for the indefinite pronouns.

0 There's some... in the backyard. Do you know him?
(a) one b where

1 I looked every... for a nice woolen sweater, but I couldn't find one.
a thing b where

2 Does any... want this cardboard box?
a one b thing

3 I ate the last slice of pizza because no... wanted it.
a one b where

4 This bag is very heavy. I want to carry some... lighter.
a thing b where

5 The tables in this café are all dirty. Let's go some... different.
a thing b where

6 It's a hot day for that thick jacket. Do you have any... thinner?
a one b thing

4 ★★ Rewrite the sentences with the correct indefinite pronoun.

0 There are people **in all the places**.
There are people __everywhere__.

1 I need to sit down **in a place**.
I need to sit down ______________.

2 There are **no items** inside this box.
There is ______________ inside this box.

3 I can't find **a place** to leave my bike.
I can't find ______________ to leave my bike.

4 Did you see any nice cotton T-shirts **in the stores**?
Did you see any nice cotton T-shirts ______________?

5 I love my new canvas backpack. It carries **all my things**.
I love my new canvas backpack. It carries ______________.

5 ★★ Complete the dialogue with the correct indefinite pronouns.

Ali What did you do this weekend?

Joe I went shopping. I wanted to buy a gift for my cousin.

Ali What were you looking for?

Joe I wanted [0] __something__ special because it's her 18th birthday. Maybe a nice leather bag.

Ali Did you find [1] ______________?

Joe No! I looked [2] ______________, but I couldn't find anything I liked. I came home with [3] ______________.

Ali Oh no! What can you do now?

Joe Well, my mom knows [4] ______________ with a really cool online store. She makes [5] ______________ from natural materials. I'm sure I can find [6] ______________ there.

Ali Cool.

LO Use indefinite pronouns to talk about people, places, and things

✓ This is easy ☺ OK ☺ hard ☺ for me.

Reading Skills

← Student Book p.28

2

Reviews

1 ★ **Skim-read the reviews A–C quickly. Match them with the emojis.**

0 😃 C   1 😕 ____   2 ☹ ____

Review

A White Sands Hotel, Dublin

Everything in the White Sands Hotel was terrible. The food was horrible, there was never anyone at the reception desk, and the bedroom was dirty! The room was dark, the bed was hard, and the walls were so thin, we could hear everything the people in the next room were saying! We'd like to say something positive about White Sands, but, sadly, there's nothing good that we can think of.

Jenny Paige

Review

B Wolfson cardboard bookcase

I bought this bookcase because I needed something cheap to put all my books and magazines on. Also, it's easier to build than most wooden bookcases. When it arrived, I was surprised by how light it was, and wasn't sure it could hold anything. But the cardboard looked thick, so I decided to keep it. It doesn't hold everything, but it's OK for the price. But I'd like to know how long these bookcases last. Probably not very long because my books are really heavy!

Isaac Pereira

Review

C Pobble water bottle

I bought this metal water bottle because my plastic water bottles didn't keep liquids cold. Also, you can't put anything hot in them. This water bottle is amazing. It keeps hot drinks hot for hours. And it keeps cold drinks cold for hours, too! Also, it isn't heavy, it's easy to take everywhere, and it looks great! I think everyone needs one! I'd like to buy them as gifts for my friends.

Alice Roberts

2 ★★ **Read the text again and highlight any words which you find difficult. Use a bilingual dictionary to check the meaning of each word.**

3 ★★ 🔊172 **Read and listen to the reviews again and choose the correct answers.**

0 Jenny Paige couldn't find ...
   (a) a worker at the reception desk.
   b anything to eat.
   c her room in the hotel.

1 She wanted ...
   a to talk to the people in the next room.
   b to sleep in a softer bed.
   c to say something bad about the hotel.

2 Isaac Pereira wanted something ...
   a light.
   b wooden.
   c cheap.

3 He couldn't ...
   a put his books and magazines on the bookcase.
   b see the price of the bookcase.
   c put all his things on the bookcase.

4 Before Alice Roberts bought the Pobble water bottle, ...
   a she used plastic water bottles.
   b she never drank anything hot.
   c she thought plastic water bottles were amazing.

5 Her metal water bottle ...
   a is very light and easy to carry.
   b is heavy, but looks great.
   c was a gift from her friends.

4 ★★ **Answer the questions. Write complete sentences.**

0 What did Jenny like about White Sands Hotel?
   She didn't like anything.

1 How did she know there were people in the next room?
   ____

2 Why was Isaac worried that the bookcase wasn't strong?
   ____

3 What does he think about the price?
   ____

4 What does Alice put in her metal water bottle?
   ____

5 Who does she think the metal bottle is good for?
   ____

LO Skim read reviews to understand the main idea

✓ This is **easy** 😀 **OK** 🙂 **hard** 😐 for me.

3 Responsible shopper

Vocabulary

← Student Book p.35 p.38

Money

1 ★ Choose the correct answers.

0 You can have $5, but don't ... it on candy and soda!
a afford b owe (c) waste d lend

1 Can I ... this T-shirt online?
a spend b order c earn d lend

2 I can't buy anything today. I'm trying to ... .
a owe b waste c spend d save

3 You ... me $10. I gave it to you last week, remember?
a lend b borrow c owe d order

4 I want to be a dentist because they ... a lot of money.
a borrow b order c earn d owe

5 Can you ... me some money for the subway?
a lend b save c pay d spend

6 I want these pants. Where do I ... for them?
a owe me b pay c afford it d borrow

2 ★★ Complete the second sentences so that they have the same meaning as the first ones. Use the correct form of the verbs in the box. You may need to add extra words.

not afford borrow earn lend ~~pay~~ spend

0 Can you buy this coffee for me?
Can you ___pay for___ my coffee?

1 She wastes a lot of money.
She ________________ a lot of money on stupid things.

2 Can I borrow $10 from you, please?
Can you ________________ $10, please?

3 We don't have enough money to go out for a meal.
We ________________ go out for a meal.

4 His parents give him $5 an hour for doing chores.
He ________________ $5 an hour by doing chores for his parents.

5 I lent my brother some money last week.
My brother ________________ some money from me last week.

Shopping

3 ★ Match the words with the pictures.

change counter coupon ~~price~~ receipt sale

0 ___price___

1 ________

2 ________

3 ________

4 ________

5 ________

4 ★★ Complete the words in the advertisement.

Don't miss **Skate Style's** *winter sale this weekend!*

We have 100s of ⁰b_a_r_g_a_i_n_s_ with 50% off everything in our store!

And you can save another 10% with our special ¹c_ _ _ _ _. Just print it from our website and present it at the ²c_ _ _ _ _ _ in store. You can use it when you pay with ³c_ _ _ or ⁴c_ _ _ _ _ c_ _ _. For the best skater clothes at amazing ⁵d_ _ _ _ _ _ _ _, come to Skate Style!

LO Talk about money
✓ This is easy 😁 OK 🙂 hard 😐 for me.

LO Talk about shopping
✓ This is easy 😁 OK 🙂 hard 😐 for me.

Grammar

← Student Book p.37

3

be going to (plans and intentions): affirmative and negative

Affirmative

Subject + **am** / **is** / **are** (**'m** / **'s** / **'re**) (**not**) + **going to** + infinitive

I	'm		
He / She / It	's	going to	save.
We / You / They	're		

We use **be going to** to talk about our plans and intentions for the future.

He's **going to** buy a new bike.

I'**m not going to** waste my money this month.

Negative

I	'm not		
He / She / It	isn't	going to	save.
We / You / They	aren't		

We often use future time expressions with **be going to**:

later tomorrow tonight this morning / afternoon / evening
this weekend next week / month / year
on Saturday (morning / afternoon)

1 ★★ Complete the sentences with the correct affirmative (✓) or negative (✗) form of *be*.

0 My parents __are__ going to buy me a new laptop. (✓)
1 Dad ________ going to lend me $20. (✓)
2 I ________ going to spend any more money. (✗)
3 We ________ going to go shopping this weekend. (✗)
4 I ________ going to order a coffee. (✓)
5 Lee ________ going to waste any money. (✗)
6 They________ going to borrow some money from their parents. (✓)

2 ★★ Order the words to make sentences.

0 to / going / we / to / concert / the / aren't / go
We aren't going to go to the concert.
1 sister / some / my / is / money / going / lend / me / to
____
____
2 going / I'm / to / for / T-shirt / pay / this
____
3 buy / she / to / anything / going / isn't
____
4 aren't / have / breakfast / they / going / to / cereal / for
____
____
5 money / going / you're / all / spend / your / to
____
6 he / money / to / 's / earn / a lot of / going
____

3 ★★ Complete the conversation with the correct form of *be going to* and the verbs in parentheses.

Leo Guess what? My parents [0] __are going to give__ (give) me a new desk for my birthday.
Seb But you wanted a guitar!
Leo I know! But they [1] ________________ (not buy) me one.
Seb Oh no! So what's the plan now?
Leo Well, I [2] ________________ (not spend) any more money on clothes or going out. I [3] ________________ (save) for a guitar. Then I [4] ________________ (practice) every day and become an amazing guitarist, like your uncle.
Seb Did I tell you? My uncle [5] ________________ (play) at a rock festival in New York next month. My brother and I [6] ________________ (see) him. Do you want to come?
Leo Yes, but I can't afford it. I'm saving for a guitar, remember?

LO Use *be going to* to talk about plans and intentions
✓ This is easy ☺ OK ☺ hard ☺ for me.

3 Grammar

← Student Book p.39

be going to (plans and intentions): questions and short answers

Questions

Am / Is / Are + subject + **going to** + infinitive?

Am	I		
Is	he she it	**going to**	save?
Are	you we they		

Short answers

Subject + **am (not)** / **are (not)** / **is (not)** (**'m not** / **isn't** / **aren't**)

Affirmative	Negative
Yes, I **am.**	No, I'm **not.**
Yes, he / she / it **is.**	No, he / she / it **isn't.**
Yes, we / you / they **are.**	No, we / you / they **aren't.**

We use questions with **be going to** to ask about plans and intentions for the future.

"Is he going to lend you any money?" "Yes, he is."

For questions which ask for more information, we use a **Wh-** question word before **am** / **is** / **are**.

What am I **going to** do?

Where are you **going to** go?

When is it **going to** start?

Why are they **going to** wait?

4 ★★ Choose the correct words to complete the questions and short answers.

0 "What ... going to have for dinner?"
"Chicken and rice."
a you (**b**) are you **c** you are

1 "Are you going to buy anything at the sale?"
"Yes, I ... ."
a go **b** 'm **c** am

2 "Dad, are you ... to buy me a motorcycle when I'm 16?"
"No way!"
a going to **b** going **c** go

3 "Where are we going ... ?"
"We're going to camp in the forest!"
a stay **b** staying **c** to stay

4 "Are your cousins going to go to the concert?"
"No, they ... ."
a don't **b** aren't going **c** aren't

5 "... going to spend $10 on a taxi?"
"Yes, she is. She always wastes her money."
a Is she **b** She's **c** Does she

5 ★★ Look at the answers in the interview and complete the questions 1–7, and the short answers a–c. Use the words in the box and *be going to*.
R = reporter; S = Sue; P = Paul.

how / you / spend   she / leave   they / go
~~what~~ / ~~they~~ / ~~do~~   when / you / get back
where / you / live   you / stay   your children / get

R Paul and Sue Jackson from Idaho won $25 million in last week's lottery. [0] *What are they going to do* with all that money?
Congratulations, both of you!
[1] ______________________ $25 million?

S Well, first we're going to go on vacation to Hawaii!

R You have two children. [2] ______________________ with you?

P No, they [a] ____________. They're at college right now.

R Your daughter is studying to be a doctor.
[3] ______________________ college now?

P No, she [b] ____________! Work is about more than money.

R [4] ______________________ from your vacation?

S At the end of April.

R [5] ______________________ when you get back?
[6] ______________________ in the same town?

S Yes, we [c] ____________. We have a lot of friends there.
But we're going to buy a much bigger house!

R [7] ______________________

S Yes, of course!

LO Use *be going to* to ask about plans and intentions

✓ This is easy 😊 OK 🙂 hard 😐 for me.

 ← Student Book p.40

A magazine article

Smart spenders

Rita and David Grant and their children, Jack, 14, and Sophie, 15, had a problem with money: they wasted [0]it. "We spent all our money before the end of the month," says Rita. "David and I are hard-working – [1]he has two jobs, and [2]mine has long hours – but we never saved anything, and we couldn't afford a vacation."

Last month, the Grants went on a TV show called "Smart spenders". For four weeks, TV cameras followed them to see how [3]they spent their money. The results were interesting:

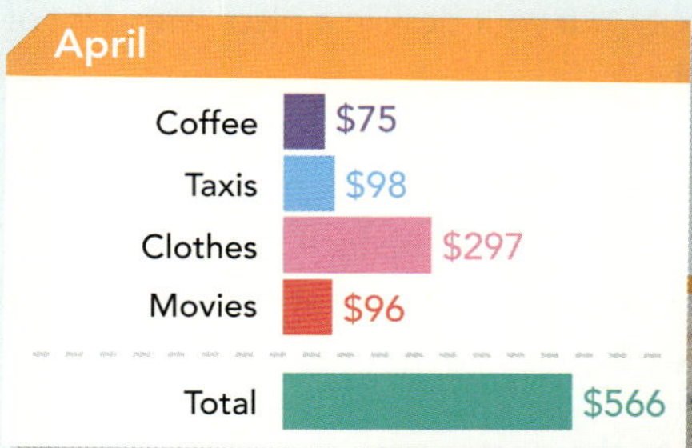

Now the Grants understand why they never have any money! "We're going to stop wasting it on unnecessary things," says Rita. "We don't need [4]them! We're going to buy clothes on sale when the prices are cheaper, and David isn't going to go out for expensive coffee – he can make [5]some at home. I'm going to take the bus instead of taxis, and Jack and Sophie aren't going to go to the movies every weekend."

"We're going to save money for the children's college education," says David. "And next year, we're going to go on a cheap vacation. We're going to go camping. This TV show changed our lives. [6]It taught us that what we save is very important."

1 ★ 173 **Read and listen to the article. Choose the incorrect sentence.**

a Jack and Sophie wasted money on movies.
b Rita wasted money on transportation.
c David wasted money at college.

2 ★★ **Read the text again and highlight any words which you find difficult. Use a bilingual dictionary to check the meaning of each word.**

3 ★★ **Read the text again. Complete each sentence with one word from the text.**

0 Rita and David have *children* called Jack and Sophie.
1 The Grants never had enough money for a __________.
2 TV cameras followed the family for __________ weeks.
3 Now Rita is going to start traveling by __________.
4 Rita and David are going to save money so Jack and Sophie can go to __________.
5 The family is going to go __________ for their vacation.

4 ★★ **Look at the highlighted pronouns in the text. Who or what do they refer to?**

0 it
 (a) money b problem c children
1 he
 a two jobs b David c Rita
2 mine
 a Rita b long hours c Rita's job
3 they
 a the Grants b TV show c cameras
4 them
 a the Grants b unnecessary things c money
5 some
 a David b money c coffee
6 It
 a the TV show b vacation c college education

LO Read an article and understand pronoun references
✓ This is easy ☺ OK ☺ hard ☹ for me.

4 Big issues

Vocabulary

← Student Book p.45 p.48

Human-caused and natural problems

1 ★ Match the headlines 0–7 with the problems a–h.

0 __d__ Scientists find a miracle cure.
1 ____ A region wants independence from the rest of the country.
2 ____ Experts predict we will need more homes, schools, and hospitals by 2025.
3 ____ Air quality is getting worse in many cities.
4 ____ Water levels are rising as heavy rain continues.
5 ____ Thousands of homes are destroyed following yesterday's disaster.
6 ____ Take only one shower a day to save water.
7 ____ Temperatures in Phoenix, Arizona, will reach 42°C by Thursday.

a flood
b heat wave
c overpopulation
~~d disease~~
e pollution
f drought
g earthquake
h war

2 ★★ Complete the words in the leaflet.

Humans vs. trees

Every year, we lose more of the world's original forests. Here are two very important reasons to save our trees.

- Trees keep our planet at a safe temperature. When we lose our forests, the Earth gets hotter, and there are more ⁰h__eat__ w__aves__. Hot weather sometimes causes ¹w________, and then we lose even more trees. Therefore, losing forests is both a cause and an effect of ²c________ c________.
- Trees take water from the Earth, but when there aren't many trees, rain quickly causes ³f________. It becomes difficult to grow food, and people are at risk of ⁴d________, such as cholera and malaria.
- Trees clean our air. When we cut down our trees, air ⁵p________ gets worse. In Paris, there are plans to create an urban forest to help make the city air cleaner.

Environmental problems and solutions

3 ★ Choose the correct verbs to complete the sentences.

0 In the U.S., people ... about 32% of their trash.
a protect (b) recycle

1 Every year, the world eats about 145 million tons of fish. Are we going to ... ?
a run out b throw away

2 Each year, between 0.01 and 0.1% of the world's animal species ... .
a become extinct b recycle

3 To ... electricity, put your desk in a place with a lot of natural light.
a reuse b save

4 Don't use plastic. ... fish and other ocean species!
a Protect b Reduce

5 Don't ... old clothes. Make different things from them!
a become extinct b throw away

4 ★★ Complete the poster with the verbs.

protect recycle reduce reuse ~~save~~ throw away

Don't waste paper

At Greenfields School, we're trying to ⁰__save__ paper. With your help, we can ¹________ the amount of paper we use by 30%.

Don't ²________ a piece of paper. Stop and think!

Are there words on both sides?
Yes → ³________ it! Put it in the right container.
No → ⁴________ it! Write on the other side.

Don't waste paper, and ⁵________ our forests!

LO Talk about human-caused and natural problems
✓ This is easy ☺ OK ☺ hard ☺ for me.

LO Talk about environmental problems and solutions
✓ This is easy ☺ OK ☺ hard ☺ for me.

Grammar

← Student Book p.47

will / won't (future predictions)

Long form

Affirmative

Subject + **will ('ll)** + infinitive.

I / You He / She / It We / You They	will	go.

Short form

I / You He / She / It We / You They	'll	go.

Negative

Subject + **will not (won't)** + infinitive.

I / You He / She / It We / You They	will not	go.

I / You He / She / It We / You They	won't	go.

We use **will** / **won't** + infinitive to make predictions about the future based on our opinion, not on evidence.
We often use **will** after **I think** and **I don't think**.

I think electric cars **will be** very popular.
I don't think people **will live** in space.
(NOT ~~I think people won't live in space.~~)

We can contract **will** with subject pronouns.

In 20 years, we**'ll** (= we **will**) go on vacation in space.

Won't is the contracted form of **will not**.

We probably **won't** find life on other planets.

Questions

Will + subject + infinitive?

Will	I / you he / she / it we / you / they	go?

Short answers

Yes, + subject + **will**.
No, + subject + **won't**.

Affirmative			Negative		
Yes,	I you he she it we they	will.	No,	I you he she it we they	won't.

1 ★★ **Complete the sentences with *will* / *'ll* or *won't*.**

0 I think we 'll see more floods in the next ten years. They're a big problem in a lot of places.
1 I don't think bookstores ________ close in the future. People will always enjoy reading.
2 Shopping malls ________ exist in 2025. We'll buy everything online.
3 I'm not worried about climate change. I think scientists ________ find a solution.
4 Overpopulation ________ be a big problem in the future. There are around eight billion people now!
5 Teenagers ________ go to school in 2030. In 2030, everyone will know everything!

2 ★★ **Write questions using the information in the chart. Then write short answers with *will*.**

Life in 2050	
0 people / have jobs	✓
1 the cell phone / exist	✗
2 humans / live / on Mars	✓
3 robots / be / more intelligent than humans	✓
4 climate change / be / a problem in the future	✗
5 everyone / speak / English	✓

0 "Will people have jobs?"
"Yes, we / they will."
1 "________________________________"
"________________"
2 "________________________________"
"________________"
3 "________________________________"
"________________"
4 "________________________________"
"________________"
5 "________________________________"
"________________"

LO Use *will / won't* to make predictions about the future based on opinion

✓ This is **easy** 😀 **OK** 🙂 **hard** 😐 for me.

4 Grammar

← Student Book p.49

be going to (future predictions)

Affirmative and negative

Subject + **am** / **are** / **is** / **'m not** / **isn't** / **aren't** + **going to** + infinitive.

The sky is dark. It'**s going to rain**.

She's late, and here's my train. I'**m not going to see** her today.

Yes / No questions

Am / **Are** / **Is** + subject + **going to** + infinitive?

Short answers

Yes, / **No,** + subject + **am** / **are** / **is** / **'m not** / **isn't** / **aren't**.

"**Are** the books **going to** fall?"

"**Yes, they are.**" / "**No, they aren't.**"

We use **be going to** to make predictions when we have concrete evidence. For example, something we know or can see helps us make a prediction.

The other team is winning 8–0. We'**re going to lose** the game.

Stop

We can also use **be going to** to talk about plans and intentions.

We'**re going to visit** my cousins this weekend.

3 ★ **Match 0–5 with a–f and complete the sentences with the correct form of *be going to*.**

0 Last year and the year before, it didn't rain for three months. f
1 There's a heat wave in Miami right now. ____
2 That's your seventh cookie in ten minutes! ____
3 I slept really badly last night. ____
4 Water pollution is killing the animals in our oceans. ____
5 It's 7:45 a.m. Get up! ____

a We aren't going to need our coats.
b You're going to be late for school!
c I'm going to feel terrible today.
d You're going to feel sick.
e They're going to become extinct.
~~f There's going to be another drought this year.~~

4 ★★ **Look at the pictures. Write questions and short answers with *be going to*, and the words in the box.**

he / win ~~I / fall~~ it / snow it / start / a wildfire they / run out we / be / on time

0

1

2

3

4

5

0 Am I going to fall? No, you aren't.
1 ______________________
2 ______________________
3 ______________________
4 ______________________
5 ______________________

5 ★★ **Complete the sentences with the correct form of *will* or *be going to*, and the verbs in the box.**

not arrive get live score ~~take~~ not wear

0 Leave your laptop here. I don't think anyone will take it.
1 The train left 30 minutes late, so it ______________ on time.
2 Emma ______________ that dress. I think she prefers pants!
3 Some people believe we ______________ on different planets in the future.
4 Look! Gómez has the ball. He ______________!
5 More people are buying cars. This means that air pollution ______________ worse.

LO Use *be going to* to make predictions about the future based on evidence

This is easy ☐ OK ☐ hard ☐ for me.

← Student Book p.50

A newspaper article

Green cities — *by Lucia Young*

Cities are bad for the environment in many different ways. Scientific studies show that cities are a major cause of climate change: heavy traffic creates air pollution, and the rapid growth of some cities destroys the natural habitats of wild animals. Overpopulation creates problems for housing, health, and transportation. It also causes high levels of water, electricity, and other energy usage, and resources can run out.

Some local governments are trying to find ways of making their cities greener. One example is in Paris, France. The city is going to create a park, 1.9 km long, on the city's main shopping street, the Champs-Élysées. This famous street is normally full of tourists and traffic, but city planners hope the new green spaces will bring peace and quiet, with 50% less traffic and more areas for people to shop, walk, and relax.

Studies on the effects of trees and plants show that the park will protect wild animals, and reduce energy use: trees reduce the temperature, and we can save energy that buildings need for air conditioning. Evidence also shows that the air will become cleaner, because trees reduce carbon dioxide and produce more oxygen. The park is going to cost over €260 million, and it is going to take ten years to build. But its positive effects will be far greater and longer-lasting.

1 ★ 174 Read and listen to the article. What is the writer's opinion? Choose the correct sentence.

a Green areas will help the environment in the future.
b Cities will always be dangerous places for animals.
c Paris is the cleanest and safest city in the world.

2 ★★ Read the text again and highlight any words which you find difficult. Use a bilingual dictionary to check the meaning of each word.

3 ★★ Read the text again. Choose the correct answers.

0 Air pollution is one of the causes of ...
   a heavy traffic.
   (b) climate change.
   c natural habitats.
   d rapid growth.

1 Overpopulation ...
   a is higher in older cities.
   b creates more electricity.
   c causes more water usage than some cities have.
   d is a serious health problem.

2 The park ...
   a is only for local people.
   b will make shopping more difficult in Paris.
   c is the longest park in France.
   d will be on a popular shopping street.

3 City planners hope the park will ...
   a reduce traffic.
   b increase tourism by 50%.
   c create a bigger area for stores.
   d make Paris more famous.

4 The city's plans will ...
   a reduce the numbers of wild animals.
   b create more safe places for animals.
   c reduce the number of tourists.
   d need more energy for air conditioning.

5 Evidence shows that ...
   a trees improve air quality.
   b we need more carbon dioxide in the air.
   c Paris needs more than €260 million for the park.
   d the park's positive effects aren't going to last very long.

4 ★★ Answer the questions. Write complete sentences.

0 What does the writer think about the effects of cities on the environment? *She thinks they're bad for the environment.*

1 What happens to animals when cities grow quickly?
______

2 What is the Champs-Élysées?
______

3 How will the park affect traffic on the Champs-Élysées?
______

4 Why do trees reduce the need for air conditioning?
______

5 When will they finish building the park?
______

LO Read an article and recognize opinions
✓ This is easy ☺ OK ☺ hard ☺ for me.

5 Good job!

Vocabulary

← Student Book p.57 p.60

Jobs

1 ★ Label the pictures with the words.

builder chef hairdresser ~~lawyer~~ nurse soldier

0 lawyer ______

1 ______

2 ______

3 ______

4 ______

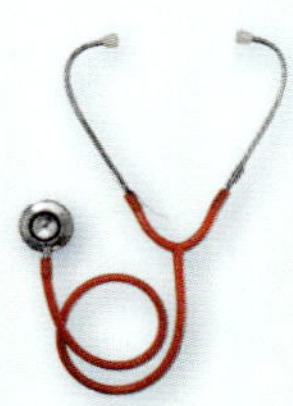

5 ______

2 ★★ What jobs do the people do? Read the descriptions and complete the jobs.

0 Liliana treats people in hospital. She's a doctor______.

1 Robert helps customers decide on cell phone plans. He's a s______.

2 Greg carries people out of dangerous buildings. He's a f______.

3 Claude creates beautiful dresses for famous actors. He's a f______ ______.

4 Sofia writes code for computer games and apps. She's a s______ ______.

5 Fiona catches criminals and protects her city. She's a p______ ______.

LO Talk about the job I want to do

✓ This is easy OK hard for me.

Personality

3 ★★ Write the opposites of the adjectives.

0 patient impatient

1 honest ______

2 reliable ______

3 helpful ______

4 careful ______

5 kind ______

6 friendly ______

4 ★★ Read the job advertisement and reply email. Complete them with the adjectives.

~~friendly~~ helpful impatient impolite kind reliable

Friends wanted!

Are you between the ages of 16 and 25? Do you enjoy the company of older people? Are you always [0] friendly, with a smile on your face? Are you [1] ______ when someone needs an extra hand? Are you [2] ______ when someone is perhaps feeling sad or alone? Are you [3] ______, and always on time? Our volunteer service puts young people together with older people when they need a friend. For more information, please email Anna Jones at the address below.

anna@silvercitizens.org

Dear Anna,

My name is Patrick Larkin, and I am 16 years old. I love talking to older people because their lives are so interesting, and they can teach me a lot. I am happy to give my time, and I am never [4] ______. These people need our respect, and I am never [5] ______ to them.

Please send me more information about your service. I look forward to hearing from you.

Best wishes,

Patrick Larkin

Reply

LO Describe people's personality

✓ This is easy OK hard for me.

Grammar

Student Book p.59

can / can't (rules and permission)

Affirmative

Subject + **can** + infinitive.

I / You He / She / It We / You / They	**can**	wear jeans.

Negative

Subject + **can't (cannot)** + infinitive.

I / You He / She / It We / You / They	**can't** (cannot)	wear jeans.

Yes / No questions

Can + subject + infinitive?

Can	I / you he / she / it we / you / they	wear jeans?

Short answers

Yes, + subject + **can**.
No, + subject + **can't**.

Yes,	I / you he / she / it we / you / they	**can**.
No,	I / you he / she / it we / you / they	**can't**.

We use **can** / **can't** to talk about rules – what is and isn't permitted.
You **can't** swim in the river. It isn't permitted.

Can has the same form for all subjects. We don't add **-s** in the **he** / **she** / **it** form.
She **can** use my cell phone. (NOT ~~She cans use my cell phone.~~)

We don't use the verb **do** in negative sentences and questions with **can**.
You **can't** sit here. (NOT ~~You don't can sit here.~~)
Can I borrow this book? (NOT ~~Do I can borrow this book~~?)

Stop

Remember that we also use **can** / **can't** to talk about ability.
Joe **can't** swim. He needs to learn.

1 ★ **Look at the rules and complete the sentences with *can* or *can't*.**

0 You <u>can't</u> eat during work hours.
1 Workers _______ use the back door after 8 a.m.
2 Everyone _______ use the back door before 8 a.m.
3 You _______ wear jeans Monday to Thursday.
4 Workers _______ wear jeans on Fridays.
5 You _______ wear sneakers.

2 ★★ **Correct the green phrases in the interview.**

Sam A firefighter's job is a great work opportunity. I'm here today with Angela, a firefighter. Angela, who does can [0] <u>can</u> become a firefighter?

Angela A person over the age of 18 cans [1] _______________ do the job. You only need a school education.

Sam What time does a firefighter's day usually start?

Angela Firefighters usually start work at 8 a.m.

Sam Do they can [2] _______________ wear their own clothes at work?

Angela No, they don't can [3] _______________. Firefighters need to wear a uniform every day. They also need to clean and check their equipment.

Sam Firefighters work long hours. You can [4] _______________ have a break during your working day?

Angela Yes, we do [5] _______________. After meals, firefighters can relax, read, or play games.

Sam You can leave [6] _______________ the station during this time?

Angela Can't we [7] _______________. Firefighters need to be prepared for an emergency at all times.

LO Use *can / can't* to talk about rules and permission
✓ This is easy OK hard for me.

5 Grammar

← Student Book p.61

(not) as ... as; too or not enough

as + adjective + **as** + noun

We use **as** + adjective + **as** to say that two things are similar or equal.

You're **as reliable as** your sister.

(= You and your sister are both reliable.)

not as + adjective + **as** + noun

We use **not as** + adjective + **as** to say that two things are different.

My dad is**n't as patient as** my mom.

(= My dad is less patient than my mom. / My mom is more patient than my dad.)

too + adjective

We use **too** + adjective to say someone / something is more careless, impatient, unreliable, etc., than is good or necessary.

I can't be a lawyer. I'm **too careless.**

not + adjective + **enough**

We use **not** + adjective + **enough** to say that someone / something is not as good, careful, patient, etc., as is necessary.

I can't be a gymnast. I'm **not good enough**.

3 ★ **Which sentence has a similar meaning to the first sentence? Choose *a* or *b*.**

0 I'm more honest than you are.
- a I'm as honest as you are.
- (b) You aren't as honest as I am.

1 You need to be more polite to people.
- a You're polite enough to people.
- b You're too impolite to people.

2 It's the same temperature in Chicago and L.A. today.
- a L.A. is as cold as Chicago today.
- b L.A. isn't as cold as Chicago today.

3 You're better at art than Jacob is.
- a Jacob isn't as good at art as you are.
- b Jacob is as good at art as you are.

4 I'm too unreliable to be a police officer.
- a I'm not reliable enough to be a police officer.
- b I'm not unreliable enough to be a police officer.

5 My sister isn't very honest. But I always tell the truth.
- a I'm not as honest as my sister.
- b My sister is too dishonest.

4 ★★ **Complete the sentences with one word.**

0 I want to be a fashion designer, but my ideas aren't original *enough*.

1 Sam __________ as tired as I am. I woke up at 5:00 a.m., and he woke up at 9:30 a.m.

2 Emilia is __________ unreliable. She needs to be on time for work!

3 You're as friendly __________ your brother. You're a nice family!

4 I'm __________ good as my sister at cooking.

5 Flying __________ as expensive as taking the train. It's cheaper!

6 Wear a jacket today. It isn't warm __________ for a T-shirt!

5 ★★ **Complete the restaurant reviews. Use *as ... as*, *too*, or *not ... enough*, and the adjectives in parentheses.**

Enzo's

Trattoria Napoli closed last year, but chef Enzo Di Matteo opened his new restaurant, Enzo's, last night.

COMMENTS:

Fantastic! Di Matteo is an awesome chef! His new restaurant is [0] *as good as* (good) the best restaurants in the city.

The restaurant isn't [1] __________________ (comfortable) the Trattoria Napoli. It's smaller, but there are more tables. It was [2] __________________ (crowded) when I was there, so it was hot and noisy.

Terrible! My soup was [3] __________________ (cold), and my pizza wasn't [4] __________________ (big). I was still hungry at the end of the meal.

Excellent! Enzo's isn't [5] __________________ (expensive) the Trattoria Napoli. The pizzas are only $8! We're going again this weekend!

LO **Use *(not) as ... as* and *too* or *not enough* to make comparisons**

✓ This is easy ☺ OK ☺ hard ☹ for me.

← Student Book p.62

A web article

The loneliest job in the world

A 2

Yellowstone National Park in the United States is one of the most beautiful parks in the world. Its 8,991 km² of mountains, lakes, and forests are home to nearly 400 species of wild animal. In the summer, Yellowstone receives over three million tourists, but in winter, heavy snow covers its roads, and they aren't safe to use. Tourists can't visit, and one of the park's only human inhabitants at that time is its caretaker, Steve Fuller. Steve is a polite, friendly man in his 70s, and he enjoys the company of friends and family. So why does he live here alone for six months of the year?

B ___

Steve started his job in 1973. The park needed a reliable caretaker to look after its buildings during the winter, and to check that the snow on the buildings wasn't too heavy. Today his job is the same: he climbs onto the buildings, and pushes the heavy snow onto the ground. Steve can't be careless or impatient.

C ___

For Steve, the park is never too quiet or boring. Years after he first became caretaker, he's as happy now as he was back then. In his free time, he takes photos of the animals and scenery, and keeps a journal. Maybe he isn't as strong as he was, but Steve isn't worried. He loves his job, and has no plans to stop!

1 ★★ 175 **Read and listen to the article. Match the headings 1–3 with the paragraphs A–C.**

1 Why he loves his job
2 One man alone with nature
3 A description of the job

2 ★★ **Read the text again and highlight any words which you find difficult. Use a bilingual dictionary to check the meaning of each word.**

3 ★★ **Read the text again. Are the sentences T (*true*), F (*false*), or NG (*not given*)? Choose the correct answer.**

0 400 species of wild animal live in Yellowstone. T ☑ F ☐ NG ☐
1 Steve is always friendly to tourists in the park. T ☐ F ☐ NG ☐
2 Steve was too unreliable for the job. T ☐ F ☐ NG ☐
3 Steve needs to be careful in his job. T ☐ F ☐ NG ☐
4 Steve became a caretaker because he wanted a quiet life. T ☐ F ☐ NG ☐
5 Steve sometimes worries that he isn't strong enough to do his job. T ☐ F ☐ NG ☐

4 ★★ **Complete each sentence with one word from the article.**

0 Yellowstone National Park is very beautiful.
1 Almost no one visits the park in winter, but in summer it is busy with ____________.
2 In winter, the roads in Yellowstone aren't safe because the snow is too ____________.
3 Steve Fuller enjoys human ____________, but doesn't mind being alone for six months every year.
4 Steve became the park's caretaker in ____________
5 Steve is never impatient in his job: one ____________ mistake can cause a serious accident.
6 His ____________ and photos tell the story of his time in the park.
7 Steve is in his 70s, but believes he is strong ____________ to do the job.

LO Read an article and understand the topic of each paragraph

✓ This is easy ☺ OK ☺ hard ☺ for me.

6 It's a crime!

Vocabulary

← Student Book p.67 p.70

Crime

1 ★ Who usually does these things: C (*criminals*), or P (*police*)?

		C	P
0	break into buildings	C ☑	P ☐
1	arrest people	C ☐	P ☐
2	commit crimes	C ☐	P ☐
3	investigate crimes	C ☐	P ☐
4	rob banks	C ☐	P ☐

2 ★★ Complete the police notes with the verbs.

arrested ~~broke into~~ caught chased steal was investigating

Date: March 12
Police officer: Officer J. Roberts

Description of incident:
The man [0] broke into a house on Pinewood Avenue this morning at around 9:35, and tried to [1] ________ a laptop computer. I was in the area because I [2] ________ another crime on the same street. I heard someone break a window, so I went over to the house. The man was just leaving, and he was carrying the laptop. He then started running, but I [3] ________ him. I [4] ________ the man on Oakland Avenue, and immediately [5] ________ him.

Safety online

3 ★ Choose the correct words to complete the computer phrases.

0 ... antivirus software
ⓐ install
b log out of

1 ... different passwords
a share
b use

2 ... on a link
a install
b click

3 ... a website
a log out of
b click on

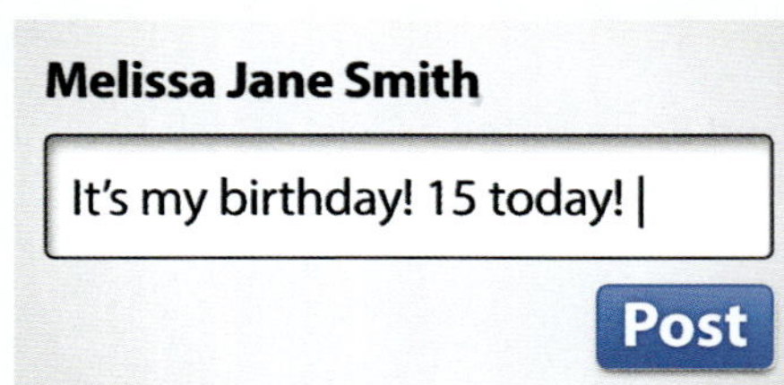

4 ... personal information
a install b share

4 ★ Complete the sentences with the verbs.

click install ~~log out of~~ share use

0 I forgot to log out of Facebook on my mom's computer, and my sister read all my messages! I'm really angry with her.
1 I'm not surprised you have a virus on your laptop. You didn't ________ antivirus software.
2 To watch the video, just ________ on this link here.
3 I hope you ________ a different password for your email, and for the app store. It isn't safe to use the same one.
4 Be careful when you ________ personal information, like your cell phone number, online. All your followers can see it.

LO Talk about crime
✓ This is easy OK hard for me.

LO Talk about safety online
✓ This is easy OK hard for me.

Grammar

← Student Book p.69

Past progressive and simple past

Past progressive

Affirmative

Subject + **was** / **were** + **-ing** form.

Negative

Subject + **wasn't** / **weren't** + **-ing** form.

Questions

Was / **Were** + subject + **-ing** form?

Short answers

Yes, + subject + **was** / **were**.

No, + subject + **wasn't** / **weren't**.

Past progressive			Simple past	
I He / She / It	**was watching** TV	**when**	I you he / she / it we you they	**heard** a noise.
We You They	**were watching** TV			

Simple past			Past progressive	
I You He / She / It We You They	**heard** a noise	**while** / **when**	I he / she / it	**was watching** TV
			we you they	**were watching** TV

We use the past progressive to talk about actions or situations that were in progress in the past. We use the past progressive and the simple past together when a short, completed action interrupts a longer action. We join the two parts of the sentence with **when** or **while**.

We use **while** or **when** before the past progressive. We use **when** before the simple past

My friend called me **while** / **when** I was having dinner.

I was having dinner **when** my friend called me.

We can change the order of the two parts of the sentence. The meaning is the same.

They were watching a movie **when** I arrived.

When I arrived, they were watching a movie.

1 ★★ **Complete the article with the past progressive or simple past form of the verbs in parentheses.**

Caught thanks to technology

In today's world of hacking and phishing, it's good to know that technology can stop crime, too.

While he [0] was robbing (rob) a supermarket, a man [1] ______________ (post) a picture of the crime on Facebook. He stole $500, and then decided to go shopping. He [2] ______________ (spend) the money in another store when the police [3] ______________ (arrest) him.

A woman [4] ______________ (show) a friend how to use a GPS app on her cell phone when a thief [5] ______________ (steal) the phone from her hand. The thief [6] ______________ (start) his motorcycle, and tried to escape, but all the time, the phone app [7] ______________ (follow) his movements, so the police quickly caught him.

2 ★★ **Look at the pictures and complete the sentences using the pairs of verbs. Use one past progressive and one simple past form in each sentence.**

~~hike~~ / ~~chase~~ score / not look steal / swim watch / eat

0

1

2

3

0 They were hiking when a bear chased them.

1 A boy ______________ my sneakers while I ______________.

2 While we ______________ a movie, the dog ______________ our dinner.

3 I ______________ a goal while the goalkeeper ______________.

LO Use past progressive and simple past

✓ This is easy ☺ OK ☺ hard ☹ for me.

 ← Student Book p.71

Adverbs of manner

Regular adverbs
adjective + **-ly**

Adjective		Adverb
slow	→	slowly
careful	→	carefully

adjectives that end in consonant + **-y**: ~~y~~ + **-ily**

Adjective		Adverb
easy	→	easily

Irregular adverbs

Adjective		Adverb
good	→	well
late	→	late
fast	→	fast

Adverbs describe verbs. There are different kinds of adverbs.
We use adverbs of manner to say how we do things.

They caught the criminal quick**ly**.
The children were playing happ**ily**.
You cook really **well**.

3 ★ Circle the correct answer.

0 You run really **fast**!
a adjective (b) adverb
1 He dances very **well**.
a adjective b adverb
2 My laptop is very **slow**.
a adjective b adverb
3 She learns languages **easily**.
a adjective b adverb
4 You need to be **careful**.
a adjective b adverb
5 My uncle drives a **fast** car.
a adjective b adverb

4 ★★ Complete Charlie's report card with the adverb from the adjectives in parentheses.

Report card

Name: Charlie Barrett
Subject: Computer science

I am pleased with Charlie's progress this year. He works [0] happily (happy) with other students, and he answers questions [1] ________ (correct) in class.

Charlie was unhappy with his exam results, but he can get a better grade next year [2] ________ (easy). He often completes activities too [3] ________ (fast), and makes mistakes. Charlie needs to work [4] ________ (slow) and [5] ________ (careful) in class. Then he can do very [6] ________ (good) next year.

5 ★★ Complete the second sentence so that it has the same meaning as the first sentence. Use the adverb that matches the word in bold.

0 My brother has a **quiet** voice.
My brother talks quietly.
1 He makes a lot of **noise** when he eats.
He ________.
2 Sarah's a **careless** driver.
Sarah ________.
3 She was **angry** when she told me the news.
She ________.
4 I'm **bad** at singing.
I ________.
5 My teacher thinks I'm a **quick** learner.
My teacher thinks ________.

LO Use adverbs of manner to talk about how we do things
✓ This is easy 😃 OK 🙂 hard 😐 for me.

 ← Student Book p.72

A blog post

The extraordinary story of Bonnie and Clyde

When Bonnie Parker met Clyde Barrow in January 1930, she was living in Texas. Soon afterwards, police arrested Clyde for different crimes, and he went to prison. However, Bonnie helped him escape, and they spent the next two years on the road.

While they were traveling, they frequently robbed banks and stole cars. They killed thirteen people, too. These crimes happened in different places, from Missouri to New Mexico. The couple quickly became the most famous criminals in the United States. The police were investigating their crimes, and everyone was reading about them in the newspapers. Bonnie and Clyde were trying to escape when police officers finally caught and killed them in Louisiana in May 1934.

At the time, the U.S. was suffering from an economic crisis, the Great Depression. People didn't have much money, and they believed the banks were responsible. Bonnie and Clyde's crimes were appalling, but for some people, they were heroes.

The story of Bonnie and Clyde continues to interest people today. They were the subject of a 1967 movie, songs, a musical, and a 2014 TV series. So why is their story so popular? Maybe it's the idea of a life of adventure on the road. However, it's important to remember that Bonnie and Clyde were real people. They committed terrible crimes, and destroyed many lives.

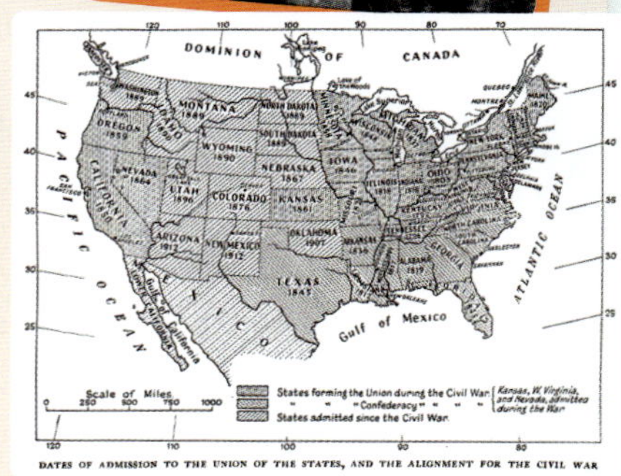

1 ★★ **Read the blog post quickly and find out …**

a two places where they committed crimes.

____

b the name of an economic crisis in the U.S. in the 1930s.

____

2 ★ 176 **Read and listen to the text again. Order the events.**

a ____ Clyde went to prison.
b ____ The police caught them.
c 1 Bonnie and Clyde met.
d ____ The couple became famous in the U.S.
e ____ There was a movie about the couple.
f ____ They started travelling around the U.S.

3 ★★ **Look at the highlighted words in the blog post. Are they nouns, verbs, adjectives, or adverbs? Write *n*, *v*, *adj*, or *adv*.**

0 frequently	adv	3 suffering	____
1 killed	____	4 appalling	____
2 couple	____	5 destroyed	____

4 ★ **Match the words with the definitions. Use the text to work out their meaning.**

0 f damaged something badly	a frequently
1 ____ made someone die	b killed
2 ____ having a bad time	c couple
3 ____ two people in a relationship	d suffering
4 ____ often, regularly	e appalling
5 ____ very bad	~~f destroyed~~

5 ★★ **Read the text again and highlight any other words which you find difficult. Use a bilingual dictionary to check the meaning of each word.**

6 ★★ **Read the text again and answer the questions. Write complete sentences.**

0 What different crimes did they commit?
They robbed banks, stole cars, and killed people.

1 How did the public know about Bonnie and Clyde?

____

2 Where did they die?

____

3 Bonnie and Clyde's bank robberies made them heroes at a difficult time in U.S. history. Why?

____

4 How did artists and writers tell the story of Bonnie and Clyde after they died?

____

5 What do we need to remember about their crimes?

____

LO Read an article and use context to guess meaning

✓ This is easy ☺ OK ☺ hard ☺ for me.

7 Bucket list

Vocabulary

← Student Book p.79 p.82

Experiences

1 ★ Match the words to make experiences.

0 __c__ race across
1 ____ appear on
2 ____ interview my
3 ____ dye my
4 ____ perform with
5 ____ make a
6 ____ sail around
7 ____ decorate my

a favorite YouTuber
b a live band
~~c a desert~~
d the world
e bedroom
f TV
g viral dance video
h hair a different color

2 ★★ What are Emilia's intentions for the year ahead? Complete the experiences.

January 1st

This year, I'm going to do a lot of different things. First, I'm going to [0]d__ecorate__ my b__edroom__. Right now, the walls are white, and I want to paint them blue.

Next, I'm going to [1]m________ a v________ d________ v________ with my friends. We're choosing our music, and we're going to make it on my new phone!

In the summer, I'm going to [2]g________ b________ for a few days with my friends – maybe in the mountains. And at night we're going to [3]c________ u________ the s________. We want to [4]g________ s________ in the ocean, too.

Finally, I'm going to [5]w________ my o________ n________. After all these amazing experiences, I'll have a great story to tell!

Phrasal verbs (movement)

3 ★ Choose the correct phrasal verbs.

0 (a) go away b get on
1 a get off b go out
2 a go out b stay in
3 a stay in b get on
4 a get back b get off
5 a go away b take off

4 ★ Complete the conversations with the phrasal verbs below.

get back   get off   go away   ~~go out~~   stay in

Tom Do you want to [0]__go out__ tonight?
Pedro I can't. I need to get up early tomorrow to [1]________. It's the beginning of my vacation.
Tom What time is your flight?
Pedro 6 a.m. So I need to [2]________ tonight.
Tom You'll be tired!
Pedro I know. And when I [3]________ the plane, there's a long bus trip to the hotel.
Tom Oh well, you can sleep when you arrive. Hey, call me when you [4]________ from your vacation. I want to hear all about it!

LO Talk about exciting experiences
This is easy ☐ OK ☐ hard ☐ for me.

LO Use phrasal verbs to talk about movement
This is easy ☐ OK ☐ hard ☐ for me.

Grammar

← Student Book p.81

Present perfect (experiences): affirmative and negative

Affirmative
Subject + **have** (**'ve**) / **has** (**'s**) + past participle.

I / You / We / They	've	traveled.
He / She / It	's	

Negative
Subject + **haven't** / **hasn't** + past participle.

I / You / We / They	haven't	traveled.
He / She / It	hasn't	

We use the present perfect to talk about experiences.
I**'ve appeared** on TV, but I **haven't acted** in a movie.

We can also add **never** to make the sentence negative. **Never** means **at no time**.
She**'s never performed** with a live band.

Negative with *never*
Subject + **'ve** / **'s** + **never** + past participle.

I / You / We / They	've	never	traveled.
He / She / It	's		

Stop

The past participle of regular verbs is the infinitive + **-ed**. The spelling changes in the same way as in the simple past.
I**'ve never sailed** on a boat.
My parents **haven't tried** Thai food.
Some verbs have irregular past participles. (See the Irregular verbs list at the end of the book.)
My brother **has seen** this movie ten times.

1 ★★ **Complete the chart with the past participles of the verbs.**

~~appear~~ carry like make perform race say see

+ -ed	+ -d	~~-y~~ + -ied	irregular
[0] *appeared*	[2] ______	[4] ______	[5] ______
[1] ______	[3] ______		[6] ______
			[7] ______

2 ★★ **Complete the present perfect sentences. Use *'ve, 's, haven't,* or *hasn't,* and the past participle of the verb in parentheses.**

0 My mom loves her bed. She *'s* never *camped* under the stars! (camp)
1 I ______ never ______ in on a Saturday night. I always go out with my friends! (stay)
2 She's run a lot of marathons, but she ______ ______ across a desert. (not race)
3 He's a very famous actor. He ______ ______ in a lot of movies and TV shows. (appear)
4 They ______ ______ on a boat before, so they know what they're doing. (sail)
5 We ______ ______ our house. We don't know how to! (not decorate)

3 ★★ **Complete the blog post with the present perfect form of the verbs.**

dye ~~interview~~ make never post paint not try write

< Previous | Forum | Next >

Tell us something you're proud of!

Poster1 I [0] *'ve interviewed* ______ my favorite YouTuber! I was at an event for YouTubers and their fans, and he was there! I was very nervous, but he was very friendly.

Poster2 I [1] ______ my hair a lot of different colors. It's pink now! My friends think I'm brave. I [2] ______ green yet. Maybe next year!

Poster3 My sister and I [3] ______ a viral dance video. We're really good dancers. I'm good at singing, too, but I [4] ______ a song online.

Poster4 I [5] ______ my own novel. It's the story of a boy who can move things with his eyes! My brother is good at art, and he [6] ______ some really cool pictures for children's books. He's going to do some for my book, too.

LO Use the present perfect to talk about life experiences
This is easy OK hard for me.

7 Grammar

← Student Book p.83

Present perfect (experiences): questions

Questions

Have / **Has** + subject + **ever** + past participle?

Have	I / you / we / they	**ever**	**performed?**
Has	he / she / it		

Short answers

Affirmative	Negative
Yes, I / you / we / they **have.**	**No,** I / you / we / they **haven't.**
Yes, he / she / it **has.**	**No,** he / she / it **hasn't.**

We use questions with the present perfect and **ever** to ask about experiences.

"**Have** you **ever** raced across the desert?"

"Yes, I **have**. It was awesome!"

We use **been** and **gone** as the past participles of **go**.

been = I went and came back.

gone = I went and I am there now.

"Have you ever **been** to Russia?" "Yes, I went there last year."

"Where has your dog **gone**?" "I don't know. I can't find him anywhere!"

4 ★★ **Complete the mini-dialogues with *have, has, haven't,* or *hasn't*.**

0 "__Have__ you ever gotten off a train at the wrong station?"
"Yes, I ________! I've done it two or three times!"

1 "________ your parents ever given you a really expensive present for your birthday?"
"No, they ________. But they always buy me nice things."

2 "________ your brother ever been snorkeling?"
'No, he ________. He doesn't like water!"

3 "________ I ever told you about the time I sailed around the world? "
"Yes, you ________. Hundreds of times!"

5 ★★ **Find and correct one grammar mistake in each conversation.**

0 "~~Has~~ you ever been away without your parents?"
"Yes, I have." __Have__

1 "Have your parents ever saw this movie?"
"Yes, they have." ________

2 "Has Tom ever appeared on TV?"
"No, he haven't." ________

3 "You have and your friends ever camped under the stars?"
"Yes, we have." ________

4 "Have you ever wrote a novel?"
"No, I haven't." ________

5 "Has your sister performed with a live band?"
"No, she has." ________

6 ★★ **Complete questions 1-3 with the present perfect form and *ever*. Write short answers for a-d.**

Abel 0 __Have I ever told__ you about my backpacking vacation? (I / tell)

Mia a ________ ✗. It sounds great.

Abel It was great! We camped on a beach and spent all day in the ocean. What about you?
1 ________ under the stars with your family? (you / camp)

Mia b ________ ✗. But we want to! I'm also hoping to go snorkeling this summer.

Abel 2 ________ it before? (you / do)

Mia c ________ ✓. And I want to take my little sister.

Abel 3 ________ it? (she / try)

Mia d ________ ✓. She loves snorkeling.

LO Use the present perfect to ask about life experiences

✓ This is easy ☺ OK ☺ hard ☺ for me.

← Student Book p.84

A profile

1 ★★ 177 Read and listen to the blog post. Match headings 0–3 with paragraphs A–D.

0 C Greta's experiences
1 ____ A famous young woman with an important message
2 ____ Greta's influence on others
3 ____ How Greta became an environmental activist

The Greta effect

A Have you ever heard of Greta Thunberg? She's the young environmental activist whose face has become famous all over the world. She has appeared on TV to ask governments for their help in stopping climate change. Reporters have interviewed her for her opinions. She's met politicians to discuss the environment. But who is Greta? And why has she become so famous?

B Greta was born in Stockholm, Sweden. Her parents aren't activists, but Greta became very worried about the environment at a young age. In 2018, when she was 15, she stopped going to school, and started protesting outside the Swedish Parliament. Soon, thousands of students around the world were protesting, too.

C As a result of her work, Greta has had many exciting experiences. She has sailed across the Atlantic to attend a climate change conference in the United States. She has been to other countries, spoken in front of thousands, and written a book with her family. Young people are inspired by her simple, clear message.

D Millions of children and teenagers around the world left their classrooms to go and protest in the streets against climate change. Many started their own environmental projects, too. These included campaigns to reduce carbon emissions and the use of plastic, to remove trash from our environment, and to recycle. A new generation wants to protect our planet. And this is thanks to the "Greta effect."

2 ★ Read the text again. Find two examples for each of the following topics.

How Greta's message has become public
She's appeared on TV.
____

Exciting things she has done
____

Ways other young people are trying to protect the environment
____

3 ★★ Read the text again and highlight any words which you find difficult. Use a bilingual dictionary to check the meaning of each word.

4 ★★ Answer the questions with a maximum of four words.

0 What does Greta want from governments in her fight against climate change?
their help
1 What do reporters want from Greta?
____
2 What was she missing while she was outside the Swedish Parliament?
____
3 Where did she sail to?
____
4 Which group of people have listened to her the most?
____
5 What has Greta taught them about?
____

LO Read an article and recognize examples
✓ This is easy ☺ OK ☺ hard ☺ for me.

8 Creativity

Vocabulary

← Student Book p.89 | p.92

Creativity: adjectives

1 ★ Choose the best adjectives to complete the sentences.

0 The gallery is very … . It sells hundreds of paintings every year.
a original   (b) successful   c enormous

1 This designer makes jewelry from parts of old computers and other … materials.
a old-fashioned   b smart   c recycled

2 I don't like modern art. It's …, and I don't understand it.
a strange   b original   c ancient

3 This painting is … ! I finished it this morning!
a delicate   b tiny   c brand new

4 That's a very … idea! Let's include it in our project.
a smart   b recycled   c old-fashioned

5 The … microchip in this pen allows it to play music while you are writing.
a ancient   b strange   c tiny

2 ★★ Replace the green words with the adjectives.

ancient   delicate   ~~enjoyable~~   enormous   old-fashioned   original

The Metropolitan Museum of Art

The Metropolitan Museum in New York City's famous Fifth Avenue offers an exciting experience that is **fun** [0] enjoyable for all ages. You can see 5,000 years of art there, from **really old** [1] ________ civilizations to the present day.

There are thousands of beautiful things, from **new and different** [2] ________ modern paintings and sculptures to **not modern** [3] ________ furniture and **small and intricate** [4] ________ jewelry.

With a total area of more than 1,800,000 square meters, the museum is **really big** [5] ________, and you can easily spend all day there.

LO Describe works of art

✓ This is easy ☺ OK ☺ hard ☺ for me.

Creativity: verbs

3 ★ Match the verbs 0–6 with a–g to make phrases.

0	c design	a	a house
1	___ sew	b	a company
2	___ discover	c	a poster
3	___ build	d	a new product
4	___ direct	e	clothes on a machine
5	___ invent	f	a cure for an illness
6	___ set up	g	a movie

4 ★★ Complete the timeline with the simple past form of appropriate verbs.

2000s: NASA [0] discovered water on Mars.

1900s: Tim Berners-Lee [1] c________ the first web page.

1800s: Gustave Eiffel [2] d________ the Eiffel Tower in Paris.

1700s: Mozart [3] c________ the opera *The Magic Flute*.

1600s: The artist Velázquez [4] p________ *Las Meninas*.

1500s: Galileo Galilei [5] i________ the first thermometer.

1400s: The Inca people [6] b________ the ancient city of Machu Picchu.

LO Talk about creative activities

✓ This is easy ☺ OK ☺ hard ☺ for me.

Grammar

← Student Book p.91

Relative pronoun:s *who*, *that*, *which*, and *whose*

We use a relative clause beginning with **who**, **that**, **which**, or **whose** to give more information about a noun.
We use a relative clause beginning with ...

- **who** to give more information about people.
  A software developer is a person **who** creates computer programs.
- **that** to give more information about people, places, and things.
  A 3D printer is a machine **that** makes objects from a digital file.
- **which** to give more information about places and things.
  I like cities **which** have a lot of parks in them.
- **whose** to give information about possession.
  Van Gogh was a painter **whose** pictures are known around the world.

1 ★ Choose the correct relative pronoun.

0 A stylus is a thing ... you use to write on a tablet.
  a where (b) which
1 Barbara Hepworth was a British artist ... sculptures are made of stone, wood, and metal.
  a who b whose
2 A chef is a person ... cooks meals in a restaurant.
  a which b who
3 Impressionism is a style ... artists developed in the 19th century.
  a where b that
4 Slinkachu takes photos ... show tiny figures of people.
  a which b whose

2 ★★ Complete the relative clauses with relative pronouns and the correct form of the verbs.

Original gift ideas for people who have everything

With this smart device, you can create your own movie theater! All you need is a room 0 that / which has (have) a big white wall. It's the perfect gift for a person 1 ____________ (love) movies.

This fun pink ball is a robot 2 ____________ (move) around your house and cleans the floor. It's great for people 3 ____________ (hate) chores. Cats love it, too!

Do you know someone 4 ____________ (passion / be) reading? Give them a reading tent, and they'll always have a place 5 ____________ (they / can) relax in.

3 ★★ Write answers to the questions. Use a relative clause and the words.

0 Who was Jørn Utzon?
  (the architect / designed the Sydney Opera House.)
  Jørn Utzon was the architect who / that designed the Sydney Opera House.
1 What is the Louvre?
  (a museum / is in Paris)
  ____
2 What is Apple?
  (a company / makes computers)
  ____
3 Who is Billie Eilish?
  (a singer from the U.S. / first album went to number one)
  ____
4 Who is J. K. Rowling?
  (the author / created Harry Potter)
  ____

LO Use relative pronouns to describe people, places, things, and possessions
✓ This is easy 😀 OK 🙂 hard 😐 for me.

8 Grammar

← Student Book p.93

Subject and object questions

In a subject question, the question word (**who**, **what**, etc.) refers to the person or thing that does the action.
Who painted "The Scream"?
Edvard Munch painted "The Scream".

In subject questions, we don't use the auxiliary verb **do** / **does** in the simple present, or **did** in the simple past.
In the simple present, the verb after the question word is always the third person singular.
Who **makes** these bags?

In an object question, the question word (**who**, **what**, etc.) refers to the object of the action.
What did Alexander Graham Bell invent?
Alexander Graham Bell invented **the telephone**.

In object questions, we use the auxiliary verb **do** / **does** in the simple present, and **did** in the simple past.

4 ★ Are these S (*subject*) or O (*object*) questions?

0 What does a sculptor do? S ☐ O ☑
1 Who invented the television? S ☐ O ☐
2 Who did you meet at the party? S ☐ O ☐
3 What did you do last weekend? S ☐ O ☐
4 Who plays Batman in the movie? S ☐ O ☐
5 What do you do on weekends? S ☐ O ☐

5 ★★ Complete the questions in the interview with the correct form of the verbs.

Paul What [0] *do you do* (you / do)?
Anna I'm a pastry chef in a five-star hotel. I make desserts.
Paul Who [1] ________ (help) you in the kitchen?
Anna I have a team of five chefs who help me.
Paul What [2] ________ (you / cook) last night?
Anna Chocolate mousse and strawberry cheesecake.
Paul Who [3] ________ (eat) at your restaurant?
Anna A lot of movie stars – although they don't all have dessert!
Paul What [4] ________ (you / enjoy) most about your job?
Anna It's very creative. I love making desserts look beautiful.
Paul Who [5] ________ (you / admire)?
Anna I've always admired the French chef Gaston Lenôtre.

6 ★★ Read the answers and write the questions.

0 *What does an interior designer do?*
An interior designer chooses paint, furniture, carpets, etc., to decorate the inside of a building.

1 ________
Suzanne Collins wrote "The Hunger Games".

2 ________
Harry Styles won **an American music award** in 2019 for his album "Fine Line".

3 ________
Commercial architects design **offices and stores**.

4 ________
____
Adele sang the song for the movie "Skyfall".

5 ________
My hairdresser, Dianne, cuts my hair. She's very original and creative!

6 ________
We visited **my grandparents** last weekend. They live near the beach!

7 ________
Painting makes me happy. I love it!

LO Use subject and object questions to ask about people and events
✓ This is easy ☺ OK ☺ hard ☺ for me.

← Student Book p.94

A blog post

Home About Articles Archive

Young artists' shopping list

These days there are more and more ways of creating beautiful art. And these come in the form of exciting products. We've chosen a few which we think you will love.

A The "Ojee" stylus is a fantastic product which will change the way you draw and design forever. This digital pen looks delicate, but it is amazingly strong. It works on all tablets, will last a long time, and now comes in a brand new range of colors. Who needs pencils and paper?

B The "Crystal" graphics tablet makes drawing more enjoyable than ever before. The 16.5 x 10 cm screen is big, but very light. In addition, this smart product doesn't need electricity, which means you can use it for as long as you want!

C The "Giotto" leather painting case looks old-fashioned, but it is a useful case where you can keep your paintbrushes clean and dry. It is easy to carry, and looks great. At $45, it isn't cheap, but will last a long time.

D Origami is an ancient east Asian art form which practices patience and precision. "The Little Book of Origami" contains over 50 beautiful objects that you can make from paper. All you need besides paper is your scissors!

E When we discovered The "Kaleidoscope" 3-D printing pen, we got excited! This amazing product can create anything you want: from tiny creatures to enormous buildings! With 18 cool colors to choose from, what are you waiting for?

1 ★ **Read the blog post quickly. What is the purpose of it?**

- **a** to recommend products
- **b** to review products
- **c** to compare products

2 ★★ **Read the text again and highlight any words which you find difficult. Use a bilingual dictionary to check the meaning of each word.**

3 ★★ 178 **Read and listen to the blog post again. Use the highlighted phrases from the text to complete the second sentence so that it has the same meaning as the first sentence.**

0 It costs a lot.
At $45, it ______ isn't cheap ______.

1 You can use it all day.
It will ____________________.

2 It can make a lot of different things.
This product can ____________________.

3 You need to be patient to use this product.
This product ____________________.

4 This isn't heavy at all.
It's big, but ____________________.

4 ★★ **Write the correct products (A–E) next to the sentences. You can use a product more than once.**

0 This product gives you the freedom of space and time. __B__

1 You can design and build your own products in any size and shape. ____

2 You need to cut paper to do this activity. ____

3 It isn't a modern product, but it is very helpful for artists. ____

4 This product is thin, but it won't break. ____

5 This product will teach you about something that started over a thousand years ago. ____

LO Read an article and recognize paraphrasing

✓ This is easy ☺ OK ☺ hard ☹ for me.

OXFORD
UNIVERSITY PRESS

Great Clarendon Street, Oxford, OX2 6DP, United Kingdom

Oxford University Press is a department of the University of Oxford. It furthers the University's objective of excellence in research, scholarship, and education by publishing worldwide. Oxford is a registered trade mark of Oxford University Press in the UK and in certain other countries

First published in 2023
2026 2025 2024
10 9

ISBN: 978 0 19 426687 1
Student Book & Workbook Online Practice Pack Component

Printed in China

This book is printed on paper from certified and well-managed sources

ACKNOWLEDGEMENTS

Cover photographs reproduced with permission from: Getty Images (kali9); Shutterstock (Coleman photographer, wavebreakmedia).

Illustrations by: Sara Lynn Cramb pp11, 47 (robot, car, Mars), 49; Denis Cristo p77; Joanna Kerr pp8, 30, 54 (climate change, drought, wild fire, heat wave, flood, overpopulation, earthquake, disease), 145; Sean Longcroft p82; Alejandro Mila/Silvie Poggio pp7, 32, 59, 129, 142; Paul Moran pp6, 16, 67, 110, 113, 128, 133, 149; Andrew Painter pp15, 39, 47 (cinema, goal, house, computer), 61, 69 (pick pocket, police, bird, robbery), 72, 144, 152; Andy Parker pp19, 36, 38 (buying t-shirts and trainers in a sale), 70, 105, 116, 117, 132, 136, 148, 159; Adriana Perlez/Lemonade Illustration p5; Ben Scruton / Meiklejohn p38 (pay with cash, bargain, coupon, receipt); Paul Williams pp4, 37, 54 (shopping x5), 68, 69 (detective and woman in café), 71; Tom Wooley pp48, 140.

Video stills by: Digital Learning Associates

Commissioned photography by: Gareth Boden pp.4, 12, 21, 22, 31, 34, 43, 44, 53, 65, 66, 75, 78, 87, 88, 97.

The publisher would like to thank the following for their permission to reproduce photographs: alinabradford.com (Alina Bradford); Alamy Stock Photo (Album, Aleksandr Kichigin, Alex Segre, Aliakseu Matsiushkou, Ben Molyneux , BIOSPHOTO, Boscorelli , David J. Green, Eric James, GL Archive, GL Archive , Greg Balfour Evans , Hero Images Inc., Image Source, imageBROKER, Jeffrey Isaac Greenberg 2+, Jim Holden, Libby Welch, Martin Norris Travel Photography 2, Maurice Savage, Mira, nicolae claudiu paizan, nik wheeler, PA Images, picture that , Pillyphotos, Rob Wilkinson, robertharding, SeventyFour Images, Sueddeutsche Zeitung Photo, ton koene, Uwe Deffner , Valerii Honcharuk, Wavebreak Media ltd, Xinhua, Zoonar GmbH); carabrookins.com (Cara Brookins); FilmMagic (Fred Duval); Getty Images (Adrian Peacock, Antony Jones, as3d, Barcroft Media, Blend Images, brightstars, Carlos Osorio , CasarsaGuru, Chanwichit Khuyngerm, Darryl Leniuk, David Madison, Edgar Mueller, Fuse, guvendemir, Heritage Images , Hero Images, Hulton Archive , Jitalia17, Jordan Siemens, Jouni Pirhonen, Jupiterimages, Kingfisher Productions, Klaus Vedfelt, Layne Kennedy, Lew Robertson, Lonely Planet Images, LordHenriVoton, MarioGuti, Maskot, Morsa Images, Multi-bits, Nick David, Onne van der Wal, pastorscott, Peter Cade, Phil Walter, Philippe PETIT, poladamonte, Print Collector, Purestock, Robyn Beck, Ryan McVay, soulsurfing - Jason Swain, SolStock, svetikd, TERADAT SANTIVIVUT, Tim P. Whitby, Tom Werner, Tommaso Altamura, William West, Windmill Books, WYSIWYG, Yellow Dog Productions, YinYang); Jolanda Sotkkerman (demealprepper); OUP (Aleksandar Levai, Benjamin Norman, Gareth Boden, PCA-STREAM, Wavebreak Media LTD); Shutterstock (2happy, ad-foto, Africa Studio, AlinaStreltsova, Andrey Bayda, Andrey Lobachev, Andrey_Popov, Andy Dean, ANL, Anna Kucherova, Anton Sterkhov, Antonio Guillem, aphotostory, Art Konovalov, Artiom Photo, atm2003, August_0802, AVAVA, Balate Dorin, BearFotos, bezikus, Billion Photos, Bisual Photo, Bizroug, Boris Stroujko, boxstock, Bruno Morand, canbedone, Catarina Belova, Chepko Danil Vitalevich, Chinnapong, critterbiz, Daniel Samray, Danilova Janna, Dean Drobot, Dean Fikar, Dean Gradella, DenPhotos, Det-anan, DNCC/EPA-EFE, donsimon, Dragon Images, EA Given, Eakachai Leesin, EldoradoSuperVector, Elena Rostunova, Elgub, Elnur, EQRoy, eurobanks, Everett Collection, Evgeniia Ozerkina, Evok20, feeling lucky, fizkes, FloridaStock, Foodio, FOTOGRIN, FXQuadro, g-stockstudio, GagliardiPhotography, Gary Blakeley, GG6369, Giovanni G, Glevalex, Guaxinim, Holli, HomeArt, Hunor Focze, Iakov Filimonov, Iam_Anuphone, Ian 2010, Ilya Studio, Inside Creative House, Irina Boldina, Irina Kozorog, Iryna Mylinska, Isabelle Ohara, ItzaVU, Iurii Stepanov, Jacek Chabraszewski, Jacob Lund, Jacquelyn Martin, Jaroslav Monchak, JeniFoto, JNP, Jorge A. Russell, joyfull, kamui29, kaprik, King Ropes Access, Kiselev Andrey Valerevich, koko-tewan, Kristina Kokhanova, Kseniya Ivanova, Kues, Kuz_com, l i g h t p o e t, Laborant, LeManna, LightField Studios, Ikunl, lovelyday12, M. Shcherbyna, MACHKAZU, Makhh, Marc Venema, Margaret.Wiktor, Maridav, Maryia_K, Master1305, Matej Hudovernik, Matej Kastelic, Mega Pixel, mezzotint, Mia2you, michaeljung, Michelle Aleksa, michelmond, Mikael Damkier, MikeDotta, Milan Ilic Photographer, Milos Luzanin, Minerva Studio, mironov, Monkey Business Images, Motortion Films, muratart, myphotobank.com.au, N8Allen, Nata Bene, natalia_maroz, New Africa, Nick Beer, Nightman1965, nine_far, Nolichuckyjake, Nomad_Soul, Nor Gal, Nutta L, Oliver Britton, Oliver Denker, oliveromg, Pablo Hidalgo, perfectlab, Peter Gudella, Phase4Studios, Phototasty, Phovoir, Pierre Vinet, pio3, Pixel-Shot, PKphotograph, ppl, Prostock-studio, puhhha, Quality Stock Arts, Racefotos2008, Rawpixel.com, REDPIXEL.PL, Richard P Long, Richard Whitcombe, Robert Kneschke, Roman Samborskyi, Romariolen, Romolo Tavani, rvlsoft, santypan, savanterpro, Sawat Banyenngam, Scott Alan Photo, sdecoret, SeaMountain, Sergey Novikov, sladkozaponi, Slavun, snowblurred, solarseven, Soloviova Liudmyla, Song_about_summer, Songquan Deng, SpaceKris, SpeedKingz, SS pixels, Stanislav Fosenbauer, Stas Tolstnev, Stasique, StockCo, stockphoto-graf, Strejman, Studio Romantic, StudioByTheSea, Sumire Jonathan, Supachai Panyaviwat, Syda Productions, T.Den_Team, Tattoboo, Tema_Kud, Tereshchenko Dmitry, Terry Yarrow, The Sturdy Table, Tihylrina, Tom Wang, Torsak Thammachote, Tribalium, tulpahn, Twinsterphoto, VAKS-Stock Agency, ValeStock, VALUA STUDIO, VH-studio, Victoria Chudinova, Victoria Labadie, Vincent St. Thomas, vinnstock, vvoe, wavebreakmedia, Wendy Nero, Wirestock Creators, Xinhua, xpixel); Wikkelhouse (Yvonne Witte).

The authors and publisher are grateful to those who have given permission to reproduce the following extracts and adaptations of copyright material: p.40 Text about Hannah Rupp, www.theoutfitrepeater.com, is included with kind permission of Hannah Rupp; pp.48 & 49 Text about The Ocean Cleanup, https://theoceancleanup.com/, is included with kind permission.

The authors and publishers would like to thank all the teachers and schools whose feedback, comments, and suggestions have contributed to the development of *Metro Second Edition*.

With thanks to the United Nations for granting permission to use the Sustainable Development Goals (SDGs): https://www.un.org/sustainabledevelopment/. The content of this publication has not been approved by the United Nations and does not reflect the views of the United Nations or its officials or Member States.

Although every effort has been made to trace and contact copyright holders before publication, this has not been possible in some cases. We apologise for any apparent infringement of copyright and, if notified, the publisher will be pleased to rectify any errors or omissions at the earliest possible opportunity.